Student Notes and Problems

CHEMISTRY 20
Alberta

CASTLE ROCK
RESEARCH CORP

Publisher
Gautam Rao

Contributors
O.J. Fleming
 Rob Schultz

Rao, Gautam, 1961 –

STUDENT NOTES AND PROBLEMS – Chemistry 20 Workbook Alberta

1. Science – Juvenile Literature. I. Title

Published by
Castle Rock Research Corp.
2340 Manulife Place
10180 – 101 Street
Edmonton, AB T5J 3S4

2 3 4 5 FP 12 11 10 09

Dedicated to the memory of Dr. V. S. Rao

STUDENT NOTES AND PROBLEMS WORKBOOKS

Student Notes and Problems (SNAP) workbooks are a series of support resources in mathematics for students in grades 3 to 12 and in science for students in grades 9 to 12. SNAP workbooks are 100% aligned with curriculum. The resources are designed to support classroom instructions and provide students with additional examples, practice exercises, and tests. SNAP workbooks are ideal for use all year long at school and at home.

The following is a summary of the key features of all SNAP workbooks.

UNIT OPENER PAGE

- summarizes the curriculum outcomes addressed in the unit in age-appropriate language
- identifies the lessons by title
- lists the prerequisite knowledge and skills the student should know prior to beginning the unit

LESSONS

- provide essential teaching pieces and explanations of the concepts
- include example problems and questions with complete, detailed solutions that demonstrate the problem-solving process

NOTES BARS

- contain key definitions, formulas, reminders, and important steps or procedures
- provide space for students to add their own notes and helpful reminders

PRACTICE EXERCISES

- include questions that relate to each of the curriculum outcomes for the unit
- provide practice in applying the lesson concepts

REVIEW SUMMARY

- provides a succinct review of the key concepts in the unit

PRACTICE TEST

- assesses student learning of the unit concepts

ANSWERS AND SOLUTIONS

- demonstrate the step-by-step process or problem-solving method used to arrive at the correct answer

Answers and solutions for the odd-numbered questions are provided in each student workbook. A *SNAP Solutions Manual* that contains answers and complete solutions for all questions is also available.

NOTES

CONTENTS

Matter as Solutions, Acids, and Bases

Quantitative Relationships in Chemical Changes

Answers and Solutions

REVIEW OF SCIENCE 10 CHEMISTRY

When you are finished this unit, you will be able to...

- describe the basic particles that make up the underlying structure of matter
- investigate technologies that are related to structure and composition of matter
- outline the role of evidence in the development of the atomic model
- compare and discriminate between protons, electrons, and neutrons
- use the periodic table to explain how elements combine to form compounds
- follow IUPAC guidelines for naming ionic compounds and similar molecular compounds
- explain how and why elements combine to form compounds in specific rations, using the periodic table
- classify ionic and molecular compounds, acids, and bases on the basis of their physical properties
- predict whether an ionic compound is relatively soluble in water, using a solubility chart
- relate the molecular structure of simple substances to their properties
- write word and balanced equations for significant chemical reactions
- interpret balanced chemical equations in terms of moles of chemical species, and relate the mole concept to the law of conservation of mass

PREREQUISITE SKILLS AND KNOWLEDGE

Prior to starting this unit, you should be able to...

- summarize the history and the concepts underlying the particle model of matter
- describe the characteristics of pure substances, mixtures, and solutions
- discuss chemical nomenclature with relation to the periodic table
- use atomic theory to contrast acids, bases, elements, compounds, and the conservation of mass
- translate between written and algebraic expressions
- add, subtract, multiply, and divide decimal numbers
- solve problems using ratios and proportions
- employ scientific notation with the help of a calculator
- recognize WHMIS symbols

Lesson 1 REVIEW OF ATOMS AND IONS

The atom is the building block of all substances since it cannot be broken down into a smaller unit. At present, around 109 elements have been isolated or synthetically prepared, and each has its own chemical symbol. The symbol is usually made up of the first and second letter of the element's name, except for a few elements. These are elements that have been isolated and used for a long period of time, and they take their symbols from their Latin names. These elements are:

Na	sodium	natrium
Cu	copper	cuprum
Sn	tin	stannum
Au	gold	aurum
Pb	lead	plumbum
K	potassium	kalium
Ag	silver	argentum
Sb	antimony	stibium
Hg	mercury	hydrargyrum
Fe	iron	ferrum
W	tungsten	wolfram (German origin)

Protons

The number of protons in an element is the same as its atomic number.

 # proton = atomic number.

Protons are located in the nucleus of the atom and have a positive charge. Each element has a different number of protons, and the number of protons in an element is its atomic number.
The number of protons in an element is the same as its atomic number.

Electrons

Electrons are located outside the nucleus and have a negative charge to balance the protons' positive charge. There is exactly the same number of electrons as protons, so that each atom is electrically neutral.
Electrons do not have a specific orbit around the nucleus, but occupy different energy levels.

Neutrons

The third fundamental particle of an atom is the neutron. A neutron has mass but does not carry an electrical charge. It is located inside the nucleus with the protons, and has roughly the same mass as a proton.

Atoms

Number of protons = number of electrons

The number of neutrons varies.

An atom is always electrically neutral; it always has the same number of protons and electrons. Atoms are represented by two basic models.
A sodium atom is used as an example.

2

Energy Level Model   **Bohr Model**

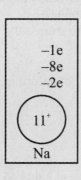

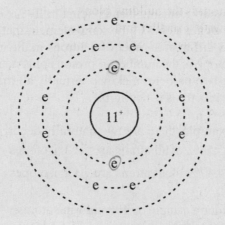

1st energy level 2e

2nd energy level 8e

3rd energy level 8e

4th energy level 2e
up to element 20

The 11$^+$ represents 11 protons in the nucleus, and the 11 electrons are distributed in three energy levels: 2e in the first, 8e in the second, and 1e in the third.

Only elements to atomic number 20 are represented in this manner.

Atomic Mass

All three particles (electrons, protons, and neutrons) make up the atom's mass, but because of the electron's small mass

(roughly $\dfrac{1}{2\,000}$th of a proton), they are ignored. Therefore, to calculate

the mass of an atom, add the protons and neutrons.

For elements with atomic numbers over 20, a different method is used, and is not required for Chemistry 20.

The number of neutrons is given in these diagrams.

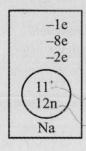

Using the sodium atom as an example, it has 11 protons (11$^+$) and 12 neutrons (12n), the atomic mass is 23.
The units of atomic mass are atomic mass units (amu).

Proton = Atomic #

neutron

Atomic mass units
= Proton + neutron
= 11 + 12 = 23.

You would not be expected to put this number in unless it was given in the question.

NOTES

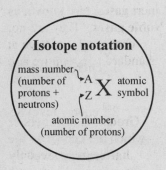

Isotope notation

mass number
(number of
protons +
neutrons)

$_Z^A X$

atomic
symbol

atomic number
(number of protons)

The symbol μ is often used to represent atomic mass units

μ is atomic mass unit

Atomic mass = Weighted Average of Atomic number + neutrons, for all natural isotopes of an element

Isotopes

Almost all elements that exist naturally have two or more isotopes. Isotopes are atoms of the same element that differ in mass because they have a different number of neutrons in the nucleus. The mass number of an isotope is the number of protons plus neutrons in the nucleus. These two particles make up virtually all the mass of the atom—the mass of the electrons is negligible.

For example, there are two naturally occurring isotopes of chlorine:

75.53% of all atoms are $_{17}^{35}$Cl isotopes

24.47% of all atoms are $_{17}^{37}$Cl isotopes

Consider a sample of 100 chlorine atoms,

Mass of 35 Cl isotopes = 75.53 atoms × 35 μ   = 2 643.55 μ
Mass of 37 Cl isotopes = 24.47 atoms × 37 μ   = 905.39 μ
Total mass of all 100 atoms   = 3 548.94 μ
Average mass of each atom   = 35.49 μ

This average mass of each atom is what is recorded for each element in the Periodic Table. The value for chlorine above differs from the value in the Periodic Table because of rounding off of the mass of each isotope.

Periodic Table

Many elements show similar regularities through physical and chemical properties, which led to the development of the periodic table.
All the elements in the periodic table can be grouped into three categories: metals, nonmetals, and metalloids. The metals are by far the most common; followed by nonmetals, and finally by metalloids.

The following page shows the full periodic table of elements, complete with the atomic number, atomic mass, and atomic radius of each element.

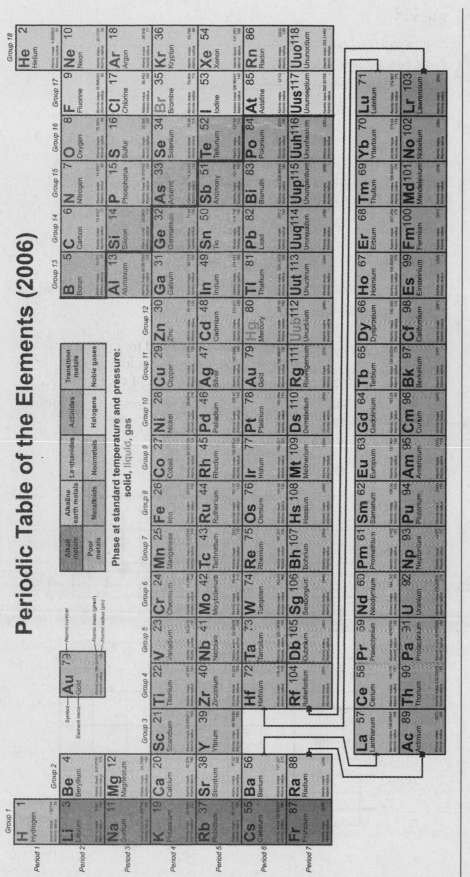

Periodic Table of the Elements (2006)

Group 18 is comprised of inert gases, also known as **Noble gases**. They are not chemically reactive at standard temperature and pressure.

Group 17, members of which are known as the **halogens**, is the only group to have elements that as a solid, liquid, and gas at standard temperature and pressure.

Any element with an atomic number higher than 92 is known as a transuranic element.

Bromine, mercury and ununbium are the only elements found in a liquid phase at standard temperature and pressure.

***See the data pages for Periodic Table of Electronegativity Using the Pauling Scale

NOTES

Metals

- are good conductors of heat
- are conductors of electricity
- are solids at room temperature, except mercury
- form positive ions

Nonmetals

- are poor conductors of both heat and electricity
- are either a solid, liquid or gas at room temperature
- form negative ions

Metalloids

- are elements that have properties that fall between metals and nonmetals
- may or may not form ions

The energy level of electrons gives the structure to the periodic table. The number of electrons in the outside energy level gives the group number (vertical columns) while the number of energy levels gives the period number (horizontal row). To show these properties, a simplified periodic table is being used.

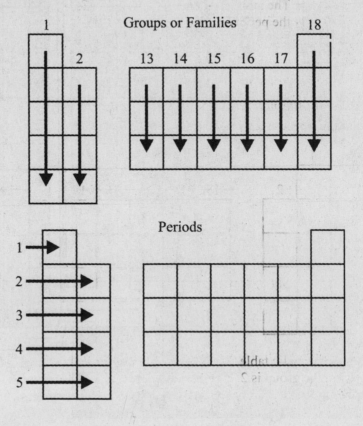

Some families of elements have historical names as shown in the periodical table below:

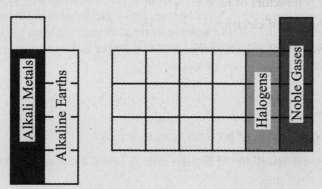

Hydrogen is not a member of the alkali metal family.

Example

Give the group and period number for magnesium (Mg)

Solution A

Draw the representation diagram for magnesium

— all element 1st level is 2, except hydrogen is 1 electrons *electron.*

Energy level = 3

The number of electrons in the outside energy level is 2. Therefore the group number is 2.

The number of energy levels is 3 (2e, 8e, 2e), therefore the period number is three.

Solution B (Alternate Method)

Using the periodic table

Group

Period

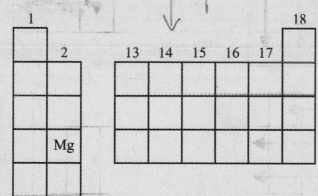

From the periodic table, Mg is located in the vertical column 2, therefore the group is 2. The horizontal row is 3. Therefore the period number is 3.

NOTES

Ions

When atoms combine to form compounds, one common way is to transfer electrons between atoms. When a transfer of electron(s) is completed, the resulting atom (with extra or fewer electrons than normal) is called an ion. An ion will always have a charge, either positive or negative, depending upon whether electrons are gained or lost.

As ions are formed, a complete outside energy level results.

A negative ion has an "ide" ending

Negative Ions

If electrons are added to the highest energy level, a negative ion is formed.

Example

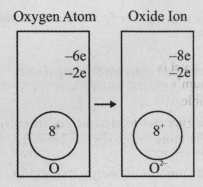

Oxygen Atom   Oxide Ion

−6e   −8e
−2e   −2e

8^+ 8^+

O O^{2-}

The outside energy level of the oxygen atom gained 2e to become an oxide ion (O^{2-})

If the outer electron level is more than half full a negative ion will result. In the example for oxygen, the outside energy level contains 6e, which is over half of its total possible of 8e.

Negative ions are also called anions.

Positive Ions

If electrons are lost from the highest energy level, resulting in the emptying of the highest energy level, a positive ion is formed.

Positive ions are also called cations.

Example

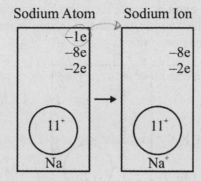

The outside energy level of the sodium atom lost its only electron to become a sodium ion (Na$^+$)

If the outer electron level is less than half full a positive ion will result. In the example, sodium's outside energy level contains 1e which is under half of its total possible of 8e.

An ion will have complete energy levels, by either gaining or losing electrons and will always have a negative or positive charge.

An ion will result when an atom gains or loses electrons.

PRACTICE EXERCISES

1. Complete the representations for the following atoms.

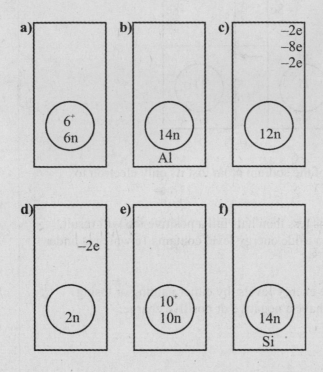

a)
6^+
$6n$

b)
$14n$
Al

c)
−2e
−8e
−2e
$12n$

d)
−2e
$2n$

e)
10^+
$10n$

f)
$14n$
Si

2. Complete the following diagrams and name the atoms.

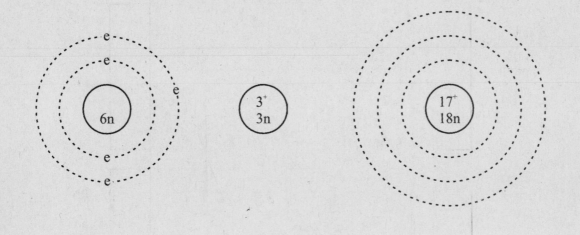

e
e
e
$6n$
e
e

3^+
$3n$

17^+
$18n$

3. Using atomic masses rounded to the nearest whole number
    (e.g. sodium (Na) 22.99 rounds to 23, sulfur (S) 32.07 rounds to 32), fill in the table:

Isotope	Atomic Number	Protons	Electrons	Neutrons	Mass Number
$^{40}_{18}$Ar	18	18	18	22	40
$^{7}_{3}$Li					7
		8			16
			24		52
$^{1}_{1}$H				0	
	13			14	
$^{28}_{13}$Al			13	15	
	29			34	

4. Given an unknown element X,
    35.60% of all atoms are $^{92}_{42}$X isotopes
    64.40% of all atoms are $^{96}_{42}$X isotopes
    What is the average mass of each X atom?

5. Using your periodic table, complete the following energy level diagrams.
    Do not include neutrons in these diagrams as their number varies.

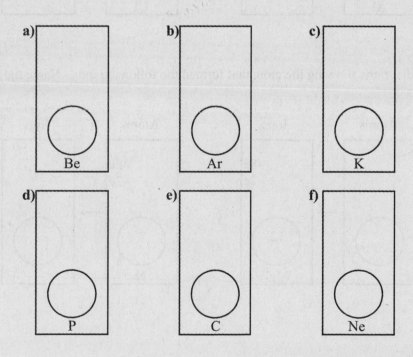

a) Be   b) Ar   c) K

d) P   e) C   f) Ne

6. Using the periodic table below, determine the group and period for the following atoms:

a) He   **b)** Al   **c)** N   **d)** Na   **e)** Cl   **f)** Ca

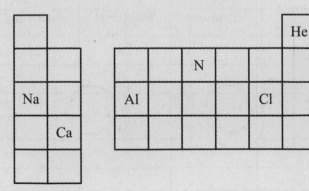

7. Complete the diagrams showing the atom to ion transformations. Name the atom and ion.

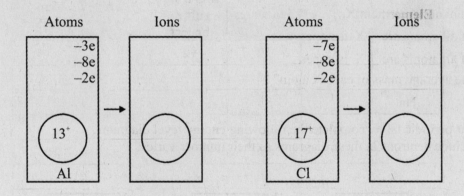

8. Complete the diagrams showing the atom that formed the following ions. Name the atom and ion.

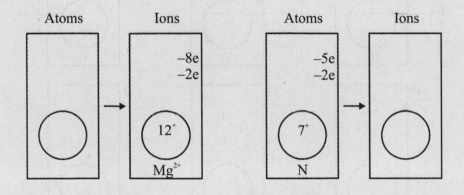

9. Complete the following diagrams. Name the atom and ion.

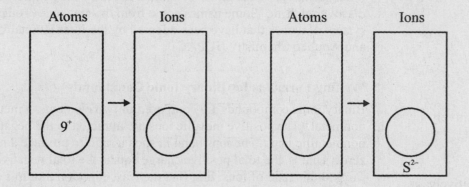

Atoms   Ions   Atoms   Ions

10. Fill in the following table:

Element	Protons	Electrons	Electrons gained or lost	Ion Charge	Ion Symbol
O	8	10	+2	2^-	O^{2-}
	9	10			
Na		10			
	13		-3		
		36			Br^-
	7	10			
	12			2^+	
		2			Li^+
	30	28			
		18	—	1^-	

Lesson 2   REVIEW OF CHEMICAL NOMENCLATURE

Chemical compounds have been named in various ways over time. Most substances were given a common name by the people who discovered them. Some names come from the ancients. Today we use a system of names that have been adopted by the International Union of Pure and Applied Chemistry (IUPAC).

Writing Formulas for Binary Ionic Compounds

Binary ionic compounds are composed of two elements–a metal and a nonmetal. The positive metallic ions are attracted to the negative nonmetallic ions. The ions bond in such a ratio to produce a net charge of zero. That is, the total positive charge equals the total negative charge. To find this ratio of ions, first find the least common multiple of the magnitude of the ion charges. The subscript for each ion can be determined by dividing the least common multiple by the charge magnitude.

Cations – positively
charged ions

Anions – <u>negatively</u>
charged ions

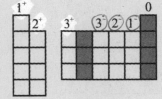

Example 1

What is the formula for aluminium oxide?

> *Solution*
> Aluminium ion is Al^{3+} and oxide ion is O^{2-}
> The least common multiple of 3 and 2 is 6.
> $$\frac{6}{3} = 2 \text{ and } \frac{6}{2} = 3$$
> Therefore, the formula is Al_2O_3.

Ion charges for the
simplified periodic table.

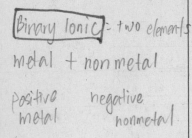

Example 2

What is the formula for magnesium chloride?

> *Solution*
> Magnesium ion is Mg^{2+} and chloride ion is Cl^-
> Least common multiple of 2 and 1 is 2.
> $$\frac{2}{2} = 1 \text{ and } \frac{2}{1} = 2$$
> Therefore, the formula is $MgCl_2$.
> (**Note:** a subscript of 1 is not shown in the formula.)

Example 3

What is the formula for magnesium oxide?

Solution

Magnesium ion is Mg^{2+} and oxygen ion is O^{2-}.
Least common multiple of 2 and 2 is 2.

$$\frac{2}{2} = 1 \text{ and } \frac{2}{2} = 1$$

Therefore, the formula is MgO.
(The subscript of 1 is not shown in the formula.)

Example 4

Write the two ions, placing the positive ion first, followed by the negative ion. The numerical value becomes the subscript of the opposite ion. Do not use the + or – charge in the formula. If the two subscripts have a common factor, divide each subscript by the common factor.

a) aluminium oxide

b) magnesium chloride

c) magnesium oxide

Solution
a) Al^{3+} O^{2-} Al_2O_3
b) Mg^{2+} Cl^{1-} $MgCl_2$
c) Mg^{2+} O^{2-} MgO

One ionic compound that is an exception to the common multiple rule is Na_2O_2, sodium peroxide.

Naming Binary Ionic Compounds

When naming compounds, the metal ion is named first followed by the nonmetal ion. Note that the suffix of the nonmetal ion is -ide.
All binary ionic compounds end in "-ide"

Example 5

What is the name of K_2S?

Solution

K is the symbol for potassium and S is the symbol for sulfur.
Therefore, the name is potassium sulfide.

NOTES

Example 6

What is the name of $CaBr_2$?

Solution

Ca is the symbol for calcium and Br is the symbol for bromine
Therefore, the name is calcium bromide.

Polyvalent Cation.

Naming and Writing Formulas with Ions that have Multiple Charges

Some metals form two ions with different charges. The IUPAC system distinguishes between these two ions by using a Roman numeral in the name of the compound to indicate the ion.

Example 7

What is the formula for iron (III) oxide?

This method is also known as the STOCK system.

Solution

Iron (III) ion is Fe^{3+} and oxide ion is O^{2-}.
The least common multiple of 3 and 2 is 6

$$\frac{6}{3} = 2 \text{ and } \frac{6}{2} = 3$$

Therefore the formula is Fe_2O_3.

Example 8

What is the name of SnI_4? *— oxygen* $Sn^{4+, 2+}$ $Sn^{4+} \ I^-_4$

$4(1)=4$

$\frac{4}{4}=1 \quad \frac{4}{1}=4 = SnI_4$

Solution

I^- is the symbol for an iodide ion and Sn^{4+} is the symbol for tin (IV) ion. (The charge must be 4+ to "balance" the negative charge.)
Therefore, the name is tin (IV) iodide.

more than 1 ionic *Tin (IV) iodide*
can be positive/negative ion

Naming and Writing Formulas Involving Complex (Polyatomic) Ions

Polyatomic ions are groups of atoms bonded together that collectively carry a charge because of an excess or deficiency of electrons. The more common polyatomic ions are listed in a data table or in your textbook. Negative polyatomic ions will generally have a suffix of -ate or -ite. If more than one polyatomic ion is bonded to another ion or ions, the formula of the polyatomic ion must be bracketed.

Polyatomic ions
with (oxygen) (o).

Net charge must be zero

"ate" – high oxygen
"ite" – low oxygen

② Complex Polyatomic Ions Compound.
(+)   (-)
Metal + Non metal
Ion   Polyatomic
Ions..
(ate, ite).
– if more than one polyatomic (bracket).

16

Example 9

What is the formula for magnesium nitrate?

Solution

Magnesium ion is Mg^{2+} and nitrate ion NO_3^-
The least common multiple of 2 and 1 is 2.

$$\frac{2}{2} = 1 \text{ and } \frac{2}{1} = 2$$

Therefore, the formula is $Mg(NO_3)_2$

Example 10

What is the name of Na_2SO_4?

Solution

Na^+ is the symbol for sodium and SO_4^{2-} is the formula for a sulfate ion.
Therefore, the name is sodium sulfate.

Naming and Writing Formulas for Molecular Compounds

Not all compounds are composed of positive and negative ions.
Nonmetal atoms can bond together to form compounds composed of
molecules. Some of these compounds are given special names.
Latin and Greek prefixes are used to indicate the number of atoms per
molecule of each element.

Molecular hydrogen
compounds do not use
prefixes.

e.g. H_2Se – hydrogen
selinide

Number	Prefix		Number	Prefix
1	mono		6	hexa
2	di		7	hepta
3	tri		8	octa
4	tetra		9	nona
5	penta		10	deca

The prefix mono is usually used for the second element only in the
compound name. No prefix means "mono".

Example 11

What is the formula for nitrogen dioxide?

Solution

Mono (1) N with di (2) O
The formula is NO_2

17

Example 12

What is the name for P_2O_5?

Solution

The prefix for 2 is di and the prefix for 5 is penta.
The name is diphosphorus pentaoxide. (To avoid the double vowel, diphosphorus pentoxide is also acceptable.)

Molecular Compounds to be Memorized

Some molecular compounds have traditional names that do not conform to the IUPAC naming system. The names and formulas for the following compounds need to be memorized:

nonmetal + nonmetal. A.

Ammonium NH4
Ethane C2H6

(+) $NH_{3(g)}$	ammonia
$C_6H_{12}O_{6(s)}$	glucose
$C_{12}H_{22}O_{11(s)}$	sucrose
$CH_{4(g)}$	methane
$C_3H_{8(g)}$	propane
$CH_3COOH_{(aq)}$	acetic acid
$H_2O_{(l)}$	water
$O_{3(g)}$	ozone
$CH_3OH_{(l)}$	methanol
$C_2H_5OH_{(l)}$	ethanol
$H_2O_{2(l)}$	hydrogen peroxide

The following elements only exist in molecular form and their formulas also need to be memorized:

$P_{4(s)}$	phosphorous
$S_{8(s)}$	sulfur
$H_{2(g)}$	hydrogen gas
$O_{2(g)}$	oxygen gas
$N_{2(g)}$	nitrogen gas
$F_{2(g)}$	fluorine gas
$Cl_{2(g)}$	chlorine gas
$Br_{2(l)}$	bromine
$I_{2(s)}$	iodine

hydrogen + non metal
hydrogen + oxygen (less + more)

Naming and Writing Formulas for Acids

Acids are compounds that contain <u>hydrogen</u> and are in aqueous solution (dissolved in water). To name or write a formula for acids it is easiest to write or name the compound as if it were an ionic <u>hydrogen compound</u>. See the notes above for naming and writing formulas for ionic compounds.

① **Binary Acids:** Consist of two elements, the <u>first one</u> always being <u>hydrogen</u>. The <u>second element</u> will be a <u>nonmetal</u> and always ends in "ide".

② **Oxy Acids:** Consist of two ions, the first one being <u>hydrogen</u>. The second ion is a <u>complex ion</u> that contains <u>oxygen</u> and will end with "ate" or "ite".

The following table summarizes acid names.

Binary acid = (two elements)
hydrogen + non-metal "ide"
(1st) + (2nd)
element   element.

Oxy Acid = two ions.
hydrogen + Complex ion
that contains
OXYGEN
"ate" or "ite"

Compound Name		Acid Name		Acid Type
hydrogen_____ide		hydro_____ic acid		binary acid
hydrogen_____ate		_____ic acid		oxy acid
hydrogen_____ite		_____ous acid		oxy acid

Binary Acid *OXY Acids*

non metal

hydrogen + non metal "ide"
hydrogen + more oxygen
hydrogen + less oxygen
(E) monatomic anion (single ion)

Simply fill in the base part of the <u>nonmetal element name</u>. The *exceptions are <u>sulfur</u> and <u>phosphorus acids</u> where the "ur" or "or" must be added.

Example 13

Binary

What is the formula for <u>hydrosulfuric acid</u>?

Solution
Hydrosulfuric acid becomes hydrogen sulfide
Hydrogen ion is H^+ and sulfide ion is S^{2-}
The formula for hydrosulfuric acid is $H_2S_{(aq)}$

Hydrogen ___ide

Example 14

What is the name of $HClO_{3(aq)}$?

Solution
H^+ is a hydrogen ion and ClO_3^- is a chlorate ion
Therefore, hydrogen chlorate becomes chloric acid

with oxygen = Polyatomic (more than 1 ion)
Negative
stay
H^+ ClO_3^-
H ___ Cl ↓
Acid.

hydrogen ___ ate
hydrogen ___ ite

(A) Acid Compound

(a) Binary Acids: (2 elements)
(+)   (-)
Hydrogen + Non metal
(element)   (element) (ide)
⇒ Hydro___ic Acid with change

(b) Oxy Acids: (2 ions)
(+)
Hydrogen + complex ion with Oxygen
negative Polyatomic ⇒ (ate, ite)
more oxy   less oxy

(i) More oxy. (ate)
___ ic acid.

(ii) Less oxy (ite).
___ ous acid.

PRACTICE EXERCISES

1. Write the formula for the given compounds.
    (The first is done as an example):

Binary Ionic Compound: two elements *"ide"*
non metal.
metal

Compound Name	Metal Ion (+)	Non Metal Ion (−)	Formula
sodium nitride	Na^+, sodium	N^{3-}, nitride	Na_3N
lithium oxide			
zinc chloride			
silver bromide			
potassium nitride			
aluminium sulfide			

2. Write the name for the following formulas:

Formula	Compound Name
NaI	
$MgCl_2$	
ZnO	
$AlBr_3$	
BaS	

3. Write names for the following compounds:

Formula	Metal Ion Charge	Non-Metal Charge	Name
$NiCl_3$			
MnO			
Cr_2O_3			
$CuCl_2$			
PbO_2			

4. Write formulas for the following compounds:

Name	Formula
nickel (II) iodide	
lead (II) nitride	
tin (IV) oxide	
antimony (III) chloride	
copper (II) oxide	

5. Write the formulas of the following compounds:

Polyatomic Ion with oxygen
"ate"
"ite"

Net charge = zero.

Name	Positive Ion Charge	Negative Ion Charge	Formula
sodium chlorate			
aluminium sulfate			
copper (II) sulfate *Nitrate*			
lithium hydroxide			
magnesium nitrate			

6. Write the names of the following compounds:

Formula	Name
$Ba_3(PO_4)_2$	
Na_2CO_3	
$Fe(NO_3)_3$	
$MgSO_4$	
Ag_2CO_3	

7. Write the formulas of the following compounds:

Nonmetal + non metal. (Molecular Compound).

Name	Formula
sulfur dioxide	
carbon monoxide	
* hydrogen sulfide	
sulfur dichloride	
tetraphosphorus decaoxide	

hydrogen no prefix

8. Write the names of the following compounds:

Formula	Name
SiO_2	
OCl_2	
SO_3	
CO_2	
NO_2	

9. Write the names of the following acids:

Formula	Binary or Oxy	Name
$HCl_{(aq)}$		
$H_2SO_{4(aq)}$		
$H_3BO_{3(aq)}$		
$HNO_{2(aq)}$		

10. Write the formulas of the following acids:

Name	Binary or Oxy	Formula
hydrofluoric acid		
nitric acid		
sulfurous acid		
phosphorous acid		

All of the preceding naming and writing formulas have been mixed in the following two exercises.

11. Write formulas for the following compounds and indicate whether
    they are ionic (i), molecular (m) or acid (a):

Name	Formula	Type
sodium bromide		
iron (II) chloride		
calcium hydroxide		
potassium sulfite		
magnesium sulfide		
phosphorus trichloride		
glucose		
ammonium sulfate		
cobalt (II) nitrate		

Name	Formula	Type
dinitrogen tetraoxide		
sulfurous acid		
hydrochloric acid		
ammonia		
hypochlorous acid		
hydrobromic acid		
phosphoric acid		
chloric acid		
carbon monoxide		

12. Write names for the following compounds and indicate whether they are ionic (i), molecular (m) or
    acid (a):

Formula	Name	Type
K_2SO_3		
$Fe(NO_3)_3$		
$K_2Cr_2O_7$		
$Ca(NO_2)_2$		
$KMnO_4$		
$H_2CO_{3(aq)}$		
N_2O_3		
$(NH_4)_2SO_3$		
$Ca(C_{17}H_{35}COO)_2$		

Formula	Name	Type
$NaHCO_3$		
$C_{12}H_{22}O_{11}$		
N_2O		
CH_4		
$H_2SO_{4(aq)}$		
$HI_{(aq)}$		
$Na_2S_2O_3$		
$NaCN$		
P_2O_5		

Lesson 3   CHEMICAL EQUATIONS

Chemical equations are the chemist's way of representing chemical reactions by using symbols and formulas to represent the elements and compounds involved. Equations must be "balanced" to ensure that atoms (and, therefore, mass) are conserved.

For example, dinitrogen pentaoxide decomposes into the two elements: nitrogen and oxygen.

Step 1: Represent the reactant and products with formulas.

$$N_2O_{5(s)} \rightarrow N_{2(g)} + O_{2(g)}$$

(handwritten: odd · even · (balance oxygen by multiplying 5) 5×2=10)

Step 2: When there is an odd number of atoms of an element on one side and an even number on the other side, find a common multiple. For oxygen, the common multiple of 5 and 2 is 10.

Step 3: Multiply each formula by a coefficient to represent the same number of atoms of oxygen on both sides.

$$2N_2O_{5(s)} \rightarrow N_{2(g)} + 5O_{2(g)}$$

(handwritten: odd even· 2×5=10 = 5×2=10 BALANCED)

Step 4: Add coefficients to the remaining formulas to "balance" the remaining atoms. There must be 4 atoms of nitrogen represented on both sides.

(handwritten: 2×2=4 2×2=4 = BALANCED ·)

$$2N_2O_{5(s)} \rightarrow 2N_{2(g)} + 5O_{2(g)}$$

Step 5: Check to make sure all atoms are balanced.

Left side: 4 N and 10 O   Right side: 4 N and 10 O

(handwritten working:
$$2N_2O_5 \rightarrow 2N_2 + 5O_2$$
2×2 2×5   2×2=4N 5×2=10 O
=4N =10 O)

Remember when the following elements are alone, they are represented as:

H₂ *Hydrogen*   N₂ *Nitrogen*

O₂ *Oxygen*   F₂ *Florine*

Cl₂ *Clorine*   Br₂ *Bromine*

I₂ *Iodine*   At₂ *Ashtine*

S₈ *Sulfur*   P₄ *Phosphorus*

They never exist as single atoms.

Types of Reactions

All reactions can be classified as being one of six types:

1. Simple Composition (SC) or Formation (F). Two elements combine to form a compound. For example:

   $2Na_{(s)} + Cl_{2(g)} \rightarrow 2NaCl_{(s)}$

   1 + 1 → 1

2. Simple Decomposition (SD). A compound decomposes into two elements. For example:

   $2HgO_{(s)} \rightarrow 2Hg_{(l)} + O_{2(g)}$

   1 → 1 + 1

3. Single Replacement (SR). An element and compound react to form a different element and compound. For example:

   an element

   $Zn_{(s)} + Cu(NO_3)_{2(aq)} \rightarrow Zn(NO_3)_{2(aq)} + Cu_{(s)}$

   element + compound → compound + element. element

   1 + compound → compound + 1 element

4. Double Replacement (DR). Two compounds form two new compounds. For example:

   $HCl_{(aq)} + NaOH_{(aq)} \rightarrow NaCl_{(aq)} + H_2O_{(l)}$

   Compound + compound → compound + compound

   (hydrocarbon + oxygen gas) or (g) + (g)

5. Hydrocarbon Combustion (HC). A hydrocarbon reacts with oxygen gas to form carbon dioxide gas and water vapour. For example:

   $CH_{4(g)} + 2O_{2(g)} \rightarrow CO_{2(g)} + 2H_2O_{(g)}$

   Hydrocarbon + oxygen gas → carbon dioxide gas + water vapour.

6. Others (O). This category is for all reactions that do not fit into the categories listed above. For example:

   $2KClO_{3(s)} \rightarrow 2KCl_{(s)} + 3O_{2(g)}$

Writing and Balancing Equations When Only One Side Is Given

Knowing the five predictable types of equations, the product or reactant side of an equation can be obtained when only products or reactants are given.

Example

$$Mg_{(s)} + O_{2(g)} \rightarrow$$

Solution

In this case, analyze the two reactants: both elements, therefore it is a formation reaction which forms only one compound, which is $MgO_{(s)}$.

$$Mg_{(s)} + O_{2(g)} \rightarrow MgO_{(s)}$$

Now balance the equation:

$$2Mg_{(s)} + O_{2(g)} \rightarrow 2MgO_{(s)}$$

Example

$$Na_{(s)} + ZnCl_{2(aq)} \rightarrow$$

Solution

Look at the two reactants: an element and a compound which indicates that it is a single replacement. $Na_{(s)}$ is a metal (+ ion); therefore it will replace the metal in the compound, Zn, to produce $NaCl_{(aq)}$.

(element) + (compound) =

$$Na_{(s)} + ZnCl_{2(aq)} \rightarrow NaCl_{(aq)} + Zn_{(s)}$$

(metal) (metal)   (replaced metal)   (metal)

Now balance the equation:

$$2Na_{(s)} + ZnCl_{2(aq)} \rightarrow 2NaCl_{(aq)} + Zn_{(s)}$$

Single replacement: metal replaces the positive ion in the compound; non-metal replaces the negative ion in the compound

In single replacement reactions, the element must be analyzed to determine whether it is a metal or a nonmetal. A metal element will replace the metal in a compound, while a nonmetal will replace the non-metal in a compound.

ACTIVITIES

Activity 1

Title

Types of Chemical Reactions: Simple Composition

Problem

What are the properties of the compound produced by the reaction of magnesium burning in air?

Materials

magnesium ribbon	tongs
beaker	Bunsen burner
water	

Procedure

1. Use tongs to hold the magnesium ribbon while igniting it in the Bunsen burner.
2. Hold the burning magnesium in a beaker to collect a sample of the product.
3. Observe the product. Note its color, phase, texture, and solubility in water.
4. Safcty Precaution: **Avoid Looking Directly At The Burning Magnesium.**

Observations

	Colour	Phase	Texture	Solubility in Water
Before $Mg_{(s)}$				
After Product				

Conclusion

Analysis

1. What evidence did you observe that indicated that a chemical reaction occurred?

2. Write the balanced chemical equation for the observed chemical reaction.

3. Name the product formed in this chemical reaction.

4. Suggest another possible chemical reaction that might be occurring in this experiment.
    Write a balanced equation for this reaction.

Activity 2

Title
A Single Replacement Reaction

Problem
What products form when calcium metal is added to water?

Prediction
Write a balanced equation (including state of matter subscripts) for the reaction you expect to occur.

Materials

water	splint
$Ca_{(s)}$	matches
test tubes	scoopula
test tube rack	litmus paper

Procedure
1. Fill a test tube half full with tap water.
2. Add a "pinch" of calcium metal tailings to the test tube of water and quickly invert a second test tube over the reaction vessel to capture any reaction product formed as a gas.
3. Perform any diagnostic tests possible to verify the identity of the products formed.
4. Safety Precaution: **Avoid Skin Contact With Both Reactants And Products.**

Observations

1. Describe any products observed being formed.

2. Describe the results of any diagnostic tests performed.

Conclusion

Write a conclusion for this experiment.

Activity 3

Title

Types of Chemical Reactions: Double Replacement

Problem

What properties are formed when the given aqueous ionic compounds are mixed?

Prediction

Make a predication based on the generalizations you have learned about double replacement reactions.

Materials

Either aqueous calcium chloride and aqueous sodium carbonate
or, aqueous nickel (II) nitrate and aqueous sodium hydroxide and

2 test tubes	filter funnel
test tube rack	filter paper
ring stand	glass rod
utility clamp	50 mL beaker

Experimental design

The two aqueous ionic compounds provided will be mixed together in one of the test tubes and the properties of any products formed described. Any insoluble products formed are to be separated from the reaction mixture by filtration. If the set of reagents are used first, diagnostic tests to be described by the teacher are to be performed.

Procedure

Write up a step by step procedure for this experiment.

Observations

Design a means of reporting the observations to be recorded in this experiment.

Analysis

1. Write a balanced equation for the reaction observed (use your solubility table to verify the identity of any insoluble products).

2. State any evidence you have to verify the identify of the products formed. (e.g., diagnostic tests preformed, agreement with the solubility table, etc.)

3. State a conclusion for the experiment.

PRACTICE EXERCISES

1. For each of the following equations, identify the type of reaction and add coefficients to balance the equation. Use initials for reaction type.

    Type

    a) ____ ____ $N_{2(g)}$ + ____ $H_{2(g)} \rightarrow$ ____ $NH_{3(g)}$

    b) ____ ____ $Na_{(s)}$ + ____ $Cl_{2(g)} \rightarrow$ ____ $NaCl_{(s)}$

    c) ____ ____ $H_2O_{(l)} \rightarrow$ ____ $H_{2(g)}$ + ____ $O_{2(g)}$

    d) ____ ____ $Na_{(s)}$ + ____ $H_2O_{(l)} \rightarrow$ ____ $NaOH_{(aq)}$ + ____ $H_{2(g)}$

    e) ____ ____ $Zn_{(s)}$ + ____ $HCl_{(aq)} \rightarrow$ ____ $ZnCl_{2(aq)}$ + ____ $H_{2(g)}$

    f) ____ ____ $CH_{4(g)}$ + ____ $O_{2(g)} \rightarrow$ ____ $CO_{2(g)}$ + ____ $H_2O_{(g)}$

    g) ____ ____ $P_{4(s)}$ + ____ $Cl_{2(g)} \rightarrow$ ____ $PCl_{5(s)}$

    h) ____ ____ $CoCl_{2(aq)}$ + ____ $Na_{(s)} \rightarrow$ ____ $NaCl_{(aq)}$ + ____ $Co_{(s)}$

    i) ____ ____ $Na_3PO_{4(aq)}$ + ____ $MgCl_{2(aq)} \rightarrow$ ____ $Mg_3(PO_4)_{2(s)}$ + ____ $NaCl_{(aq)}$

    j) ____ ____ $C_4H_{10(g)}$ + ____ $O_{2(g)} \rightarrow$ ____ $CO_{2(g)}$ + ____ $H_2O_{(g)}$

    k) ____ ____ $P_2O_{5(s)} \rightarrow$ ____ $P_{4(s)}$ + ____ $O_{2(g)}$

    l) ____ ____ $Al_{(s)}$ + ____ $Cu(NO_2)_{2(aq)} \rightarrow$ ____ $Cu_{(s)}$ + ____ $Al(NO_2)_{3(aq)}$

    m) ____ ____ $CaCl_{2(s)}$ + ____ $H_2SO_{4(aq)} \rightarrow$ ____ $CaSO_{4(s)}$ + ____ $HCl_{(aq)}$

2. For each of the following word equations or descriptions, write and balance an equation to represent the reaction. Identify the type of reaction.

    a) Magnesium metal reacts with hydrochloric acid to form magnesium chloride and hydrogen gas, H_2.

    b) Aluminium metal reacts with iron (III) oxide to form iron metal and aluminium oxide.

    c) Barium hydroxide solution reacts with sulfuric acid to produce solid barium calcium sulfate and water.

d) Elemental sulfur, S_8, reacts with oxygen gas, O_2, to form sulfur trioxide gas.

e) Lead (II) oxide is decomposed into lead metal and oxygen gas, O_2.

f) Propane gas, C_3H_8, burns by combining with oxygen gas to produce carbon dioxide gas and water vapour.

In doing the next few problems, refer to the classifications of reactions.
Remember to balance the equation.

3. ___ $H_{2(g)}$ + ___ $O_{2(g)}$ →

4. ___ $KCl_{(s)}$ →

5. ___ $MgCl_{2(aq)}$ + ___ $Al_2O_{3(s)}$ →

6. ___ $Cl_{2(g)}$ + ___ $NaI_{(aq)}$ →

7. ___ $KCl_{(aq)}$ + ___ $AgNO_{3(aq)}$ →

8. ___ $Pb_{(s)}$ + ___ $ZnBr_{2(aq)}$ →

Lesson 4 MOLES

Since individual atoms or molecules are far too small to be counted individually, chemists use "moles" to represent the amount of a pure substance. One mole is 6.02×10^{23} particles.

Activity 1

Measure out 18.0 mL of water using a graduated cylinder.
The cylinder contains 1 mol of water, which is made up of 6.02×10^{23} water molecules.

The symbol for mole is mol

Activity 2

How long will it take to count a mole of marbles?   If a machine counts 1 marble per second, and it counts 24 hours per day and 365 days per year, how many years will it take?

6.02×10^{23} is known as Avogadro's number.

A mole is like a dozen, only much larger.

Example 1

Using the two above activities as models, why do scientists use mass or volume measurements to calculate the number of moles?

Solution

Molar mass is the mass in grams of one mole of a pure substance. Using moles allows us to change the unit of mass from atomic mass units μ, per atom to grams per mole, g/mol. It remains numerically the same.
For a compound, molar mass is the sum of the masses of all moles of each element represented in the formula.

Example 2

What is the molar mass of sucrose, $C_{12}H_{22}O_{11}$?

In calculating molar mass, always use two digits after the decimal point.

Solution

Each mole of sucrose consists of 12 moles of C atoms, 22 moles of H atoms, and 11 moles of O atoms.

$$12 \text{ mol C} \times 12.01 \text{ g/mol} = \quad 144.12 \text{ g}$$
$$22 \text{ mol H} \times 1.01 \text{ g/mol} = \quad 22.22 \text{ g}$$
$$11 \text{ mol O} \times 16.00 \text{ g/mol} = \quad 176.00 \text{ g}$$
$$1 \text{ mol of } C_{12}H_{22}O_{11} \quad = \quad 342.34 \text{ g}$$

The molar mass of sucrose is 342.34 g/mol.

Dimensional Analysis

Any mathematical relationship can be converted into two "unit conversion" multipliers that allow one to easily convert between the two units in the mathematical relationship.

Example 3

How do we find unit conversion multipliers?

Solution

1 000 g   =   1 kg can be written

$$\frac{1\,000\,g}{1\,kg} \quad \text{or} \quad \frac{1\,kg}{1\,000\,g}$$

The first form can be used to convert kg amounts to g; the second to convert g to kg. "Bottom" units are always being converted into the "top" units.

Example 4

5.3 kg = _____ g   576 g = _____ kg

Solution

$$5.3\,kg \times \frac{1\,000}{1\,kg} = 5\,300\,g \qquad 576\,g \times \frac{1\,kg}{1\,000\,g} = 0.576\,kg$$

Chemistry conversions can be done this way.

Example 5

Find the number of particles in 0.56 moles of $Cl_{2(g)}$.

Solution

Since 1 mol = 6.02×10^{23} particles

$$0.56\,mol \times \frac{6.02 \times 10^{23}\,molecules}{1\,mol}$$

$$= 3.37 \times 10^{23}\,molecules$$

Example 6

Find the number of moles in 6.50 g of NaCl(s).

Solution

For $NaCl_{(s)}$, 1 mol = 58.44 g of NaCl

$$\begin{array}{ll} 22.99 & (Na) \\ +\,35.45 & (Cl) \\ \hline 58.44\,g/mol \end{array}$$

$$6.50\,g \times \frac{1\,mol}{58.44\,g} = 0.111\,mol$$

Example 7

Find the mass of 4.25 mol of $NaCl_{(s)}$.

Solution

$$4.25 \text{ mol} \times \frac{58.44 \text{ g}}{1 \text{ mol}} = 248 \text{ g}$$

Several unit conversions can be used in sequence.

Example 8

How many atoms are there in 7.95 g of $NO_{2(g)}$?

Solution

$$\begin{array}{cc} 14.01 & (N) \\ \text{Molar mass of } NO_2 \quad + 2(16.00) & (O) \\ \hline 46.01 \text{ g/mol} \end{array}$$

$$7.95 \text{ g} \times \frac{1 \text{ mol}}{46.01 \text{ g}} \times \frac{6.02 \times 10^{23} \text{ molecules}}{1 \text{ mol}} \times \frac{3 \text{ atoms}}{1 \text{ molecule}}$$

$$= 3.12 \times 10^{23} \text{ atoms}$$

We used these relationships in the above example:

for $NO_{2(g)}$ 1 mol   = 46.01 g
for any molecular substance 1 mol   = 6.02×10^{23} molecules
in $NO_{2(g)}$ 1 molecule   = 3 atoms

Finding the Number of Moles or the Mass of a Sample

Let n represent the number of moles of a pure substance
          m represent the mass of a sample of a pure substance, and
          M represent the molar mass

Then,   the number of moles, $n = \dfrac{m}{M}$

        the mass of a sample, $m = nM$, and

        the molar mass, $M = \dfrac{m}{n}$

NOTES

Example 9

Calculate the number of moles of NaCl in 205 g of the compound.

Solution

Molar mass of NaCl:
1 mol of Na × 22.99 g/mol = 22.99 g
1 mol of Cl × 35.45 g/mol = 35.45 g
1 mol = 58.44 g

$$n = \frac{m}{M} = \frac{205 \text{ g}}{58.44 \text{ g/mol}} = 3.51 \text{ mol}$$

Alternatively, this step can be set up as a proportion.

$$\frac{x \text{ mol NaCl}}{205 \text{ g}} = \frac{1 \text{ mol NaCl}}{58.44 \text{ g}}$$
$$x = 3.51 \text{ mol}$$

Example 10

Calculate the mass of a 0.750 mol of $K_2SO_{4(s)}$.

Solution

Molar mass of K_2SO_4:
2 mol K × 39.10 g/mol = 78.20 g
1 mol S × 32.06 g/mol = 32.06 g
4 mol O × 16.00 g/mol = 64.00 g
1 mol = 174.26 g

$$m = nM = 0.750 \text{ mol} \times 174.26 \text{ g/mol} = 131 \text{ g}$$

Alternatively, this step can be set up as a proportion.

$$\frac{x \text{ g of } K_2SO_4}{0.750 \text{ mol}} = \frac{174.26 \text{ g } K_2SO_4}{1 \text{ mol}}$$
$$x = 131 \text{ g}$$

PRACTICE EXERCISES

1. Calculate the molar mass of the following compounds:

Formula	Name	Molar Mass (g/mol)
Na_2SO_4		
$Ca(NO_3)_2$		
N_2O_5		
$K_2Cr_2O_7$		
Al_2O_3		
$(NH_4)_2SO_4$		

2. Fill in the blanks of the following table:

Compound	Numbers of Atoms or Molecules	Number of Moles	Mass (g)
$NaCl_{(s)}$	6.02×10^{25}		
$AgNO_{3(s)}$		0.650	
$K_{(s)}$	1.50×10^{23}		
$Zn_{(s)}$			200 g
$Cl_{2(g)}$		3.20	
$NaOH_{(aq)}$			60.0 g
$HCl_{(g)}$	1.20×10^{25}		

3. Complete the following table:

	Compound	Name	Molar Mass (g/mol)	Number Of Moles (mol)	Mass (g)
1	$CH_{4(g)}$				34.7
2	$CuCl_{2(s)}$				115
3	$Ca(NO_3)_{2(s)}$				455
4	$CO_{2(g)}$				6.75
5	$ZnS_{(s)}$				885
6	$(NH_4)_2SO_{4(s)}$				75.0
7	$C_2H_{6(g)}$	ethane		2.55	
8	$MgBr_{2(s)}$			25.5	
9	$NiCl_{2(s)}$			33.4	
10	$Fe_2O_{3(s)}$			0.115	
11	$HCl_{(g)}$			5.75	
12	$K_2Cr_2O_{7(s)}$			0.012 5	

REVIEW SUMMARY

- Atoms consist of protons, neutrons and electrons. The number of protons in an element is the same as its atomic number.

- In an electrically neutral atom, the number of protons must always equal the number of electrons. The number of neutrons can vary. Protons and neutrons make up the majority of the mass of the atom.

- Electrons exist at different energy levels in an atom. The number of electrons in each level goes up in a pattern: 2, 8, 8, 16 and so on.

- Isotopes are atoms that can have varying numbers of neutrons in the nucleus of the atom.

- The Periodic Table is constructed to show organization amongst the elements, that are grouped according to shared characteristics.

- Ions are atoms that lost or gained electrons when they combined with other atom(s) to form an ionic compound.

- The loss of electrons creates a positive ion (cation) whereas the gain of electrons forms a negative ion (anion).

- Ionic compounds form when a metallic ion combines with a non-metallic ion to form a compound.

- The formula for an ionic compound is based on balancing the charges of the ions, which forms an electrically neutral compound. The number of positive charges balances the number of negative charges.

- Nonmetals can combine to form molecular compounds.

- Acids contain hydrogen and are compounds that are dissolved in water.

- Binary acids consist of hydrogen and one other non-metallic element. The name for the nonmetal is written last and ends in the suffix "ide".

- Oxy acids consist of hydrogen and a complex (polyatomic) ion that has to have oxygen in it. The name for the complex ion is written last and ends in either "ate" or "ite".

- Chemical reaction equations can be balanced to ensure that the same number of atoms of each element appear on the right hand side of the equation as did on the left. This makes sense when considering that atoms are only being rearranged in a reaction, and are not being created nor destroyed in the process.

- Six reaction types were presented in this course: Simple Composition of Formation, Simple Decomposition, Single Replacement, Double Replacement, Hydrocarbon Combustion, and Other.

- Reaction products can be predicted based on knowing the reactants and estimating what is likely to happen.

- The mole is an amount of a pure substance. One mole consists of 6.02×10^{23} particles of the substance. In calculations, the symbol for a mole is mol.

- Molar mass is the mass of one mole of the substance. The periodic table presents masses for each element, which effectively is the number of grams per mol of the element.

PRACTICE TEST

1. Without using your periodic table, give either the name or symbol of the following elements:

Symbol	Name
	carbon
Al	
Li	
	fluorine
	neon
	oxygen
Au	

Symbol	Name
Ag	
	magnesium
Cl	
Ni	
Na	
	iron
	potassium

2. Draw an atom representation for:
   a) sulfur

   b) potassium

3. Complete the ion representation

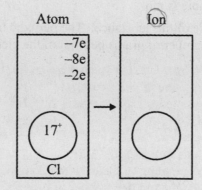

4. Fill in the blanks in the following table for each isotope:

Atomic Number	Protons	Electrons	Neutrons	Mass Number	Isotope Symbol
	12			24	
					$_{1}^{1}\text{H}$
		17	18		
				39	

5. Place the letter identifying the element in the appropriate space on the following table. Shade in the halogen family.

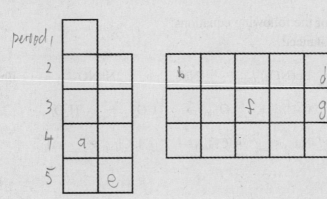

a) An alkali metal in period 4
c) A noble gas in period 1
e) An alkaline earth in period 5
g) A gas in group 17 period 3

b) Found in group 13 period 2
d) A halogen in period 2
f) A metalloid in period 3

6. Match the following:

_____ isotope	**a)** polyatomic ion
_____ cations	**b)** the total possible electrons in the first energy level
_____ sodium	**c)** molecular compound
_____ ide	**d)** an element that contains differing number of neutrons in the nucleus
_____ two	**e)** acid
_____ lose	**f)** positive ions
_____ $HCl_{(aq)}$	**g)** an alkali metal
_____ electrons	**h)** the ending of binary ionic compound
_____ gains	**i)** in an atom the number of protons and _____ are equal
_____ SO_4^{2-}	**j)** fluorine _____ one electron to become an ion
_____ $CO_{2(g)}$	**k)** to become a positive ion, an atom will _____ electrons

7. Fill in the table:

Formula	Name
$CH_{4(g)}$	
	ammonia
$H_2SO_{4(aq)}$	
	hydrofluoric acid
$Cu(ClO_3)_{2(s)}$	
$CH_3OH_{(l)}$	
	sucrose

Formula	Name
$Al_2O_{3(s)}$	
	iron (III) oxide
$Na_2CO_{3(s)}$	
$Mg(NO_3)_{2(s)}$	
	tetraphosphorous decaoxide
$HCl_{(aq)}$	
	ozone

8. Balance and indicate the type of the following equations:

Type   Balanced

a) _____   ___ $Pb(NO_3)_{2(aq)}$ + ___ $NaI_{(aq)}$ → ___ $NaNO_{3(aq)}$ + ___ $PbI_{2(s)}$

b) _____   ___ $C_2H_{6(g)}$ + ___ $O_{2(g)}$ → ___ $CO_{2(g)}$ + ___ $H_2O_{(g)}$

c) _____   ___ $Na_{(s)}$ + ___ $AlCl_{3(aq)}$ → ___ $NaCl_{(aq)}$ + ___ $Al_{(s)}$

9. Given the word equation, write and balance the equation that represents the reaction. Identify the reaction type.

Type:

a) _____ Aqueous sodium hydroxide reacts with sulfuric acid to produce aqueous sodium sulfate and water.

b) _____ Water decomposes into hydrogen gas and oxygen gas.

c) _____ Phosphorous solid reacts with chlorine gas to form solid phosphorous pentachloride.

Use the following information to answer the next question.

- 20.0 g of $NaOH_{(s)}$
- 2.00×10^{23} molecules of $H_2O_{(l)}$
- 0.400 mol of $CH_{4(g)}$

10. Which of the above has the greatest mass?

11. Given 0.50 mol of $C_{12}H_{22}O_{11(s)}$

    a) The mass of the sample is _____

    b) The number of sugar molecules in the sample is _____

    c) The number of carbon atoms present in the sample is _____

12. Complete the following table?

Compound	Formula	Molar Mass (g/mol)	Number of Moles (g/mol)	Mass (g)
calcium oxide			5.00	
	$NaNO_{3(s)}$			150
nickel (II) chloride			0.750	
	$CH_3OH_{(l)}$			60.0
water			2.60	

13. The element Q is found to have three naturally occurring isotopes in the following quantities. What is the average mass of Q?

    $^{122}_{?}Q$ –   16.0%

    $^{118}_{?}Q$ –   72.6%

    $^{115}_{?}Q$ –   11.4%

NOTES

THE DIVERSITY OF MATTER AND CHEMICAL BONDING

When you are finished this unit, you will be able to...

- recall principles for assigning names to ionic compounds
- explain why formulas for ionic compounds refer to the simplest whole-number ratio of ions that result in a net charge of zero
- define valence electron, electronegativity, ionic bond, and intramolecular force
- use the periodic table and electron dot diagrams to support and explain ionic bonding theory
- explain how an ionic bond results from the simultaneous attraction of oppositely charged ions
- explain that ionic compounds form lattices and that these structures relate to the properties of the compounds
- conduct investigations into relationships among observable variables and use a broad range of tools and techniques to gather and record data
- explain that scientific knowledge and theories develop through hypotheses, the collection of evidence, investigation, and the ability to provide explanations
- integrate technology into experiments, measurements, and calculations
- verify the value and validity of scientific evidence

PREREQUISITE SKILLS AND KNOWLEDGE

Prior to starting this unit, you should be able to...

- follow IUPAC guidelines for naming ionic compounds and similar molecular compounds
- interpret balanced chemical equations in terms of moles of chemical species, and relate the mole concept to the law of conservation of mass
- write word and balanced equations for significant chemical reactions
- graph and interpret data
- manipulate and solve basic linear equations
- understand SI units of measurement, scientific notation, rates, ratios, and proportions

Lesson 1   WHAT IS A CHEMICAL BOND?

NOTES

One of the central themes in the study of chemistry is the chemical bond. Most of the chemistry that you will study will involve the formation or the breaking of chemical bonds.

A bond is an electrostatic attraction between particles

A chemical bond is an electrostatic attraction between two particles, such as atoms, ions or molecules.   Electrostatic refers to positive and negative charges.   Therefore, a bond is a net attractive force which holds two particles together because of their electrical charges.

THE NOBLE GAS ATOMS

The noble gases do not form compounds.

The noble gases include helium, neon, argon, krypton, xenon, and radon. With the exception of a few isolated situations, these elements do not form compounds and bond to other atoms.   Chemists theorize this is because of the number of electrons in the outermost energy level in atoms of these elements.   They have "stable octets" (or "stable duet" in the case of helium) of valence electrons.   Other atoms form bonds to attempt to acquire electron arrangements or configurations like these atoms.

Atoms attempt to achieve the electron structure of the nearest noble gas.

The electron structure model for chemical bonding suggests that each atom attempts to achieve the electron structure of the nearest noble gas. For example, chlorine has room for one more electron.   If it could gain this one electron, its electron structure would resemble that of argon, the nearest noble gas.   Similarly, if sodium could lose a single electron, its electron structure would resemble that of neon, the noble gas closest to sodium.   Since some atoms attempt to lose electrons and some atoms attempt to gain electrons, electrons can be transferred or shared between atoms satisfying the electron structure requirements of both.   When there is a transfer or sharing of electrons a chemical bond results.

Loss of electrons:

      oxidation – LEO

Gain of electrons:

      reduction – GER

When a chemical bond is formed, the atoms have a more stable energy level.

ENERGY MODEL OF BOND FORMATION

As we know from experience, most everything tends toward a minimum energy. For example, a ball rolls down a hill and an apple falls to the ground. The energy model suggests that when a chemical bond is formed, the atoms involved have reached a lower, and therefore, more stable energy level.

Consider the formation of a hydrogen molecule, $H_{2(g)}$, from two hydrogen atoms, $H_{(g)}$. When this reaction occurs, a large amount of energy is released.

$$H_{(g)} + H_{(g)} \rightarrow H_{2(g)} + 435 \text{ kJ}$$

We can represent this change on a potential energy diagram. The vertical axis represents potential energy, and the horizontal axis represents the distance separating the two hydrogen atoms.

Graph of Potential Energy vs. Distance for the Separation of H Atoms

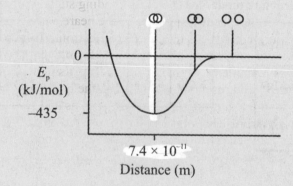

As two hydrogen atoms approach each other, they experience a net attractive force. The closer they come together, the stronger the force becomes until they reach a separation of 7.4×10^{-11} m. At this distance, the molecule is most stable, and at the lowest energy. If the atoms are forced closer together, they begin to overlap excessively and a net repulsive force pushes them apart. The point at which they are most stable represents the point at which a chemical bond is formed.

Atoms can be represented with **dot diagrams**.

The Octet Rule:

Electron form pairs to a maximum of eight.

Unpaired electrons are bonding electrons

Electron-Dot Diagrams or Lewis Diagrams

Atoms can be represented by electron-dot diagrams.
To construct an electron-dot diagram for an atom, do the following:

1. Write the atomic symbol for the atom. This represents the nucleus and the filled inner energy levels which do not participate in bonding. This is sometimes referred to as the "kernel" of the atom.

2. Dots (•), one per outer energy level (valence) electron, are arranged around the atomic symbol.

*   One electron is placed in each of the four available orbitals before any electron pairing occurs.
*   Beginning with the fifth electron, pairing may occur to a maximum of eight electrons. This is called the octet rule.

H •							:He:
Li •	Be •		• B •	• C •	• N •	• O •	:F •	:Ne:
Na •	Mg •		• Al •	• Si •	• P •	• S •	:Cl •	:Ar:
K •	Ca •						

For example:

Calcium	Carbon	Chlorine
Ċa • not Ca:	• Ċ • not :C: or Ċ:	:Ċl •

Unpaired electrons in the dot diagrams are called bonding electrons, because they are involved in bond formation.
Paired electrons are called "lone pairs" and are generally not involved in bond formation. However, in some complex molecules and ions they do become involved in bond formation.

Lone pairs ⟨ :Ċl • → Bonding electron (unpaired electron)

48

Rules for Electron Dot Diagrams, Structural Formulas and Lewis Structures

1. Electron Dot Diagrams for Elements
    *   Fill the "four sides" first
    *   Unpaired electrons are available for bonding

    Na •   Ca •   • N •   • C •   • P •

The chemical symbol represents the nucleus and inner electrons.

2. Electron Dot Diagrams for Ionic Compounds
    *   Electrons are transferred from metal to non-metal (i.e. no electron dots shown on metal)
    *   "Charged" species are enclosed in brackets

    Na • Cl : represented by [Na]⁺ [: Cl :]⁻

    metal non metal.

3. Structural Formulas
    *   A shared pair of electrons between two atoms is represented by a single line
    *   If an atom shares two or three pairs of electrons, a double or triple line is used.

    Single bond   : Cl : Cl :   or   Cl – Cl

    Double bond   : O :: O :   or   O = O

    Triple bond   : N ::: N :   or   N ≡ N

If single bonds do not satisfy the requirement, try a double or triple bond

4. Lewis Structures for Covalently Bonded Compounds
- Sum the valence electrons for all the atoms in the molecule.
- Determine if necessary which atom can form the most number of bonds – this is the "central atom".
- Bonds between atoms are represented by a "—" this represents two electrons, usually one from each atom.
- Any electrons left over are distributed in pairs such that each atom obeys the "octet rule"—except hydrogen which obeys the "duet" rule.
- The exact number of valence electrons must be used—no more, no less.

Some examples are illustrated below.

Molecule	Total Valence e⁻		Electron Dot Diagram	Structural Formula	Lewis Structures
$HF_{(g)}$	H	1	H $:\ddot{F}:$	H–F	H–$\ddot{F}:$
	F	$\frac{7}{8}$			
CF_4	C	4	$:\ddot{F}:\ddot{C}:\ddot{F}:$ with $\ddot{F}$ above and below	F–C–F with F above and below	$:\ddot{F}:$ $:\ddot{F}–\ddot{C}–\ddot{F}:$ $:\ddot{F}:$
	$4 \times F$	$\frac{4(7)}{=\frac{28}{32}}$			
CH_3F	C	4	$:\ddot{F}:\ddot{C}:H$ with H above and below	H–C–F with H above and below	H–C–$\ddot{F}:$ with H above and below
	H	$\frac{3(1)}{=3}$			
	F	$\frac{7}{14}$			

Lewis Structures Involving Multiple Bonds, Ions and Resonance

Multiple bonds

Consider the Lewis structure for CS_2,

Atom	e⁻
C	4
$2 \times S$	12
Total	16 e⁻

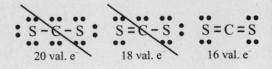

20 val. e⁻   18 val. e⁻   16 val. e⁻

In a double covalent bond, two pairs of electrons are shared between atoms.

Ions

Consider CN⁻ (cyanide ion).

NOTES

(Add 1 for excess negative charge)

Atom	e⁻
C	4
N	5
−1	1
Total	10 e⁻

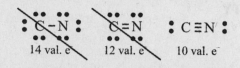

14 val. e⁻   12 val. e⁻   10 val. e⁻

In a triple covalent bond, three pairs of electrons are shared between atoms.

Resonance

Consider SO_3 (sulfur trioxide).

Atom	e⁻
S	6
3 × O	18
Total	24 e⁻

All three structures are required to describe SO_3 ("RESONANCE"). The Real Lewis Structure is the average of these three.

Resonance structures:

Sometimes more than one Lewis structure is necessary to accurately represent a molecule.

NOTES

ACTIVITIES

ACTIVITY

Title
Properties of Ionic and Molecular Compounds

Problem
What are some characteristic properties of ionic and molecular compounds?

Variables
List the appropriate variables.

Materials

$NaCl_{(s)}$	$C_{12}H_{22}O_{11(s)}$
$C_3H_4OH(COOH)_{3(s)}$ (citric acid)	$KMnO_{4(s)}$
canola oil	$CuSO_4 \cdot 5H_2O_{(s)}$
$C_3H_5(OH)_{3(l)}$ (glycerol)	$CaSO_{4(s)}$

Procedure
Write a procedure to obtain observations of the following properties:
- solubility in water
- electrical conductivity of aqueous solution (if formed)
- state

Observations

Complete the following data table:

Formula	Name	State at Room Temp	Colour in Solution	Conductivity	Solubility	Type Ionic or molecular
NaCl						
$C_3H_4OH(COOH)_3$						
Canola oil						
$C_3H_5(OH)_3$						
$C_{12}H_{22}O_{11}$						
$KMnO_4$						
$CuSO_4 \cdot 5H_2O$						
$CaSO_4$						

Analysis

Write operational (empirical) definitions for the following:
- ionic compound
- molecular compound

Empirical definition
- evidence that you can see and measure
- visible observation

Conceptual definition
- explanation of theory
- abstract

PRACTICE EXERCISES

1. Fill in the following table.

Name	Electron Dot Diagram	Number of Lone Pairs	Number of Bonding Electrons
Na			
C			
N			
Ar			

2. Complete the following tables.

Name	Formula	Electron Dot Diagram	Structural Formula
ammonia			
bromine liquid			
		H $\colon$ H	
hydrogen chloride			
nitrogen triiodide			
			H⟍ ⟋H N–N H⟋ ⟍H
	$N_{2(g)}$		
carbon dioxide			
ethane	C_2H_6		
ethene	C_2H_4		
acetylene		H $\colon$ C $\vdots\vdots$ C $\colon$ H	

Name	Formula	Electron Dot Diagram	Structural Formula
water			
			H | H–C–O–H | H
chlorine			
		H : C : H (with H above and below)	
oxygen difluoride			
hydrogen peroxide			
difluoroethyne			F – C ≡ C – F
dichloroethane	$C_2H_4Cl_2$		
formaldehyde	H_2CO		
		H : C ::: N	
dichloroethyne	C_2Cl_2		
	H_3O^+		
	NO_3^-		
nitrosyl	NO^+		
	PO_4^{3-}		

Lesson 2 IONIC, COVALENT, AND METALLIC BONDING

NOTES

Electrons present in an atom's outer energy level are termed bonding electrons or valence electrons.   It is these electrons and any vacancies in the outer energy level which determine how the element will bond.

It must be emphasized that according to our model, all bonds are alike in that atoms are attempting to gain a completely filled outer energy level of electrons.   The differences which may appear in the descriptions that follow are differences of degree rather than kind.

Ionic Bonding (Transfer)

An ionic bond is the bond that results from the electrostatic attraction between a positive and a negative ion.   The positive ion is formed when an atom loses one or more electrons thus achieving the electron structure of the nearest noble gas.   The negative ion is formed when an atom gains one or more electrons in order to achieve the electron structure of its nearest noble gas.   The resulting positive and negative ions are then attracted to each other and held together by the electrostatic force.   We can think of an ionic bond as being one that is formed by the transfer of electrons from one atom to another.   For example,

An ionic bond is an
attraction between positive
and negative ions.

$$\text{Na} \bullet \; + \; \overset{\bullet\bullet}{\underset{\bullet\bullet}{\text{Cl}}} \, \colon \; \rightarrow \; \text{Na}^+ \; \colon \overset{\bullet\bullet}{\underset{\bullet\bullet}{\text{Cl}}} \, \colon^- \; \rightarrow \; [\text{Na}]^+ \left[\colon \overset{\bullet\bullet}{\underset{\bullet\bullet}{\text{Cl}}} \, \colon \right]^-$$

$$\text{Li} \bullet \; + \; \bullet \, \overset{\bullet\bullet}{\underset{\bullet\bullet}{\text{O}}} \, \colon \; \rightarrow \; \begin{matrix} [\text{Li}]^+ \\ [\text{Li}]^+ \end{matrix} \; + \; \left[\colon \overset{\bullet\bullet}{\underset{\bullet\bullet}{\text{O}}} \, \colon \right]^{2-}$$

Covalent Bonding (same type sharing) Non metal elements (molecules)

Sharing

A covalent bond is the
result of a mutual sharing
of electrons.

A covalent bond is the bond which results from the electrostatic attraction between the electrons of one atom and the nucleus of another atom and vice versa.   Two atoms approach close enough to each other to allow the nucleus of each atom to attract the electrons of the other.
The result is a mutual sharing of electrons between the two nuclei.
Each nucleus, by reason of its sharing of another's electrons, is able to achieve its completely filled outer energy level.
For example,

$$\colon \overset{\bullet\bullet}{\underset{\bullet\bullet}{\text{Cl}}} \, \bullet \; + \; \bullet \, \overset{\bullet\bullet}{\underset{\bullet\bullet}{\text{Cl}}} \, \colon \; \rightarrow \; \colon \overset{\bullet\bullet}{\underset{\bullet\bullet}{\text{Cl}}} \, \colon \overset{\bullet\bullet}{\underset{\bullet\bullet}{\text{Cl}}} \, \colon$$

56

Covalent bonds may be classified as single, double, or triple bonds, depending on the number of pairs of electrons shared between nuclei. For example, chlorine atoms share one pair, oxygen atoms share two pairs, and nitrogen atoms share three pairs of electrons.

Single bond $:\overset{\cdot\cdot}{\underset{\cdot\cdot}{Cl}}:\overset{\cdot\cdot}{\underset{\cdot\cdot}{Cl}}:$ or $Cl-Cl$

Double bond $:\overset{\cdot\cdot}{O}::\overset{\cdot\cdot}{O}:$ or $O=O$

Triple bond $:N:::N:$ or $N\equiv N$

Metallic Bonding (just metal)

A metallic bond is the type of bond which holds pure metals together. It results from the electrostatic attraction between the freely moving valence electrons of many atoms in the metal and the positive ions which have been formed when these electrons leave in order for the ion to have the electron structure of the nearest noble gas.

In many ways the metallic bond falls somewhere between the ionic bond and covalent bonds. Like the ionic bond, positive ions are formed in metallic bonding. Like the covalent bond, electrons are shared between atoms. One important difference is that the electrons in a metal are free to move. This is unlike both ionic and covalent substances. It is this factor which is responsible for the important metallic property of electrical conductivity. For example,

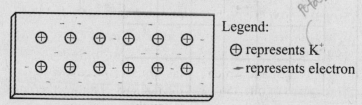

Potassium

Legend:

$\oplus$ represents K^+

— represents electron

"Instantaneous" position of electrons in a metal

Some Generalizations

What types of elements are involved in ionic, covalent, and metallic bonding? First, it is reasonable that all metals in their elemental states would display metallic bonding. Second, ionic bonding takes place between an element which forms positive ions and a second element which forms negative ions; that is, between a metal and a nonmetal. (Ionic bonding) More specifically, ionic bonding occurs between metals in Group 1 and 2 with nonmetals in Groups 16 and 17. Third, from the examples we have considered, we can conclude that the non-metallic elements which form diatomic molecules (H_2, N_2, O_2, F_2, Cl_2, Br_2, and I_2) exhibit covalent (Non-metal element) bonding. From this we can generalize that nonmetals bond covalently to all other nonmetals.

NOTES

Covalent bonds may be single, double or triple.

A **metallic bond** is an attraction between electrons and positive ions.

PRACTICE EXERCISES

1. Use electron dot diagrams to predict the formula of

   a) aluminium and fluorine

   b) magnesium and nitrogen

2. Draw the electron dot and structural formula representations for the following:

   a) Br_2

   b) H_2

3. Draw electron dot diagrams for the elements in the first three rows (periods) of the Periodic Table of Elements.

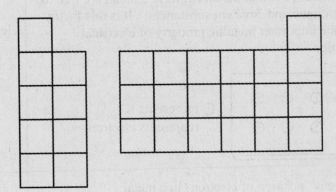

4. a) Why are the elements, in Group 17 of the Periodic Table called the "Noble Gases"?

   b) What evidence is there that the electron structure in these elements is stable?

   c) Why do other elements try to obtain the electron structure of the nearest noble gas by bonding to one another?

58

5. Define:

a) Bonding electrons. Give an example.

b) Lone pair. Give an example.

6. a) Give a conceptual definition of an ionic bond.

b) State a generalization of which groups of elements in the Periodic Table of Elements form ionic bonds.

7. a) Complete the following table,
   - state the group number of each atom
   - state whether it must gain or lose electrons to achieve the electron structure of the nearest noble gas and how many electrons are involved
   - name and write the formula of the resulting ion after the electron loss or gain

Atom	Group Number	Gain or Loss	Name of Ion	Formula of Ion
Na				
Mg				
S				
Cl				

b) Name and write the formula for every possible binary ionic compound that could result from ionic bonding between the ions in the table.

8. For the element carbon, C:

   a) State its group number.

   b) State whether it must gain or lose electrons to achieve the electron structure of the nearest noble gas and how many electrons are involved.

   c) Considering your answer to part **b**, is there an alternative way for carbon atoms to gain a noble gas-like structure or configuration? Explain.

9. **a)** Give a conceptual definition of a covalent bond.

   b) State a generalization of which groups of elements in the Periodic Table will likely form covalent bonds.

10. a) Give a conceptual definition of a metallic bond.

   b) State a generalization of which groups of elements in the Periodic Table will likely form metallic bonds.

11. Based on positions of the elements in the Periodic Table, predict whether the bonding between atoms in the following substances would be <u>ionic</u>, <u>covalent</u>, or <u>metallic.</u> Place checkmarks in the column which correctly identifies the type of bond involved in the corresponding substance.

Molecule	Covalent	Ionic	Metallic
$KCl_{(s)}$			
$Mg_{(s)}$			
$CaO_{(s)}$			
$O_{2(g)}$			
$NO_{2(g)}$			
$Ag_{(s)}$			
$BaCl_{2(s)}$			
$S_{8(s)}$			
$SO_{2(g)}$			
$CsF_{(s)}$			

12. Using the law of charges, tell whether attraction or repulsion will take place in each case.

a)

_____

b)

_____

c)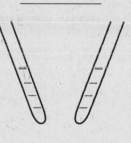

_____

d)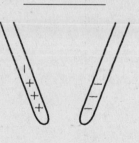

_____

Lesson 3   BOND TYPES AND ELECTRONEGATIVITY

Electronegativity is a measure of an atom's attraction for electrons in a bond

Electronegativity

Electronegativity is defined as a measure of an atom's attraction for electrons in a chemical bond.   The most electronegative element is fluorine, and it is assigned a value of 4.0.   Other elements are assigned a value relative to this standard.   For example, chlorine atoms have about three-fourths the attraction as fluorine atoms, so chlorine is assigned a value of $\frac{3}{4} \times 4.0$ or 3.0.   The values for electronegativities are listed in your **Periodic Table**.   The difference in electronegativity values for two elements can be used to describe the nature of the bond.   A difference of 1.7 produces a bond of 50% ionic character.

Electronegativity Difference Between the Two Atoms	Type of Bond Between Atoms	Descriptions of the Electrons in the Bond
≥ 1.7	Ionic	Transfer of electrons between metal and non-metal to form ions.
< 1.7	Polar Covalent	Electrons shared unequally between unlike atoms.
0	Non-polar Covalent	Electrons shared equally between identical non-metallic atoms. (molecules)
0	Metallic	Electrons moving freely between metallic (positive) ions.

Examples:

Atoms	Electronegativities	Difference	Bond Type
Li – F	Li = 1.0 F = 4.0	3.0	Ionic Li^+ F^-
Sc – Cl	Sc = 1.3 Cl = 3.0	1.7	Ionic Sc^{3+} $Cl-$
Ba – I	Ba = 0.9 I = 2.5	1.6	Polar Covalent
N – O	N = 3.0 O = 3.5	0.5	Polar Covalent
N – Cl	N = 3.0 Cl = 3.0	0	Polar covalent (because of different atom sizes)
O – O	O = 3.5 O = 3.5	0	Non-polar covalent

(handwritten notes in margin:) N^{3-} , O^{2-} Non metal non metal. (different size atom) => Non equal sharing (molecules only) identical atom. => Equal sharing

Electronegativity and Covalent Bonding

If a bond is formed between two identical atoms, then the electrons making up that bond will be shared equally between the atoms. *(Non Polar)*
For example, the electrons in a hydrogen molecule, H_2, are shared equally by two hydrogen atoms. If a bond is formed between two atoms of different elements, then the electrons will not be shared equally.
The more electronegative element will attract the electrons with greater force. The result will be a bond with a negative end (the end closest to the more electronegative atom) and a positive end (the end closest to the less electronegative atom). For example, the electrons in the bond between a hydrogen atom and a chlorine atom in a hydrogen chloride molecule, HCl, will be pulled closer to the chlorine atom. The chlorine end of the bond will be negative and the hydrogen end will be positive.

A polar covalent bond is a bond formed between unlike atoms with an electronegativity difference of less than 1.7. The word "polar" implies an overall charge separation. One end of the bond is positive and the other end is negative due to the differing electronegativities of the atoms sharing the electrons. This is called a bond dipole. For example,

$$\overset{2.1}{H} - \overset{3.0}{Cl} \quad \text{Electonegativity difference} = 0.9$$

The element with the greater electronegativity attracts the electrons more strongly.

Polar covalent bonds form when there is an unequal sharing of bonding electrons.

NOTES

$\delta+$ $\delta-$
H – Cl

H – Cl

Same non metal element.

Non-polar covalent bonds form when there is an equal sharing of bonding electrons.

Since the chlorine atom pulls the electron closer to it, the chlorine end of the bond is negative as compared to the hydrogen end. This can be symbolized two ways:

• using $\delta+$ and $\delta-$
The Greek letter delta (δ) implies the existence of a difference in charge that is real but small. We do not use + and – signs alone since this would be confused with the ions present in an ionic bond.

• using bond dipoles
A dipole is represented by an arrow over the molecule, with the tip of the arrow pointing towards the negative end.

A non-polar covalent bond will only exist between two atoms of the same non-metallic element. For example, Cl_2, H_2, O_2, all have non-polar covalent bonds. The electrons in the bonds of these molecules are shared equally by the atoms since their electronegativities are equal. There is no overall charge separation and the covalent bond is non-polar.

Coordinate Covalent Bonds

Coordinate covalent bonds are a special type of polar covalent bond in which one atom supplies both electrons to the covalent bond.

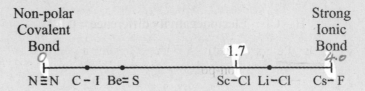

| Hydrogen ion | Ammonia molecule | | Ammonium complex ion |

Other examples: H_3O^+, Nh_3, Bf_3, HCN

Generalizations

The difference between ionic and covalent bonds is a difference of degree. At one end of a continuum lies a covalent bond between two identical atoms. At the other end of the continuum lies an ionic bond between two atoms with a large difference of electronegativity (Fr and F). Most bonds fall in the middle, and they have some ionic and some covalent character.

Non identical non-metallic atoms with the same electronegativity will not usually form a non-polar bond because of the difference in size.

Non-polar Covalent Bond   Strong Ionic Bond

0   1.7   4.0

N ≡ N   C – I   Be= S   Sc–Cl   Li–Cl   Cs– F

PRACTICE EXERCISES

1. Define electronegativity.

2. State the generalization that exists between electronegativity and atomic number:
   a) within a group

   b) within a period

   c) for the transition elements (B group elements)

3. On the basis of electronegativity difference state a generalization for:
   a) the formation of an ionic bond between two elements

   b) the formation of a covalent bond between two elements

4. Conceptually define:
   a) non-polar covalent bonds

   b) polar covalent bonds

5. On the basis of electronegativity difference state a generalization for:
   a) the formation of a non-polar covalent bond

   b) the formation of a polar covalent bond

6. Identify the positive end and the negative end of a bond between the following pairs of atoms by either δ+, δ–or dipoles:

a) C–H

b) N–O

c) P–Cl

d) S–H

7. Predict on the basis of electronegativity difference whether the bond between the following pairs of atoms will be ionic, non-polar covalent, polar covalent, or metallic:

Pairs of Atoms	Electronegativity Difference	Type of Bond
H–H		
C–H		
K–K		
Li–Br		
C–S		
Zn–Br		
S–S		
N–I		
Fr–F		
V–V		

66

(Non metal & non metal).

Lesson 4 MOLECULAR SHAPES (STEREOCHEMISTRY) AND POLARITY

All discrete molecules have a definite three dimensional shape.
The number of electron pairs surrounding the central atom(s) can be used to predict the stereochemistry of a molecule. The electron pairs repel each other and take up positions as far from one another as possible.

This theory of molecular shapes is known as the Valence-Shell Electron-Pair Repulsion (VSEPR) Theory.   When determining the shape of molecules, the electron pairs of a multiple bond (double or triple) count as only one pair of electrons for stereochemistry purposes

Bonding Electrons and Molecular Shapes

Valence Electrons of Central Atom

Number of Bonding Electrons	Number of Lone Pairs	Molecular Shape	Example
1	3	Diatomic Linear	HCl
2	2	V-shaped (bent)	H_2O
3	1	Trigonal Pyramidal	NH_3
4	0	Tetrahedral	CH_4
3	0	Trigonal Planar	BI_3
2	0	Triatomic Linear	CS_2

To represent the three-dimensional shape of the atom, we often use the following conventions:

1. Covalent bonds between those atoms in the same plane are represented with solid lines (___).

2. Covalent bonds between atoms behind the plane of the paper are represented with dotted lines (_ _ _).

3. Covalent bonds between atoms in front of the plane of the paper are represented with a wedge (Δ).

NOTES

The VSEPR Theory can be used to predict molecular shapes.

The number of lone pairs and bonding e⁻ will give shape to a molecule.

Boron does not usually obey the octet rule.

Summary of Shape Diagrams

Molecular Shape	Example	Dot Diagram	Shape Diagram
Diatomic linear	HCl	H :Cl: *Polar*	H−Cl
V-shaped	H_2O	H H O *Polar*	H O H
Pyramidal	NH_3	H :N: H H *Polar*	H N H H
Tetrahedral	CH_4	H H :C: H H *non polar*	H C H H H
Trigonal Planar	BI_3	I B I I *non-Polar*	I B I I
Triatomic Linear	CO_2	:O: :C: :O: *non Polar*	O=C=O

Asymmetrical molecules are generally polar.

POLARITY OF MOLECULES

Molecular dipoles

A polar molecule refers to a molecule which has an overall charge separation; i.e., a positive and negative end.   A non-polar molecule, on the other hand, has no net charge separation.   If a molecule is polar, it is said to have a molecular dipole.   *Equal /=0*   *unequal.*

A molecular dipole is the result of an unequal sharing of electrons in a molecule.   If one end of a molecule appears to be negative compared to the other end, it is because, overall, the electrons in the bonds are being shared unequally.

If, however, the molecule is symmetrical, and all the bond dipoles cancel each other, the molecular dipole will be zero. That is, there will be no net charge separation on the molecule, and it will be non-polar. Some examples follow.

Symmetrical molecules are non-polar if all bonds are identical

Molecules		Structural Formula Showing Dipole	Polarity
H_2	H **:** H		non-polar
HCl	H **:** C̈l **:**	H $\overrightarrow{Cl}$	polar
CO_2	**:** Ö **::** C **::** Ö **:**	O $\overleftarrow{=}$ C $\overrightarrow{=}$ O	non-polar

Polarity of Water Molecules

Consider the water molecule. There are two possibilities for a structural diagram.

H $\overrightarrow{O}\overleftarrow{}$ H   H $_{\searrow O \swarrow}$ H   or   H $\downarrow$ H   Symmetrical = non polar

Whether water is polar or non-polar depends on the shape of the molecule. Experimental evidence indicates water is a polar molecule; hence it has a bent or "V"-shape rather than a linear shape. Also, since the oxygen in a water molecule has 2 lone pairs and 2 bonding electrons, the VSEPR theory would also predict it to be V-shaped. The second representation is correct.

If the molecule is symmetrical in all planes and all bonds are identical, the bond dipoles will cancel, and the molecule will be non-polar. If the molecule is not symmetrical in all planes or symmetrical with non-identical bonds, there will generally be a net dipole, and the molecule is polar.

NOTES

Example 1

Is carbon tetrachloride (CCl_4) a polar or non-polar molecule?

Solution

Central atom (C) has 4 bonding pairs of electrons. Therefore, the shape is tetrahedral. There is a dipole between C and Cl.

Intermolecular bonds are attractions between molecules.

Intramolecular bonds are attractions within a molecule

Since this is a symmetrical molecule, the two horizontal and the two vertical dipoles will cancel each other out.

Intermolecular Bonds (Bond within molecules)

An intermolecular bond is a bond between molecules.
Until now we have considered the bonding between atoms within molecules. The intermolecular bond involves the electrostatic attractive forces between molecules. Ionic substances and metallic substances do not form molecules. Ionic compounds in solid state exist as crystal lattices made up of anions and cations held together by ionic bonding.

The crystal lattice is shaped such that each cation has only anions as its nearest neighbours. The ratio of cations of anions in the lattice is the same as the formula we write for an ionic compound. In sodium chloride, there is Na^+ for every 1 Cl^- in the lattice. The formula is NaCl.
In calcium chloride, there are 2 Cl^- for every Ca^{2+}. The formula is $CaCl_2$.
There are no molecules of ionic substances! The smallest unit of an ionic compound is called a formula unit, not a molecule.

Therefore, intermolecular bonding only occurs in substances that form covalent bonds. Intermolecular bonds are much weaker than ionic, covalent, or metallic bonds.

Forces of attraction btw molecules

TYPES OF INTERMOLECULAR BONDING

NOTES

Van der Waals forces are named after a Dutch physicist.

1. Van der Waals Forces

Van der Waals bonds are present between all chemical species. They are divided into two types: dipole-dipole forces and London dispersion forces.

Dipole-Dipole Forces *(Polar molecules)* *unequal*

If the substance contains polar molecules, then the positive end of one molecule will be attracted to the negative end of a neighboring molecule. This will extend in all directions involving many molecules.

Dipole-dipole attractions exist between polar molecules.

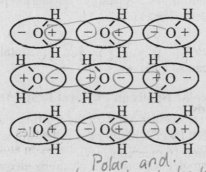

London Dispersion Forces *(Polar and Non polar molecules) exist in all molecules*

In substances with non-polar molecules, no permanent dipoles exist. The intermolecular force which holds these molecules together in the solid and liquid states of matter is the London Dispersion Force. The force is due to the electrostatic attraction between temporary dipoles in neighboring molecules.

If we consider the hydrogen molecule as an example, the two electrons which form the bond may, at a particular instant, be found closer to one of the hydrogen nuclei than to the other.

Dispersion forces exist between all molecules

Hydrogen bonds are the strongest of the intermolecular bonds.

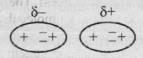

Induction is the process by which a temporary or permanent dipole causes a temporary dipole to form in a neighboring molecule. The result will be a temporary dipole with one end slightly negative. This temporary dipole then may be attracted to a dipole which has been induced in a neighboring molecule. For larger molecules containing more electrons, a stronger dipole can be formed. As a result, these bonds usually increase in strength as the molecules become larger.

In a London Dispersion force there is no net shift of electrons. Therefore, there is not a permanent molecular dipole, and the molecule is non-polar. However, a dipole-dipole interaction can result for an instant as a result of temporary shifts in electrons.

NOTES

$H + (F, O, N) = $ Hydrogen Bonding

2. Hydrogen Bonding

When hydrogen is bonded to highly electronegative elements (fluorine, oxygen, and nitrogen), the bond is strongly polar. The hydrogen end of the bond takes on a strong positive charge, because of the exposed positive hydrogen nucleus.

If there is a neighboring molecule containing a highly electronegative atom with a lone pair of electrons, the hydrogen atom is attracted to this electron pair.

$$\overset{\delta+ \ \ \delta-}{H-F} \qquad \overset{\delta+ \ \ \delta-}{H-F}$$

The hydrogen atom, in fact, appears to be sharing pairs of electrons on different molecules. For example, $HF_{(g)}$

$$H \ \vdots \ \overset{\bullet\bullet}{\underset{\bullet\bullet}{F}} \ \vdots \ H \ \vdots \ \overset{\bullet\bullet}{\underset{\bullet\bullet}{F}} \ \vdots$$

Effect of Intermolecular Bonds on Physical Properties

The effect of the intermolecular bond on the melting and boiling points of compounds can be seen by considering the following list of compounds of hydrogen and the Group 16 elements.

Melting and boiling points can be a measure of intermolecular bond strength.

Compound	Molecular Mass	Melting Point (°C)	Boiling Point (°C)
H_2O	18 g/mol	0	100.0
H_2S	34 g/mol	−85.5	−60.7
H_2Se	81 g/mol	−60.4	−41.5
H_2Te	130 g/mol	−48.9	−2.2

Normally, as the molecular mass increases (and hence the number of electrons), the melting points and the boiling points will also increase. This trend is found to be followed for the compounds H_2S to H_2Te, but as we can see from the following graph and the preceding table, three compounds (NH_3, H_2O and HF) do not fit the trend. In fact, the hydrogen bonding is so strong in water, ammonia and hydrogen fluoride that the melting point and the boiling point are much higher than would have been predicted.

72

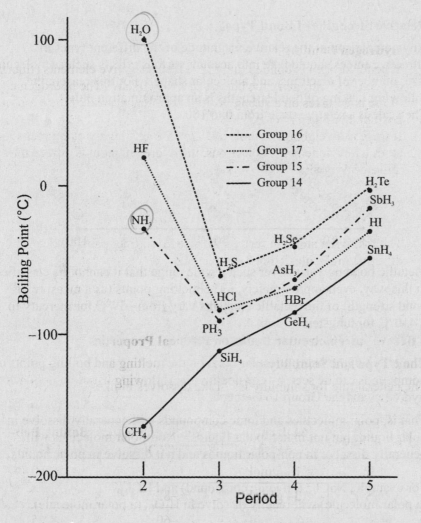

In general, the greater the intermolecular bond strength between the molecules of a compound, the higher the melting point and boiling point of that compound. This is due to the increased energy which must be supplied to break the strong intermolecular bonds between the molecules to allow the compound to melt and eventually boil. The additional energy that must be supplied increases the temperature.

The more complex the molecule is, the stronger the intermolecular bonds will be.

NOTES

"Like dissolves like."

Relative Strengths of Bond Types

Any comparison of the relative magnitude of the different types of attractive forces should take into account various effects such as molecular size, number of electrons, and molecular shape. For this reason, the following ranking of bond strengths is an approximation only.
The scale is a relative scale from 0 to 100.

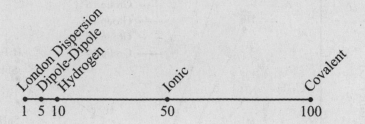

Metallic bonding varies over such a wide range that it cannot be classified in this way, even approximately. The melting points (as a measure of bond strength) of the metallic elements vary from $-39°C$ for mercury to $3\,410°C$ for tungsten.

Bond Type and Solubility

The general rule for solubility is: "Like dissolves in like."

That is, polar molecules and ionic compounds will generally dissolve in polar liquids but not in non-polar liquids. Non-polar molecules will generally dissolve in non-polar liquids and not dissolve in polar liquids.

For example, $NaCl_{(s)}$ (an ionic compound) and $HCl_{(g)}$ (a polar molecule) will readily dissolve in $H_2O_{(l)}$ (a polar molecule).

$C_{14}H_{30(s)}$ (grease, a non-polar molecule) will dissolve in benzene, $C_6H_{6(l)}$ (a non-polar molecule) but will not dissolve in water.

Types of Solids

Type of Solid	Examples	Particles Making Up Solid	Force of Attraction Between Particles	Relative Melting Point	Hardness	Electrical Conductivity
Atomic	helium neon	atoms	London dispersion	low	soft	poor
Molecular	Cl_2 H_2O $C_{12}H_{22}O_{11}$	molecules	London dispersion may also be: dipole-dipole induction, hydrogen bonding	low	usually soft	poor
Network	diamond quartz SiO_2	atoms or molecules in covalent crystal	Covalent bonds	very high	hard	poor, exception: graphite which is good
Metallic	sodium magnesium	positive ions in electron cloud	Metallic bonds	moderate to high	soft to hard	good
Ionic	NaCl CaF_2	positive and negative ions in crystal lattice	Ionic bonds	high	hard	poor, except when aqueous or liquid (molten)

PRACTICE EXERCISES

1. Complete the following table.

Molecule	Lewis Structure	Molecular Shape	Shape Diagram	Polarity
NF_3				
CH_2Cl_2				
CS_2				
CBr_4				
HCl				
H_2Te				
O_2				
$CHCl_3$				
CH_3OH				
CO_2				

2. Complete the following table.

Polarity	Molecular Substance with Phase at Room Temperature	Molar Mass	Melting Points (°C)	Boiling Points (°C)	Types of Intermolecular Forces		
					van der Waals		hydrogen bonding
					dipole-dipole	London dispersion	
	$F_{2(g)}$		−220	−188			
	$Cl_{2(g)}$		−101	−35			
	$Br_{2(l)}$		−7	59			
	$I_{2(s)}$		114	184			
	$ClF_{(g)}$		−154	−101			
	$BrF_{(g)}$		−33	−20			
	$BrCl_{(g)}$		−66	5			
	$ICl_{(g)}$		14	97			
	$IBr_{(s)}$		42	116			
	$H_2O_{(l)}$		0	100			
	$H_2S_{(s)}$		−86	−61			
	$H_2Se_{(s)}$		−60	−42			
	$H_2Te_{(s)}$		−49	−2			
	$CF_{4(g)}$		−184	−129			
	$CCl_{4(g)}$		−23	77			
	$CBr_{4(s)}$		40	189			
	$CH_3F_{(g)}$		−149	−78			
	$CH_3Cl_{(g)}$		−98	−24			
	$CH_3Br_{(g)}$		−94	4			
	$CH_3I_{(l)}$		−66	43			
	$CH_3OH_{(l)}$		−100	65			
	$C_2H_5F_{(g)}$		−143	−38			
	$C_2H_5Cl_{(g)}$		−136	13			
	$C_2H_5Br_{(l)}$		−119	38			
	$C_2H_5I_{(l)}$		−108	72			
	$C_2H_5OH_{(l)}$		−117	78			

3. Complete the following table by

   a) drawing the Lewis structure
   b) describing the shape of the molecule or ion
   c) describing the polarity of the molecule
   d) describing the intermolecular bonds as: London dispersion force, dipole-dipole attraction, or hydrogen bond.

Formula	Lewis Diagram	Shape	Polarity	Types of Intermolecular Bond
NH_3				
CBr_4				
H_2S				
PCl_3				
BCl_3				
NH_4^+				
HBr				
OCl_2				
NI_3				
SO_4^{2-}				
SBr_2				
GeH_4				
H_2Te				
NF_3				
H_2Se				
$SnBr_4$				
SO_3^{2-}				
CO_2				
PO_4^{3-}				

4. Carbon, hydrogen, and oxygen form these three compounds represented by their structural formulas:

$$
\begin{array}{ccc}
\text{H\ \ H\ \ H} & \text{H\ \ H\ \ H} & \text{H\ \ H\ \ H}\\
\text{H-C-C-C-O-H} & \text{H-O-C-C-C-O-H} & \text{H-O-C-C-C-O-H}\\
\text{H\ \ H\ \ H} & \text{H\ \ H\ \ H} & \text{H\ \ O\ \ H}\\
 & & \text{H}
\end{array}
$$

1-propanol   1, 3-propanediol   1, 2, 3-propanetriol

Which compound should have the highest boiling point? Explain your answer.

Use the following information to answer the next question

In an experiment, a student made these observations about five different solids:

Solid	Color	Odor	Hardness	Other Properties
A	yellow	slight	moderate	melts over burner flame
B	white	none	hard	does not melt but dissolves in water and conducts electricity
C	white	strong	soft	melts over a candle flame
D	grey	none	very hard	does not melt nor dissolve in water
E	silver	none	hard	does not melt nor dissolve in water and is often used in making cutting instruments

5. Identify the above solids as one of the following. Explain your answers with respect to the type of bonding involved.

Name	Formula	Solid	Type of Bonding
sodium chloride			
silicon carbide			
iron			
sulfur			
1,3-dichlorobenzene	$C_6H_4Cl_2$		

6. Carbon, hydrogen, and chlorine form five different molecules using only one carbon atom: CH_4, CH_3Cl, CH_2Cl_2, $CHCl_3$, and CCl_4. Which molecules are polar and which are non-polar? Explain your answers by using Lewis structure formulas or structural formulas.

REVIEW SUMMARY

- Bonds that form between atoms, ions, or molecules are all examples of electrostatic attraction.

- Noble gas atoms are so stable that they do not form compounds.

- Atoms will lose or gain electrons to try to achieve the electron structure of the noble gas that is nearest to them in the periodic table.

- When a chemical bond is formed, the atoms have a more stable energy level.

- Electron dot diagrams are a useful way to illustrate how atoms can arrange themselves in compounds to produce stable octet electron pairings.

- An ionic bond is an attraction between positive and negative ions.

- A covalent bond is the result of a mutual sharing of electrons.

- A metallic bond is an attraction between electrons and positive ions.

- Electronegativity is a measure of an atom's attraction for electrons in a bond

- If the electronegativity difference between two atoms in a bond is greater than or equal to 1.7, the bond is considered to be ionic.

- If the electronegativity difference between two atoms in a bond is less than 1.7, the bond is considered to be covalent, but has a polar quality to it.

- If the electronegativity difference between two atoms in a bond is 0, then the bond is considered to be covalent or metallic, depending on whether the atoms are nonmetals or metals.

- Polar covalent bonds form when one atom tends to attract electrons more than the other. The electrons are pulled to one side, making one end of the bond more negative, and the other end by default becomes more positive.

- The number of lone pairs and bonding e⁻ will give shape to a molecule.

- Bonds or attractions between molecules are known as intermolecular bonds.

- Intermolecular bonds such as Van der Waals forces can consist of dipole-dipole forces or London Dispersion forces.

- Hydrogen bonding is another form of intermolecular bond.

- Intermolecular bond strength can be used to help explain differences in melting points and boiling points of different substances.

- Bonding types can also be sued to predict the likelihood that one substance will dissolve in another. The expression "like dissolves like" is a useful rule.

PRACTICE TEST

1. Match the following

   _____ ionic bond
   _____ covalent bond
   _____ electronegativity
   _____ polar covalent bond
   _____ non-polar covalent bond
   _____ metallic bond
   _____ dipole-dipole attraction
   _____ London dispersion force
   _____ bonding electron
   _____ lone pair electrons

   a) single, unpaired valance electrons
   b) only attraction between non-polar molecules
   c) unequal sharing of electrons
   d) attraction between positive and negative ions
   e) paired valance electrons
   f) attraction between polar molecules
   g) equal sharing of electrons
   h) attraction when electrons are shared
   i) attraction between positive ions and electrons
   j) measure of attraction for electrons

2. Explain why atoms bond together.

3. Fill in the blanks in the following table:

Formula	Lewis Structure Diagram	Shape Diagram	Shape Description	Intermolecular Attraction
CH_4				
OF_2				
NCl_3				
BI_3				
CO_2				
C_2H_4				
H_2O				
SiH_4				
SCl_2				
C_2H_2				
PBr_3				
H_2Te				

4. Explain how melting and boiling points can be used as a measure of intermolecular bond strengths.

5. Explain how electronegativity can be used to determine bond type.

6. From the following list of substances, rank them in order of increasing melting point. Give reasons to support your answer.

_____ **a)** sodium chloride, NaCl
_____ **b)** water, H_2O
_____ **c)** methane, CH_4
_____ **d)** hydrogen chloride, HCl
_____ **e)** hydrogen gas, H_2
_____ **f)** methanol, CH_3OH

7. The combination of elements which is most likely to form an ionic bond is

A. O and F
C. F and Cl
B. K and O
D. Cl and Kr

8. A chemical bond formed by the unequal sharing of the bonding electrons is called

A. coordinate covalent
C. polar covalent
B. non-polar covalent
D. covalent

9. A molecular dipole results from

A. atoms in a molecule having the same electronegativity
B. a charge separation in the molecule
C. the bonding electrons being equally distributed
D. equal sharing of the bonding electrons

10. If a carbon atom is to become the negative end of a bond, it must be bonded to an atom of

A. hydrogen
C. chlorine
B. nitrogen
D. oxygen

11. Which diagram represents the molecule with the chemical formula C_2H_3I?

A.

$$H \; \overset{\displaystyle H}{\underset{\displaystyle H}{\overset{\cdot\cdot}{\underset{\cdot\cdot}{C}}}} :: C : \overset{\cdot\cdot}{\underset{\cdot\cdot}{I}} :$$

B.

$$H : \overset{\displaystyle \overset{\cdot\cdot}{H}}{\underset{\displaystyle H}{C}} ::: C : \overset{\cdot\cdot}{\underset{\cdot\cdot}{I}} : H$$

C.

$$H : \overset{\displaystyle H}{\underset{\displaystyle H}{C}} :: \overset{\cdot\cdot}{C} : \overset{\cdot\cdot}{\underset{\cdot\cdot}{I}} :$$

D.

$$H : \overset{\displaystyle H}{\underset{\displaystyle H}{C}} : \overset{\cdot\cdot}{C} : \overset{\cdot\cdot}{\underset{\cdot\cdot}{I}} :$$

12. The structural formula for carbon disulfide is

A. $S - C - S$

B. $C - S - C$

C. $S = C = S$

D.

$$S \overset{\displaystyle C}{\diagup\!\diagdown} S$$

$$S - S$$

13. Which statements describe water molecules?

I. Oxygen has two unshared electron pairs.
II. The water molecule is V-shaped.
III. Water molecules are an excellent solvent.
IV. Hydrogen and oxygen have different electronegativities.
V. Water can conduct electricity.

A. I, IV, and V
B. II and III only
C. III, IV, and V
D. I, II, and IV

14. Electronegativity can best be defined as

A. a measure of the electron attracting ability of atoms in a molecule
B. the energy required to remove an electron from a neutral atom
C. the negative charge on the non-metallic atom in an ionic compound
D. the negative effect electrons have when added to atoms

15. The FALSE statement concerning the nature of a chemical bond is

A. Chemical bonds can result from the simultaneous attraction for valence electrons by two or more nuclei of closely approaching atoms.
B. Separated atoms are at a lower energy condition than chemically bonded atoms.
C. Chemical bonds can form between closely approaching atoms if their valence electrons are rearranged so as to produce a net attraction between them.
D. Energy is always required to separate atoms or ions that are chemically bonded.

16. Molecules which exhibit very high intermolecular bond strengths will possess

    A. low melting and boiling points
    B. high melting and boiling points
    C. high melting and low boiling points
    D. low melting and high boiling points

17. The electronegativity of atoms always decreases as

    A. the size of atoms decrease
    B. the non-metallic property of atoms increases
    C. the metallic property of atoms increases
    D. the number of valence electrons of atoms increases

18. How many bonds must calcium form in order to achieve the electron structure of the nearest noble gas?

    A. 0   **B.** 1
    C. 2   **D.** 3

19. An ionic bond results from

    A. electrons transferring from one atom to another
    B. electrons shared between two non-metallic atoms
    C. electrons shared between two metallic atoms
    D. non-metallic complex ions sharing electrons

20. A triple covalent bond involves ____ pairs of electrons.
    A. 1   **B.** 2
    C. 3   **D.** 4

21. A bond formed between two oxygen atoms will be
    A. ionic
    B. polar covalent
    C. non-polar covalent
    D. metallic

22. The correct electron dot diagram for SF_2 is

    A.   **B.**

    C.   **D.**

23. The non-polar molecule listed below is
    A. NF_3 **C.** H_2O
    B. C_2H_6 **D.** $CHCl_3$

24. In a bond between carbon and oxygen

    A. there is no bond dipole
    B. carbon will be the positive end of the bond dipole
    C. oxygen will be the positive end of the bond dipole
    D. one cannot determine whether or not there is a bond dipole

25. The imaginary molecule that would most likely NOT have a molecular dipole is

    A. $\begin{array}{c} X-Y \\ | \\ Y \end{array}$

    B. $\begin{array}{c} Q-J-Q \\ | \\ Q \end{array}$

    C. $\begin{array}{c} R \\ | \\ M-L-M \\ | \\ M \end{array}$

    D. $Q-Z-Q$

26. The substance that exhibits hydrogen bonding is

    A. C_2H_6 B. H_2
    C. H_2S D. CH_3CH_2OH

27. The situation that does NOT involve intermolecular bonding is

    A. methane molecules attracting methane molecules
    B. the sulfur atom in an H_2S molecule attracting the hydrogen atoms
    C. the hydrogen atom of H_2O attracting the oxygen atom of CH_3OH
    D. forces of attraction holding molecules of H_2O together in ice

28. Consider the four compounds: H_2O, H_2S, H_2Se, and H_2Te. Based on the kind of molecular forces that operate between the molecules of each compound in the liquid phase, the compound with the highest boiling point is most likely

    A. H_2O B. H_2S
    C. H_2Se D. H_2Te

NOTES

FORMS OF MATTER—GASES

When you are finished this unit, you will be able to…

- describe and compare the behaviour of real and ideal gases in terms of kinetic molecular theory

- convert between the Celsius and Kevin temperature scales

- explain the law of combining volumes

- illustrate how Boyle's and Charles' laws, individually, and combined, are related to the ideal gas law ($PV = nRT$)

- express pressure in a variety of ways, including units of kilopascals, atmospheres, and millimeters of mercury

- perform calculations, based on the gas laws, under STP, SATP, and other defined conditions

- state hypotheses and make predictions based on information about the pressure, temperature, and volume of a gas

PREREQUISITE SKILLS AND KNOWLEDGE

Prior to starting this unit, you should be able to…

- describe the evidence for chemical changes, including changes in state, temperature, or energy

- solve linear equations graphically and algebraically

- evaluate appropriate instruments for collecting evidence

- assess appropriate processes for problem solving, inquiring, and decision making

Lesson 1   GAS LAWS

Molar Volume of a Gas

The molar volume of a gas is the volume occupied by one mole at the specified temperature and pressure.   At standard temperature and pressure, (STP) this volume is 22.4 L for all gases.

At STP, molar volume is 22.4 L. (STP is 273 K and 101.3 kPa)

Standard temperature is 0°C (273 K) and standard pressure is 1.00 atmospheres or 101.3 kPa.

At standard ambient temperature and pressure (SATP), 25°C (298 K) and 100 kPa, molar volume is 24.8 L.   Temperature in Kelvins (K) will be developed completely in the TEMPERATURE SCALES section of this unit.

At SATP, molar volume is 24.8 L. (SATP is 298 K and 100 kPa)

BOYLE'S LAW

In 1662, Robert Boyle proposed a relationship between the volume and pressure of a gas.   We now accept this as a law, known as Boyle's Law.

"For a constant mass of gas at constant temperature, the volume varies inversely with the pressure."

$$P \propto \frac{1}{V}$$

"$\propto$" may be substituted for "$= k$"

Let V represent volume, and
    P represent pressure, and
    k represent a constant of proportionality.

$V\uparrow\ P\downarrow$
inverse relationship
(Vol $\propto$ Pressure)

Then, $PV = k$

$$P = k\left(\frac{1}{V}\right)$$

$$P = \frac{k}{V}$$

$$PV = k$$

For two different conditions of pressure and volume of the same gas sample,

$$P_1V_1 = k$$
$$P_2V_2 = k$$

Therefore, $P_1V_1 = P_2V_2$

Two items both equal to the same value are equal to each other.

Measuring Gas Pressure

Gas pressure is usually measured by the height of liquid column supported by the collisions of gas molecules (pressure) on the liquid. Pressure is force per unit area.

$Pa = N/m^2$

One standard atmosphere of pressure (atm) will support a column of mercury 760 mm high.

1 kPa = 7.50 mm Hg

$$1 \text{ atm} = 760 \text{ mm Hg}$$

The SI unit of gas pressure is the pascal or kilopascal (kPa).

$$1 \text{ kPa} = 1\,000 \text{ N/m}^2$$
$$1 \text{ kPa} - 7.50 \text{ mm Hg}$$
$$1 \text{ atm} = 101.3 \text{ kPa}$$

Example 1

P_1

A sample of methane gas at 105.0 kPa pressure has a volume of 25.0 L. The pressure is decreased to 95.0 kPa. What is the new volume?

P_2 V_1 V_2

Solution
$$P_1V_1 = P_2V_2$$
$$V_2 = \frac{P_1V_1}{P_2}$$
$$= \frac{(105.0 \text{ kPa})(25.0 \text{ L})}{95.0 \text{ kPa}}$$
$$= 27.6 \text{ L}$$

Example 2

V_1 P_1

A sample of carbon dioxide gas has a volume of 15.0 L at 110.0 kPa. To what must the pressure be increased to the change the volume to 12.0 L?

P_2 V_2

Solution
$$P_1V_1 = P_2V_2$$
$$P_2 = \frac{P_1V_1}{V_2}$$
$$= \frac{(110.0 \text{ kPa})(15.0 \text{ L})}{12.0 \text{ kPa}}$$
$$= 138 \text{ kPa}$$

ACTIVITIES

Activity 1

Title

To calculate the molar volume of $H_{2(s)}$ using magnesium metal and hydrochloric acid.

Materials

gas tube	2.0 to 4.0 cm of magnesium metal
1.0 mol/L $HCl_{(aq)}$	water overflow container
one hole stopper	

Diagram

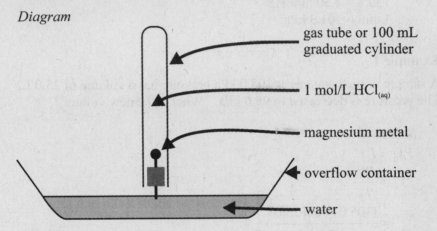

gas tube or 100 mL graduated cylinder

1 mol/L $HCl_{(aq)}$

magnesium metal

overflow container

water

Measure the mass of 1.0 m of $Mg_{(s)}$ ribbon

From this, find the mass of magnesium used.

Procedure
- Assemble apparatus as shown in diagram
- Fill tube half full of 1.0 mol/L $HCl_{(aq)}$
- Fill remainder with tap water
- Place rubber stopper with 2.0–4.0 cm of $Mg_{(s)}$ on tube.
- Invert tube in container of water
- After reaction is complete, equalize outside pressure with inside pressure by placing tube in a tall container of water.
- Read volume of gas produced.
- Clean lab area and put equipment away

Safety

1.0 mol/L $HCl_{(aq)}$ will burn skin. Wash off with water if it comes in contact with skin.

Observation

Volume of $H_{2(g)}$ _____

Analysis

$Mg_{(s)} + 2HCl_{(aq)} \rightarrow MgCl_{2(aq)} + H_{2(g)}$

Ratio between $Mg_{(s)}$ and $H_{2(s)}$ is 1:1 (Coefficients from balanced equation).

Therefore, the number of moles of $Mg_{(s)}$ will also be the number of moles of $H_{2(g)}$.

Conclusion

1 mol of $H_{2(g)}$ occupies _____ L.

$$\frac{\% \text{ difference between your value and } 24.8}{24.8} \times 100$$

Activity 2

Title

To find the constant (k) using Boyle's law.

Observation

Pressure (kPa)	Volume (L)
103.0	1.50
115.9	1.33
126.8	1.22
133.1	1.16
164.0	0.94
252.4	0.61
300.0	0.51

Analysis

Graph P vs. V where Volume is the manipulated variable and Pressure is the responding variable.

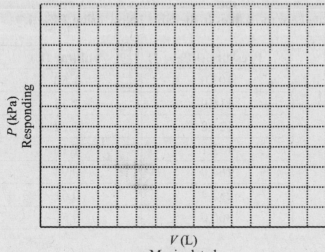

NOTES

To straighten out the above curved line graph, graph P vs. $\dfrac{1}{V}$

Pressure (kPa)	$\dfrac{1}{V}\left(\dfrac{1}{L}\right)$
103.0	
115.9	
126.8	
133.1	
164.0	
252.4	
300.0	

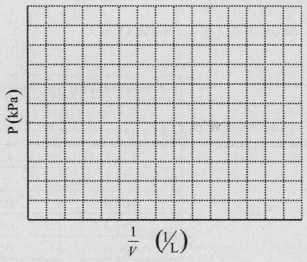

Find the slope of line for the P vs. $\dfrac{1}{V}$ graph.

This value is the constant for this data.

Slope of a line is the $\dfrac{\text{rise}}{\text{run}}$.

Calculate k for the values in the table below using $PV = k$.

Pressure (kPa)	Volume (L)	k
103.0	1.50	
115.9	1.33	
126.8	1.22	
133.1	1.16	
164.0	0.94	
252.4	0.61	
300.0	0.51	

Find the average for k. _____
How does it compare to the value of the slope?

PRACTICE EXERCISES

1. At a pressure of 75.0 kPa, a sample of gas has a volume of 450.0 mL. What is the volume at 96.5 kPa?

2. A sample of gas has a volume of 235 mL at a pressure of 115 kPa. What is the volume of the gas at 85.5 kPa?

3. A sample of gas has a volume of 3.25 L at a pressure of 775 mm Hg. What must the pressure be on this sample for the volume to change to 2.90 L?

4. A sample of gas has a volume of 24.0 L at STP. What will the volume be at a pressure of 150.0 kPa?

5. A sample of oxygen gas has a volume of 35.0 L at 85.0 kPa. What will the volume of the oxygen gas be at a pressure of 65.0 kPa?

Lesson 2   CHARLES' LAW AND TEMPERATURE SCALES

Charles' law was first published by Joseph Louis Gay-Lussac in 1802, but he used unpublished work by Charles from 1787.

Charles' Law does not work if temperatures are in Celsius. They must be in Kelvins.

In 1787 Jacques Charles summarized his observations about gas volume and temperature.

"For a constant mass of gas at constant pressure, the volume varies directly with its Kelvin (absolute) temperature."

$T \uparrow V \uparrow$
$T \downarrow V \downarrow$

Let V represent volume, and

T represent the Kelvin temperature, and

k represent a constant of proportionality.

Then, $\dfrac{V}{T} = k$

For two different conditions of temperature and volume of the same gas sample,

$$\frac{V_1}{T_1} = k$$

$$\frac{V_2}{T_2} = k$$

Therefore, $\dfrac{V_1}{T_1} = \dfrac{V_2}{T_2}$

Temperature Scales

When referring to the Kelvin scale, do not use °. Just use K.

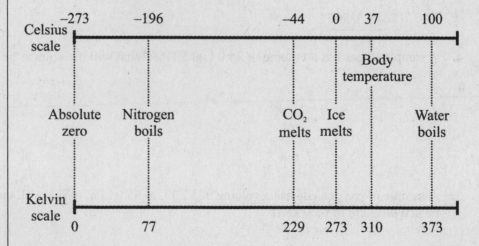

To convert from Celsius to Kelvin: K = °C + 273

94

Example 1

A sample of neon gas has a volume of 25.0 L at 25.0°C. What is the volume at 45.0°C?

Solution

$T_1 = 25.0°C = 298 \text{ K}$

$T_2 = 45.0°C = 318 \text{ K}$

$\dfrac{V_1}{T_1} = \dfrac{V_2}{T_2}$

$V_2 = \dfrac{V_1 T_2}{T_1}$

$\quad = \dfrac{(25.0 \text{ L})(318 \text{ K})}{298 \text{ K}}$

$\quad = 26.7 \text{ L}$

Example 2

A sample of helium gas has a volume of 445 L at 30.0°C. To what temperature must the helium be heated to increase the volume to 500 L?

Solution

$T_1 = 30.0°C = 303 \text{ K}$

$\dfrac{V_1}{T_1} = \dfrac{V_2}{T_2}$

$T_2 = \dfrac{T_1 V_2}{V_1}$

$\quad = \dfrac{(303 \text{ K})(500 \text{ L})}{445 \text{ L}}$

$\quad = 340 \text{ K}$

$\quad = 67.4°C$

ACTIVITIES

Activity 1

Title

To calculate Charles' Law constant.

Observations

The following data are for volumes vs. temperature at different pressures.

Pressure 1	
Volume (L)	Temperature (°C)
39.0	−50
48.0	0
57.0	50
65.5	100

Pressure 2	
Volume (L)	Temperature (°C)
30.0	−50
36.5	0
43.0	50
50.0	100

Pressure 3	
Volume (L)	Temperature (°C)
21.5	−50
26.3	0
31.1	50
36.0	100

Pressure 4	
Volume (L)	Temperature (°C)
13.0	−50
16.1	0
19.1	50
22.1	100

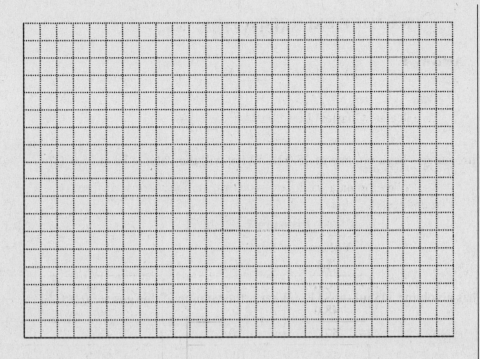

Analysis

(Hint: Temperature range should be from –300°C to 100°C.)

Graph all four sets of data on one set of axes labeling each line P_1, P_2, P_3 and P_4.
Calculate the constant for each line.

$k_1 = $ _____
$k_2 = $ _____
$k_3 = $ _____
$k_4 = $ _____

Extrapolate each line to the left until it crosses the horizontal axis.
At what point does each line cross the horizontal axis?

$P_1 = $ _____
$P_2 = $ _____
$P_3 = $ _____
$P_4 = $ _____

What do we call this point?

PRACTICE EXERCISES

1. **a)** 35°C = _____ K   **b)** −196°C = _____ K

 c) 212 K = _____ °C   **d)** 450 K = _____ °C

2. At 25.0°C, a sample of nitrogen gas has a volume of 45.0 L. What will the volume be at 75.0°C?

3. A sample of oxygen gas has a volume 345 mL at STP. What is the volume of this gas at 20.0°C?

4. A sample of gas at 110.0°C has a volume of 24.0 L. What is the volume of this gas at −45.0°C?

5. At 17.0°C, a sample of hydrogen gas has a volume of 45.0 L. To what temperature must this gas be heated to change the volume to 65.0 L?

6. A sample of argon gas has a volume of 38.0 L at 12.0°C. What is the volume of this sample at 112.0°C?

Lesson 3   COMBINED GAS LAW

What happens when both the temperature and the pressure of a gas changes at the same time?   Boyle's Law and Charles' Law can be combined into one relationship.

Boyle's Law gives this relationship: $P_1V_1 = P_2V_2$

Charles' Law gives this relationship: $\dfrac{V_1}{T_1} = \dfrac{V_2}{T_2}$

Combining these two laws: $\dfrac{P_1V_1}{T_1} = \dfrac{P_2V_2}{T_2}$

As in Charles' Law, temperature must be in Kelvins.

Example 1

A sample of ethane gas has a volume of 35.0 L at 25.0°C and 100.0 kPa. The temperature is increased to 35.0°C while the pressure drops to 85.0 kPa.   What is the volume of the gas?

Solution

$T_1 = 25.0°C = 298\ K$

$T_2 = 35.0°C = 308\ K$

$\dfrac{P_1V_1}{T_1} = \dfrac{P_2V_2}{T_2}$

$V_2 = \dfrac{P_1V_1T_2}{T_1P_2}$

$\quad = \dfrac{(100.0\ \text{kPa})(35.0\ \text{L})(308\ \text{K})}{(85.0\ \text{kPa})(298\ \text{K})} = 42.6\ \text{L}$

Example 2

A sample of neon gas has a volume of 145 mL at −10.0°C and 755 mm Hg. The temperature is increased to 45.0°C and the pressure is increased to 805 mm Hg.   What is the new volume of the neon gas?

Solution

$T_1 = -10.0°C = 263\ K$

$T_2 = 45.0°C = 318\ K$

$\dfrac{P_1V_1}{T_1} = \dfrac{P_2V_2}{T_2}$

$V_2 = \dfrac{P_1V_1T_2}{T_1P_2}$

$\quad = \dfrac{(755\ \text{mm Hg})(145\ \text{mL})(318\ \text{K})}{(263\ \text{K})(805\ \text{mm Hg})}$

$\quad = 164\ \text{mL}$

Gay-Lussac's Law (The Law of Combining Volumes)

In 1808, Joseph Gay-Lussac performed a series of experiments measuring the relative volumes of gases involved in chemical reactions.

The results led to the Law of Combining Volumes: "When measured at the same temperature and pressure, volumes of gaseous reactants and products of chemical reactions are always in simple ratios of whole numbers."

Avogadro's Theory

In 1810 the Italian scientist Amadeo Avogadro proposed an explanation for the Law of Combining Volumes: "Equal volumes of gases at the same temperature and pressure contain equal numbers of molecules and therefore the same number of moles." This means that the volume of a gas is directly proportional to the number of moles of gas present.

Kinetic Molecular Theory

The Kinetic Molecular Theory is a theory of matter with the following precepts:

- all matter is composed of particles (atoms, ions, etc.)
- there are spaces between the particles
- the particles are in constant motion
- there are forces of attraction between particles

The Kinetic Molecular Theory can be used to explain various phenomena in science, such as the states of matter.

Solids: the particles are held tightly together by strong forces of attraction and have only slight vibrational motion.

Liquids: the particles have weaker forces of attraction between them, greater spaces and greater motion. Particles can slip and slide over one another.

Gases: particles are moving rapidly, separated by large spaces with weak forces of attraction between them.

Ideal vs Real Gases

An ideal gas behaves perfectly under all conditions of pressure, temperature and volume.

For example, ideal gases do not condense into liquids.
They have particles of zero size that have no forces of attraction between them and their V vs. T and P vs. T graphs are straight lines.

Real gases deviate most from ideal gases at low temperature and high pressure. As temperature increases and pressure decreases, real gases behave more ideally.

Small gas molecules (e.g., H_2) behave more ideally than large gas molecules (e.g., I_2).

The following chart compares the theoretical nature of real and ideal gases:

Real Gas	Ideal Gas
molecules have a distinct size and are "soft"	molecules are point masses (have no size) and are "hard"
forces of attraction between molecules cause them to condense into a liquid if the temperature gets low enough	molecules do not have forces of attraction among them so there is no cause for them to condense into liquid
molecules move about randomly, but because of the attraction between them, they don't travel in straight lines—they are influenced by each other	molecules of gas move about randomly; only collisions with container walls and other molecules cause them to change direction
collisions between molecules are inelastic—kinetic energy isn't conserved	collisions between molecules are elastic—kinetic energy is conserved

An ideal gas behaves perfectly under all conditions.

Real gases deviate most from ideal gases at low temperature and high pressure

Small molecules behave more ideally than large gas molecules

PRACTICE EXERCISES

V_1 P_1

1. 24.5 L of chlorine gas at 110.0 kPa and 25.0°C is changed to 95.0 kPa and 45.0°C. What is the new volume?

$V_2 = ?$ T_1 P_2 T_2

2. A sample of fluorine gas with a volume of 45.0 L at STP is changed to 111 kPa and 35.0°C. What is the new volume of the gas?

V_1 P_1 T_1 V_2 T_2 P_2

3. A gas sample has a volume of 50.0 L at 775 mm Hg and 30.0°C. What is the volume at STP?

4. 150.0 mL of hydrogen gas at 35.0°C and 120.0 kPa is changed to 10.0°C and 140.0 kPa. What is the new volume?

V_1 T_1 P_1

5. A sample of argon gas has a volume of 775 mL at –25.0°C and 660 mm Hg. The temperature is increased to 45.0°C and the pressure to 885 mm Hg. What is the new volume?

T_2 P_2 $V_2 = ?$

For the following questions explain each of the following concepts in terms of the theoretical concepts of the kinetic molecular theory.

6. The pressure exerted by a gas increases when the temperature is increased.

7. Gases have indefinite shapes and volumes compared to solids (in an open system).

8. Gases are compressible (liquids and solids generally are not).

9. Gases fill and assume the shape of their container.

10. Real gases are most like ideal gases at high temperature and low pressure.

Lesson 4   THE IDEAL GAS LAW

Let V represent volume

P represent pressure

T represent Kelvin temperature

n represent the number of moles of gas

From: Boyle's Law PV = a constant

Charles' Law $\dfrac{P}{T}$ = a constant

Avogadro's Theory $\dfrac{V}{n}$ = a constant

Then, putting all three relationships together,

Ideal Gas Equation

$\dfrac{PV}{nT}$ = a constant, R, which is known as the universal gas constant.

$$R = 8.31 \frac{L \times kPa}{mol \times K}$$

$PV = nRT$

This relationship is usually represented as:

$$PV = nRT$$

R is the ideal gas constant

Example

$8.31 \dfrac{L \times kPa}{mol \times K}$

What is the volume of 3.35 mol of neon at 42.5°C and 96.5 kPa?

Solution

$T = 42.05°C = 315.5 \text{ K}$

$PV = nRT$

$V = \dfrac{nRT}{P}$

$= \dfrac{(3.35\,\text{mol})(8.31\,\text{L} \times \text{kPa/mol} \times \text{K})(315.5\,\text{K})}{96.5\,\text{kPa}}$

$= 91.0\,\text{L}$

Example

What is the volume of 66.4 g of $CO_{2(g)}$ at 32.0°C and 115 kPa?

Solution

Molar mass of CO_2:

(1 mol C) (12.01 g/mol) = 12.01 g
(2 mol O) (16.00 g/mol) = 32.00 g
        1 mol   = 44.01 g

Number of moles,

$$n - \frac{m}{M}$$

$$= \frac{66.4\,g}{44.01\,g/mol}$$

$$= 1.15\,mol$$

$T = 32.0°C = 305\,K$

$PV = nRT$

$$V = \frac{nRT}{P}$$

$$= \frac{(1.51\,mol)(8.31\,L \times kPa/mol \times K)(305\,K)}{115\,kPa}$$

$$= 33.3\,L$$

PRACTICE EXERCISES

1. What is the volume of 2.50 mol of methane gas at 25.0°C and 95.0 kPa?

2. What is the mass of 34.0 L of carbon dioxide gas at 30.0°C and 115 kPa?

3. What is the volume of 44.0 g of butane gas, $C_4H_{10(g)}$, at 45.0°C and 95.0 kPa?

4. To what temperature must 20.2 g of $H_{2(g)}$ be heated at 110 kPa to occupy a volume of 345 L?

5. What is the mass of 48.0 L of oxygen gas at 55.0°C and 96.5 kPa?

6. 0.575 g of an ideal gas has a volume of 350 mL at 105 kPa and 24.0°C.   What is its molar mass?

106

REVIEW SUMMARY

- STP is 273 K and 101.3 kPa.
- SATP is 298 K and 100 kPa.
- The volume of one mole of a gas at STP is 22.4 L.
- The volume of one mole of gas at SATP is 24.8 L.
- Boyle's law states that $P_1V_1 = P_2V_2$
- 1 kPa = 7.50 mm Hg
- Charles' Law states that $\dfrac{V_1}{T_1} = \dfrac{V_2}{T_2}$
- To convert from Celsius to Kelvin: K = °C + 273
- The combined gas law provides a formula that allows both pressure and temperature variables to be manipulated:

$$\frac{P_1V_1}{T_1} = \frac{P_2V_2}{T_2}$$

- Treating all gases as ideal gases simplifies calculations and can provide good approximations to help solve problems. Real gases can behave differently than the 'ideal' case, however:
    - extreme conditions of low temperatures or high pressures can cause real gases to behave differently than an ideal gas.
    - Large gas molecules are more likely to deviate from ideal gas behavior than are smaller molecules.
- The Ideal Gas Law combines Boyle's Law, Charles' Law, and Avogadro's Theory into one form, the Ideal Gas Equation:

$$PV = nRT$$

- R is the ideal gas constant $8.31\dfrac{L \times kPa}{mol \times K}$

PRACTICE TEST

1. State Boyle's Law.

2. If the pressure of a gas is doubled at constant temperature, how is the volume affected?

3. State Charles' Law.

4. State the effect on the volume of a gas when the temperature:

   a) increases by a factor of two

   b) decreases by a factor of four

5. State the variable or variables that are assumed to be constant for each of the following:

   a) Boyle's Law

   b) Charles' Law

   c) Combined Gas Law

   d) Ideal Gas Law

6. State Avogadro's Law.

7. Explain the difference between STP and SATP.

8. Calculate the volume of gas involved for each of the following:

   a) 20 L of N_2 at 100 kPa if the pressure is reduced to 75 kPa.

   b) 15 L of oxygen if the temperature is increased from 75 K to 175 K.

   c) 100 mL of gas at 25°C and 50 kPa is heated to 75°C and 100 kPa pressure.

   d) 1.50 g of gas (oxygen) at a temperature of 75°C and 60 kPa pressure

   e) 300 mL of chlorine gas at –15°C and 115 kPa if the conditions are changed to SATP.

9. Find the molar mass of nitrogen dioxide if 0.456 g occupies a volume of 150 mL at 30°C and a pressure of 150 kPa.

Use the following information to answer the next two questions.

Given the following gas laws:

1. $P_1V_1 = P_2V_2$

2. $\dfrac{V_1}{T_1} = \dfrac{V_2}{T_2}$

3. $\dfrac{P_1V_1}{T_1} = \dfrac{P_2V_2}{T_2}$

4. $PV = nRT$

10. Charles' gas law is

A. 1   B. 2
C. 3   D. 4

11. The ideal gas law is

A. 1   B. 2
C. 3   D. 4

12. −25°C when changed to K will have what numerical value?

A. 25   B. 248
C. 273   D. 298

13. What would the pressure of a gas be, originally at 760 mm of Hg, if the temperature is lowered from 95.0°C to 85.0°C at constant volume?

A. 781 mm of Hg   B. 753 mm of Hg
C. 739 mm of Hg   D. 680 mm of Hg

14. A gas sample weighing 0.528 g is collected in a flask having a volume of 126 mL.
At 75°C, the pressure of the gas is 101 kPa. The molar mass of the gas is closest to which one of the following?

A. 180 g/mol   B. 160 g/mol
C. 120 g/mol   D. 100 g/mol

15. Under what conditions do real gases deviate most from ideal gas behavior?

    A. high temperature and high pressure
    B. low temperature and high pressure
    C. low temperature and low pressure
    D. high temperature and low pressure

16. A sample of gas with a volume of 800 mL and pressure of 1.00 atm is brought to a volume of 250 mL at constant temperature. What is the final pressure of the gas?

    A. 0.313 atm   B. 1.00 atm
    C. 3.20 atm   D. 2.20 atm

NOTES

MATTER AS SOLUTIONS, ACIDS AND BASES

When you are finished this unit, you will be able to…

- recall the categories of pure substances and mixtures

- provide examples from living and nonliving systems that illustrate how dissolving substances in water is often a prerequisite for chemical change

- differentiate between electrolytes and nonelectrolytes

- determine mass or volume of a solution from the concentration of that solution

- use data and ionization/dissociation equations to calculate the concentration of ions in a solution

- define solubility and identify conditions that affect solubility

- explain saturation in terms of equilibrium and crystallization

- describe the procedures and calculations required for preparing and diluting solutions

- identify monoprotic and polyprotic acids and bases and compare their ionization/dissociation

- define neutralization as a reaction between hydronium and hydroxide ions

- explain how the use of indicators, pH paper or pH meters can be used to measure $H_3O^+_{(aq)}$

Lesson	Page	Completed on
1. Definitions of Solutions, Acids and Bases	114	
2. Aqueous Solutions	122	
3. Concentration of Solutions	131	
4. Solubility	145	
5. Acids and Bases	155	
Review Summary	169	
Practice Test	170	
Answers and Solutions	at the back of the book	

PREREQUISITE SKILLS AND KNOWLEDGE

Prior to starting this unit, you should be able to…

- recall International Union of Pure and Applied Chemistry (IUPAC) nomenclature of acids and bases

- discriminate between pure substances, mixtures, and solutions

- define potential hydrogen as a characteristic of a solution

- understand and apply the meaning of WHMIS symbols to safe laboratory practices

- compose and solve balanced chemical equations

- solve mathematical expressions involving logarithms

- interpret balanced chemical equations in terms of moles of chemical species, and relate the mole concept to the law of conservation of mass

- solve simple algebraic linear equations using ratio, proportion, and percentage to express the results

Lesson 1 DEFINITIONS OF SOLUTIONS, ACIDS AND BASES

NOTES

Definitions

A solution is a homogeneous (the same, or uniform, throughout) mixture of two or more substances. The particles in a solution are:

1. of molecular size
2. scattered randomly throughout the solution
3. in constant motion

(larger Quantity)
water

Solvent – material that dissolves the solute.

sugar
(smaller quantity)

The substance that is present in larger quantity is usually referred to as the solvent. The substance present in smaller quantity, which is dissolved in the solvent, is usually referred to as the solute.

For example, sugar dissolves in pure water to form a solution. Water is the solvent, and sugar is the solute.

Classification of Matter

To understand the nature of solutions we need to distinguish between pure substances, heterogeneous mixtures, and solutions.

Pure Substance

elements   *compounds*

• can't be broken down

• 2 or more elements

• may be decomposite into simpler substances

1. A pure substance is a homogeneous (uniform) material. It consists of only one particular kind of matter, and therefore, always has the same composition and properties throughout. Pure substances can be classified into two categories:
    • Elements are pure substances which cannot be broken down into simpler substances by ordinary chemical methods. Examples are carbon (C), oxygen (O_2), iron (Fe), and sulfur (S_8).

    • Compounds are pure substances which consist of two or more elements in combination. They may be decomposed into two or more simpler substances by ordinary chemical methods. Examples are water (H_2O), carbon dioxide (CO_2), and sodium chloride (NaCl).

2. A mixture is a combination of two or more pure substances, each of which retains its own chemical and physical properties.

Heterogeneous – mixture of more than one phase.

3. A heterogeneous mixture is a non-uniform mixture which consists of more than one phase. Phase refers to any region with a uniform set of properties. For example, a mixture of sand and water consists of two phases: the solid sand and the liquid water phases. A mixture of brown sand and white sugar consists of two phases: the solid brown sand and the solid white sugar phases.

A heterogeneous mixture is easily identified because the borderline or interface between different phases is easily seen. A salami, mushroom, and cheese pizza is a heterogeneous mixture with several identifiable components. Milk, too, is a heterogeneous mixture. On close examination, we can see that it consists of small fat droplets suspended in a water layer.

Heterogeneous mixtures are not uniform throughout. Different portions (or phases) have different sets of properties. In addition, the composition can vary. On your pizza you can ask for more salami and less mushroom, or some of the fat can be removed from milk to produce skim milk or partially skimmed milk. It is this last feature (variability of composition) that distinguishes mixtures from pure substances.

4. A homogeneous mixture has only one phase, and it is called a solution. It is uniform throughout. A solution, like a heterogeneous mixture, may have a variable composition but only within certain limits. For most solutions, the solubility of one substance in another is limited.

Homogeneous – consists <u>only of one phase.</u>

Classification of Matter

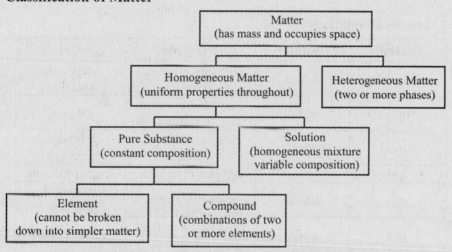

A pure liquid will boil at a fixed, constant temperature. A solution will boil over a range of temperatures that is higher than that of the solvent. The addition of a solute will always increase the boiling point.

A liquid containing a solute will boil at a higher temperature than the pure liquid.

As the solution boils, it will become more concentrated, and its boiling point will get higher.

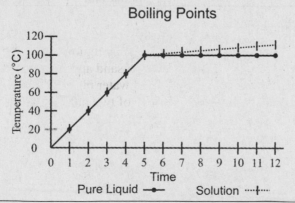

NOTES

Types of Solutions

Liquid Solutions: Liquid solutions are made by dissolving solids, liquids, or gases in liquids. Examples include:

solid in liquid – sugar dissolved in water
liquid in liquid – methanol dissolved in water
gas in liquid – carbon dioxide dissolved in water

Gaseous Solutions: Gaseous solutions are made by dissolving a gas, liquid, or solid in a gas. All gases mix in all proportions to produce solutions. Air, for example, is a solution of oxygen, carbon dioxide, and many other gases dissolved in nitrogen. It is possible for liquids and solids to dissolve in gases, but examples are rare.

Solid Solutions: Solid solutions are formed when a solid, liquid, or gas is mixed with a solid substance to produce a homogeneous mixture. (The mixing may occur only when the solid solvent has been heated to a liquid and then allowed to cool.) A solid solution of one metal (or several) in another is called an alloy. For example, brass is a solid solution of zinc dissolved in copper.

Examples of Solutions

Solvent	Solute	Example	Use
liquid	liquid	ethylene glycol in water	antifreeze solution
liquid	solid	ammonium nitrate in water	ice pack
liquid	gas	carbon dioxide in water	carbonated beverages
gas	gas	oxygen in helium	deep sea diving
gas	liquid	gasoline in air	automobile engines
gas	solid	p-dichlorobenzene in air	moth crystals
solid	solid	copper in gold	jewelry
solid	liquid	mercury in silver and copper	dental amalgams
solid	gas	hydrogen in palladium	gas stove lighter

116

ACTIVITIES

Activity 1

Title
Properties of Liquids

Problem
Which liquids are
• pure liquids
• liquids containing dissolved solids

Materials
Dropper bottles containing:
distilled water
tap water
unknown liquids
bunsen burner
glass slides
tongs

Safety Precaution
1. Glass slides will break if put in flame.
2. Hot slides will break if rinsed under tap water.
3. Hot slides will burn skin and flesh.

Procedure
1. Place 2 or 3 drops of liquid from a dropper bottle on a slide.
2. Gently heat slide with bunsen burner until liquid evaporates.
3. Examine for residue and record data

Observations

Material	Residue	No Residue

Activity 2

Title

Boiling Points of Liquids

Problem

How will the boiling points of the pure liquids differ from those of the liquid mixtures?

Materials

methanol (50 mL)	water-methanol mixture (50 mL)
ethanol (50 mL)	water-ethanol mixture (50 mL)
ethanol-methanol mixture (50 mL)	water (50 mL)
hot plate	distillation apparatus

Procedure

Data Table

Graph of Temperature, Time Data for Each Liquid

Analysis

For each liquid, state whether it is a mixture or a pure substance.

Activity 3

Title

Energy Changes During Dissolving

Problem

Does the temperature decrease, increase, or remain the same when the given solids dissolve in water?

Materials

ammonium chloride, calcium acetate, potassium nitrate, ammonium nitrate, potassium hydroxide, copper (II) sulfate-5-er or anhydrous electronic balance, beakers, scoopula, thermometer, retort stand, graduated cylinder, clamp

Procedure

• Measure 25 mL of water and record temperature.
• Dissolve 1.0 g of each compound in the water.
• Record final temperature

Observations

Material	Initial Temperature	Final Temperature	ΔT(°C)
ammonium chloride			
calcium acetate			
potassium nitrate			
ammonium nitrate			
potassium hydroxide			
copper (II) sulfate (anhydrous)			

Analysis

State whether dissolving absorbed or released energy for each substance.

PRACTICE EXERCISES

1. Operationally (empirically) define:

   a) solute

   b) solvent

   c) solution

2. Identify the solvent and solute in the following solutions:

   a) 15 mL water in 85 mL of methanol

   b) 0.1 g sugar in 100 mL of water

   c) 0.1 mol/L solution of $NaOH_{(aq)}$

3. Explain the difference between the following:

   a) a solution and a heterogeneous mixture

   b) a solution and a pure substance

4. What tests would you perform to determine whether the following homogeneous substances are solutions or pure substances?

a) a white solid

b) a colorless liquid

5. Operationally (empirically) define soluble.

6. List five solutions used in the home.

7. Classify the following solutions as solid, liquid, or gaseous:

Solution	Type
sugar and water	
air	
copper and zinc	
carbonated beverage	
alcohol and water	
table salt and water	

Lesson 2 AQUEOUS SOLUTIONS

Solutions made by dissolving solutes in water are called aqueous solutions.

The Importance of Aqueous Solutions

Chemists work mainly with liquid solutions, rather than gaseous or solid solutions. Particles in the liquid phase are relatively mobile and can easily collide with one another to cause reactions. Water is the liquid solvent most commonly used by chemists. It is sometimes referred to as the "universal solvent." It is an excellent solvent for many solutes because of its polarity.

Water is one of our most abundant chemicals. In fact, two-thirds of our body mass is water, and our life processes depend upon reactions in aqueous solution. Important chemicals such as hormones and nutrients are transported throughout the human body dissolved in blood, which is composed mainly of water.

Energy Changes in the Formation of Aqueous Solutions

If the temperature of a solution rises as a solute is dissolved, then the solution process is said to be exothermic. Heat energy is released to the solvent and surrounding matter during the dissolving process. That is, energy is a product of the dissolving process.

If the temperature of a solution decreases as a solute is dissolved, then the solution process is said to be endothermic. Heat energy is absorbed from the solvent and surrounding matter during the dissolving process. That is, energy is required to be added in order to cause dissolving to occur.

The Solution Process Model

Chemists have proposed a model describing what happens when a solute dissolves in a solvent. According to this model the solution process occurs in three simultaneous steps:

1. the solvent particles separate from each other
2. the solute particles separate from each other
3. the solute particles attract and bond to the solvent particles

Steps 1 and 2 are endothermic since energy must be supplied in order to pull apart particles in both the solvent and solute. Step 3 is exothermic since when particles attract each other energy is released as the particles achieve a more stable energy state.

Since dissolving always includes all three steps in the solution process, whether the dissolving will be endothermic or exothermic depends on the sum of the energies involved in the three steps. It is not possible to separate the steps when we investigate the dissolving process in the laboratory; we can only observe the over-all effect.

NOTES

Exothermic – heat is released.

Endothermic – heat is absorbed.

Electrolytes and Non-electrolytes

Some solutions will conduct an electric current, and the solutes in these solutions are called electrolytes. The electrical conductivity of solutions is tested with a simple apparatus consisting of a light bulb in series with a pair of electrodes. When this apparatus is connected to a source of electricity, no current can flow as long as the electrodes are separated. A current will flow (and the bulb glow) only when the electrodes are joined by a substance which will conduct electricity, such as a copper wire or a solution of an electrolyte.

In order for a solution to conduct electricity, charged particles (ions) must exist in solution. It is the movement of charged particles that allows an electric current to pass through a solution of an electrolyte. Positive ions are attracted to the negative electrode, and negative ions are attracted to the positive electrode.

There are some solutions through which an electric current will not pass. The solutes in these solutions are called non-electrolytes.

Non-electrolytes contain solutes which form neutral molecules in solution. These molecules are not affected by the presence of electrodes carrying a potential difference. No current flows and the solutions are non-conductors.

Changes in Structure in Aqueous Solution Formation

When nonelectrolytes dissolve in water, the particles of the solute are separated from each other, but their structure remains unchanged. When electrolytes dissolve in water, the particles undergo a structural change. There are two mechanisms which can be used to describe the changes that take place—dissociation and ionization.

1. **Dissociation:** The separation of ions from the crystals of ionic compounds during the solution process is called dissociation. For example, when sodium chloride dissolves in water, sodium ions and chloride ions are formed. Upon dissolving, the ions are separated and surrounded by water molecules. This process by which a solvent surrounds and attracts solution particles is called solvation. In water the process is also known as hydration.

   Water molecules are polar; that is, they have a positive and negative end. The positive end of water molecules will be attracted to the negative chloride ions, and the negative ends of the water molecules will attracted to the positive sodium ions. The water-surrounded sodium ions are called hydrated or aqueous sodium ions, and the water-surrounded chloride ions are called hydrated or aqueous chloride ions. This can be represented by an equation:

$$NaCl_{(s)} \rightarrow Na^+_{(aq)} + Cl^-_{(aq)}$$

Electrolyte—will conduct an electric current in solution.

Non-electrolyte—will not conduct an electric current in solution.

- dissolve in water, particle of solute are seperated, but structure remains unchanged

$$NaCl + H_2O \rightarrow Na^+ + Cl^- + H_2O.$$

$$Na^+_{(aq)} + Cl^-_{(aq)}$$

<u>Disassociation</u> = (separation of ions)

NOTES

Balancing

$K_2SO_{4(s)} \rightarrow 2K^+_{(aq)} + SO_4^{2-}_{(aq)}$

| $K = 2$ | $K = X2$ |
| $SO_4 = 1$ | $SO_4 = 1$ |

$Ca(NO_3)_2 \rightarrow Ca^{2+}_{(aq)} + 2(NO_3)^-_{(aq)}$

| $Ca = 1$ | $Ca = 1$ |
| $NO_3 = 2$ | $NO_3 = X2$ |

<u>Ionization</u> (formation of ions)

$HCl + H_2O \rightarrow H_3O^+_{(aq)} + Cl^-_{(aq)}$

Other ionic substances behave in a similar manner:

$$K_2SO_{4(s)} \rightarrow 2K^+_{(aq)} + SO_4^{2-}_{(aq)}$$
$$Ca(NO_3)_{2(s)} \rightarrow Ca^{2+}_{(aq)} + 2NO_3^-_{(aq)}$$

Note that the total positive charge of the ions must always equal the total negative charge. That is, the solution is always electrically neutral. The presence of ions explains why these solutes are electrolytes.

2. **Ionization:** The <u>formation of ions</u> from polar molecules by the action of the solvent is called ionization. For example, when hydrogen chloride gas dissolves in water, hydronium ions and chloride ions are formed:

$$HCl_{(g)} + H_2O_{(l)} \rightarrow H_3O^+_{(aq)} + Cl^-_{(aq)}$$

Because hydrogen is not a metal, hydrogen chloride is not an ionic substance. When dissolved in water, the molecule ionizes to produce H^+ and Cl^-. The H^+ is immediately hydrated, forming a hydronium ion, $H_3O^+_{(aq)}$.

Other molecular substances behave in a similar manner:

$$HBr_{(g)} + H_2O_{(l)} \rightarrow H_3O^+_{(aq)} + Br^-_{(aq)}$$
$$NH_{3(g)} + H_2O_{(l)} \rightarrow NH_4^+_{(aq)} + OH^-_{(aq)}$$

The presence of ions explains why these solutes are electrolytes.

ACTIVITIES

Activity 1

Title
Conducting Liquids

Problem
Which liquids conduct an electric current?

Materials

distilled water (25 mL)	methanol (25 mL)
ethanoic acid (25 mL)	hydrochloric acid (25 mL)
potassium nitrate aqueous (25 mL)	sucrose aqueous (25 mL)
sodium chloride aqueous (25 mL)	beakers
copper (II) sulfate aqueous (25 mL)	
conductivity apparatus	

Procedure
Place each solution in a beaker and test with conductivity apparatus.

Observation

Material	Conductor	Non Conductor

PRACTICE EXERCISES

1. Write dissociation equations for each of the following solid ionic compounds:

a) sodium sulfate

b) calcium chloride

c) copper (II) nitrate

d) barium chloride

e) zinc sulfate

f) lithium hydroxide

g) magnesium bromide

h) potassium sulfide

i) aluminium sulfate

j) magnesium iodide

2. Write ionization equations for each of the following compounds:

   a) $HI_{(g)}$

   b) $HNO_{3(aq)}$

   c) $HClO_{3(aq)}$

   d) $H_2SO_{4(aq)}$

3. Operationally (empirically) define the following terms:

   a) aqueous solution

   b) exothermic change

   c) endothermic change

   d) electrolyte

   e) non-electrolyte

4. Conceptually (theoretically) define the following terms

   a) electrolyte

   b) non-electrolyte

   c) solution process model

   d) hydration

   e) hydronium ion

5. Describe a solution.

6. Ammonium nitrate and water are used in cold packs. These packs can be used in place of ice to keep food cool. Propose a hypothesis to explain how a cold pack might work.

7. Describe how a solid dissolves in a liquid solvent.

8. Why do many chemical reactions occur in aqueous solution?

9. Distinguish between dissociation and ionization.

10. Write dissociation equations for the following ionic solids dissolving in water:

   a)   sodium hydroxide

   b)   magnesium bromide

   c)   potassium carbonate

   d)   aluminium nitrate

   e)   calcium phosphate

11. Write ionization equations for the following molecular compounds dissolving in water:

   a)   hydrogen bromide

   b)   methanoic acid

   c)   sulfuric acid

   d)   carbonic acid

   e)   nitric acid

   f)   chlorous acid

12. Predict whether the following solutes will be electrolytes or nonelectrolytes:

   a) potassium chloride

   b) hydrogen chloride

   c) sucrose

   d) sodium carbonate

   e) ethanoic acid

   f) carbon dioxide

   g) sulfur dioxide

Lesson 3 CONCENTRATION OF SOLUTIONS

Defining Concentration

The concentration of a solution is defined as the amount, mass, or volume of solute in a unit volume of solution. There are various ways in which concentration can be measured: the percentage of solute compared to solvent by volume, percentage of solute compared to solvent by mass, moles of solute per unit volume of solvent, and moles of solute per unit volume of solution. The most common expression used by chemists is the last—moles of solute per unit volume of solution (litre). Therefore, the units of concentration are moles per litre (mol/L).

Qualitatively, the concentration of solutions can be referred to as concentrated or dilute. A concentrated solution contains a relatively large amount of solute compared to the amount of solvent. A dilute solution contains a relatively small amount of solute compared to the amount of solvent.

Concentration is often represented by square brackets around the formula. For example, [NaCl] means the concentration of sodium chloride solution in moles per litre.

Calculation of Concentrations

Let C represent the concentration in moles per litre,

      V represent the volume of solution in litres, and

      n represent the number of moles of solute

$$\text{Concentration, } C = \frac{n}{V} \quad \frac{mol}{\ell}$$

$$\text{Number of moles of solute, } n = CV$$

$$\text{Volume of solution, } V = \frac{n}{C}$$

$$\text{Mol} = CV$$

Calculation of Ion Concentration in Electrolytes

Electrolytes form ions in solution. Often we will refer to the concentration of an electrolyte by describing the number of moles of solute that are dissolved in one litre of solution. For example, if we dissolve 0.23 mol of aluminium sulfate in 1.0 L of solution, we can say that the concentration of the aluminium sulfate solution is 0.23 mol/L. However, the solute does not exist in solution as a single entity, but rather it dissociates into ions according to the following equation:

$$Al_2(SO_4)_{3(s)} \rightarrow 2Al^{3+}_{(aq)} + 3SO_4^{2-}_{(aq)}$$

$$C = \frac{n}{V} = \frac{0.23\ mol}{1\ \ell} = 0.23\ \frac{mol}{\ell}$$

$$1 \quad : \quad 2 \quad : \quad 3$$

$$0.23\ \frac{mol}{\ell} : 0.46\ \frac{mol}{\ell} : 0.69\ \frac{mol}{\ell}$$

NOTES

Since every mole of aluminium sulfate dissociates to form two moles aluminium ion, the concentration of the aluminium ion will be two times the concentration of the aluminium sulfate.

$$\left[Al^{3+}_{(aq)}\right] = 2 \times 0.23 \text{ mol/L} = 0.46 \text{ mol/L}$$

Similarly, the concentration of the sulfate ion will be three times the concentration of the aluminium sulfate.

$$\left[SO_4^{2-}_{(aq)}\right] = 3 \times 0.23 \text{ mol/L} = 0.69 \text{ mol/L}$$

Dilution of Solutions

A more concentrated solution can be diluted to a less concentrated solution by adding more solvent.

The number of moles of solute remains the same in both solutions.

Then, $n_1 = n_2$
$C_1V_1 = C_2V_2$

$C = \dfrac{n}{V} = \dfrac{0.9 \text{ mol}}{0.5\,l}$

$= 1.8 \text{ mol/}l$

Example 1

$0.5\,l$

n

0.900 mol of $NaCl_{(s)}$ is dissolved to give 500.0 mL of solution, what is the concentration of the solution?

C

Solution

$$\text{Concentration} = \frac{\text{mol}}{\text{Volume}(L)}$$

$$= \frac{n}{V}$$

$$= \frac{0.900 \text{ mol}}{0.500 \text{ L}}$$

$$= 1.80 \text{ mol/L}$$

Example 2

n V C

How many moles of solute are in 2.00 L of a 0.0025 mol/L solution of $KMnO_{4(aq)}$?

Solution

$$\text{Concentration} = \frac{\text{mol}}{V}$$

Therefore, number of mol $= CV$

$$= (0.002\,5 \text{ mol/L})(2.00 \text{ L})$$

$$= 0.005\,0 \text{ mol}$$

$C = \dfrac{n}{V}$

$n = CV$

$= 0.0025 \text{ mol/}l \times 2\,l$

$= 0.005 \text{ mol}$

Example 3

What volume of 0.71 mol/L sodium hydrogen carbonate solution contains 0.179 mol of the solute?

Handwritten:
$C = \dfrac{n}{V}$
$V = \dfrac{n}{C} = \dfrac{0.179 \text{ mol}}{0.71 \text{ mol/L}} = 0.252 \text{ L}$

Solution

$$\text{Concentration} = \frac{\text{mol}}{\text{Volume}(L)}$$

$$V = \frac{n}{C}$$

$$= \frac{0.179 \text{ mol}}{0.716 \text{ mol/L}}$$

$$= 0.250 \text{ L or } 250 \text{ mL}$$

The volume of solution is 0.250 L or 250 mL.

Example 4

What mass of sodium carbonate decahydrate is needed to make 0.400 L of a 0.050 0 mol/L solution?

Handwritten right margin:
① $C = \dfrac{n}{V}$
$n = CV$
$= 0.05 \text{ mol} / (0.4 \text{ L})$
$n = 0.02 \text{ mol}$

② $n = \dfrac{m}{M}$
$M = n \cdot M$
$= 0.02 \text{ mol} \times 286^{\text{g}}$
$= 5.724$ g

$Na_2 CO_3 \cdot 10 H_2O$

Handwritten center:
Molar Mass.
$2 Na \ 2(22.99)$
$CO_3 \ 12.01 + 3(16.0)$
$H_2O \ 10((1.01 \times 2) + 16)$
$286.19 \ ^g/_{mol}$

Solution

Moles needed:

mol	=	(Concentration) (Volume(L))
	=	(0.050 0 mol/L) (0.400 L)
	=	0.020 0 mol

Molar mass of $Na_2CO_3 \times 10H_2O_{(s)}$:

2 Na	= 2 × 22.99 g	= 45.98 g
1 C	= 1 × 12.01 g	= 12.01 g
3 O	= 3 × 16.00 g	= 48.00 g
10 HOH	= 10 × 18.02 g	= 180.20 g
		286.19 g

Mass needed:

$$\frac{285.99 \text{ g}}{1 \text{ mol}} = \frac{y}{0.020 \ 0 \text{ mol}}$$

$$(y)(1 \text{ mol}) = (286.19 \text{ g})(0.020 \ 0 \text{ mol})$$

$$y = \frac{(286.19 \text{ g})(0.020 \ 0 \text{ mol})}{(1 \text{ mol})}$$

$$y = 5.72 \text{ g}$$

The mass required is 5.72 g.

NOTES

Alternative Solution

Number of moles $Na_2CO_3 \times 10H_2O$,

$$n = CV$$
$$= (0.0500 \, mol / L)(0.400 \, L)$$
$$= 0.0200 \, mol$$

Mass of solute,

$$m = n \times M$$
$$= (0.0200 \, mol)(286.19 \, g / mol)$$
$$= 5.72 \, g$$

Example 5

What is the concentration of the solution if 25.0 mL of 2.00 mol/L $NaCl_{(aq)}$ is diluted to a new volume of 125 mL?

Solution

$$\boxed{C_1V_1 = C_2V_2}$$
$$C_2 = \frac{C_1V_1}{V_2}$$
$$= \frac{(2.00 \, mol/L)(25.0 \, mL)}{125 \, mL}$$
$$= 0.400 \, mol/L$$

Example 6

What volume of 12.1 mol/L $HCl_{(aq)}$ is needed to make 300.0 mL of 1.25 mol/L solution?

Solution

$$C_1V_1 = C_2V_2$$
$$V_1 = \frac{C_2V_2}{C_1}$$
$$= \frac{(1.25 \, mol/L)(300.0 \, mL)}{12.1 \, mol/L}$$
$$= 31.0 \, mL$$

— Handwritten annotations —

$C = \dfrac{n}{V}$ $n = CV$
$\quad = 2 \, \text{mol} \cdot 0.025\ell$
$n_2 = 0.05 \, mol$

$C = \dfrac{0.05 \, mol}{0.125 \, \ell} = 0.4 \, mol/L$

$V_1 = 0.025 \, \ell \quad C_1$
$V_2 = 0.125 \, \ell$
$C_1V_1 = C_2V_2$

$C_1V_1 = C_2V_2$
$V_1 = \dfrac{C_2V_2}{C_1}$
$\quad = \dfrac{1.25 \, mol/L \,(0.3 \, \ell)}{12.1 \, mol/L}$
$\quad = 0.031 \, L$

$V_2 = 0.3 \, \ell$

ACTIVITIES

Activity 1

Title
Preparation of a Solution

Problem
What is the proper technique for preparing 100.00 mL of a 0.350 mol/L solution of potassium chloride?

Materials

potassium chloride   balance
volumetric flask with cap (100 mL) eyedropper
distilled water in beaker   scoopula
wash bottle with distilled water   funnel

Procedure
Write a point form procedure.

Analysis
Show the calculations that were necessary in order to determine the mass of solute required.

Expansion Exercise
Calculate the concentrations of the potassium chloride solution, the potassium ion, and the chloride ion.

NOTES

Activity 2

Title

Preparation of a solution of copper (II) sulfate pentahydrate

Problem

How is 100 mL of a 0.125 mol/L solution of copper (II) sulfate pentahydrate prepared?

Materials

Procedure

Analysis

Show all calculations.

Activity 3

Title
Dilution of a Solution

Problem
What is the proper technique for diluting 0.0100 mol/L $KMnO_{4(aq)}$ to form 100.00 mL of 0.001 00 mol/L $KMnO_{4(aq)}$?

Materials
0.010 0 mol/L $KMnO_{4(aq)}$
eyedropper
volumetric flask (100.00 mL)
wash bottle
distilled water
pipette
funnel
pipette bulb

Technique Method
Write a point form method as the activity is done.

Procedure

Observations

Analysis
Show the calculations that were necessary in order to determine the initial volume of concentrated solution that was required.

Activity 4

Title
Dilution of a Solution of $CuSO_{4(aq)}$

Problem
How are 100.00 mL of 0.050 0 mol/L $CuSO_{4(aq)}$ prepared from a
solution of 0.500 mol/L $CuSO_{4(aq)}$?

Materials

Procedure

Observations

Analysis
Show all calculations.

Activity 5

Title

Concentration

Problem

What is the concentration of an unknown solution of $KCl_{(aq)}$?

Materials

$KCl_{(aq)}$ (max. 20 mL)	beaker
Bunsen burner	retort stand, etc.
Balance	pipette

Procedure

Observations

Analysis

PRACTICE EXERCISES

1. Calculate the molar concentration (molarity) of the following solutions:

   a) 3.44 mol of NaCl in 450 mL of solution

   b) 0.766 mol of $CuSO_4$ in 675 mL of solution

   c) 7.11 mol of $C_{12}H_{22}O_{11}$ in 2.25 L of solution

   d) 8.25×10^{-2} mol of KBr in 25.0 mL of solution

2. Calculate the concentration (molarity) of the following solutions:

   a) 44.8 g of NaCl in 450 mL of solution

   b) 6.68 g of $CuSO_4$ in 675 mL of solution

c) 145 g of $C_{12}H_{22}O_{11}$ in 2.25 L of solution

d) 45.3 g of $ZnBr_2$ in 35.0 mL of solution

3. Calculate the number of moles of solute needed to make the following solutions:

a) 35.0 mL of 1.25 mol/L $HCl_{(aq)}$

b) 565 mL of 0.122 mol/L $H_2SO_{4(aq)}$

c) 85.0 mL of 2.22 mol/L $Na_2SO_{4(aq)}$

d) 125.0 mL of 0.175 mol/L $CH_3COOH_{(aq)}$

4. Calculate the mass of solute needed to make the following solutions:

a) 25.0 mL of 0.350 mol/L $Na_2CO_{3(aq)}$

b) 1.25 L of 1.50 mol/L $C_6H_{12}O_{6(aq)}$

c) 75.0 mL of 2.35 mol/L $Ca(NO_3)_{2(aq)}$

d) 125 mL of 0.850 mol/L $Na_2S_{(aq)}$

$C = \dfrac{mol}{L}$

5. For each of the following electrolytes, write a dissociation equation and calculate the concentrations of the ions present:

a) 0.091 mol/L $Na_3PO_{4(aq)}$

b) 0.014 3 mol/L $NaHCO_{3(aq)}$

c) 0.250 mol/L $Fe_2O_{3(aq)}$

d) 50.0 g of $Mn(CH_3COO)_{4(s)}$ dissolved in 3.00 L of solution

e) 100.0 g of $Ga_2(C_2O_4)_{3(s)}$ dissolved in 5.00 L of solution

6. For each of the following, write a dissociation equation and calculate the concentration of the solute needed to produce the given ion concentration.

a) $Na_2CO_{3(aq)}$ with 0.500 mol/L sodium ion

b) $(NH_4)_2SO_{4(aq)}$ with 1.20 mol/L sulfate ion

c) $K_2Cr_2O_{7(aq)}$ with 0.600 mol/L potassium ion

7. Determine the concentration of the solution when:

   a) 25.0 mL of 3.00 mol/L $HCl_{(aq)}$ is diluted to 65.0 mL

   b) 450.0 mL of 1.75 mol/L $HNO_{3(aq)}$ is diluted to 675.0 mL

   c) 35.0 mL of 6.00 mol/L $KOH_{(aq)}$ is diluted to 125 mL

   d) 1.25 L of 4.50 mol/L $NaCl_{(aq)}$ is diluted to 3.45 L

8. Calculate the volume of the original solution needed to make the new solution when:

   a) 5.25 mol/L $NaOH_{(aq)}$ is used to make 625 mL of 3.50 mol/L solution

   b) 4.75 mol/L $CaCl_{2(aq)}$ is used to make 380.0 mL of 1.25 mol/L solution

   c) 10.0 mol/L $AgNO_{3(aq)}$ is used to make 865 mL of 3.45 mol/L solution

   d) 5.00 mol/L $NaClO_{3(aq)}$ is used to make 50.0 mL of 3.75 mol/L solution

eg
Sugar

eg.
water

mol/L.

Lesson 4 SOLUBILITY

When a solute dissolves in a solution, particles from the surface of the solute move into the solvent, in a process called dissolving.
As the solute particles leave the surface of the solute, the solute crystal becomes smaller and the amount of solute dissolved in the solvent becomes larger.

However, an opposing process soon begins. Solute particles which are already dissolved begin to collide with undissolved solute particles and return to the solid from the solution. This process is called crystallization.

As more and more particles dissolve, more particles crystallize.
Finally a state of balance, or equilibrium, occurs.

A Saturated Solution

The rate at which particles dissolve equals the rate at which particles crystallize. This is called a state of dynamic equilibrium because two opposing processes (dissolving and crystallizing) occur at equal rates. When this stage is reached, undissolved solute remains visible, no matter how long the solution sits, or how hard the solution is stirred.
The solution is saturated; no more solute will dissolve.
A saturated solution contains the maximum amount of solute at a particular temperature. Particles continue to dissolve, but other particles are crystallizing at the same rate, so the concentration of dissolved solute remains the same.

Sometimes a saturated solution may be heated to dissolve extra solute and the carefully cooled to the original temperature without the extra solute reappearing. Such a solution is said to be supersaturated. This solution is not stable because addition of a small crystal or agitation of the solution may cause crystallization. A supersaturated solution contains more dissolved solute than it would if it were saturated.

If all of the solute particles are dissolved, the solution is unsaturated.
An unsaturated solution contains less than the maximum amount of solute than can dissolve in a given amount of solvent at a particular temperature.
There will be no dynamic equilibrium, because there will be no opposing forces of dissolving and crystallizing.

Dynamic equilibrium:
when the rates of
dissolution and
crystallization are equal.

The term solubility can be used in two senses, qualitatively and quantitatively.

Qualitatively: Qualitatively, solubility is often used in a relative way when substances are classed as being soluble, low solubility or insoluble. The table below lists solubility characteristics generally associated with qualitative terms:

Solubility	Qualitative Term	Examples
> 0.1 mol	soluble	$Na_2CO_{3(aq)}$
< 0.1 mol	low solubility	$CaSO_{4(aq)}$
Extremely low	insoluble	$CCl_{4(aq)}$ in $H_2O_{(l)}$

Quantitative: The qualitative use of solubility is not precise enough for many purposes. The quantitative definition of solubility has a defined meaning. Quantitatively, solubility is the concentration of a solute in a saturated solution at a given temperature.

Therefore, solubility would be the number of moles of solute needed to form one litre of saturated solution at a specified temperature, i.e. the maximum concentration of a solute.

$$\text{solubility} = \left(\begin{array}{c} C \\ \text{saturated} \\ \text{solution} \end{array} \right) = \frac{n}{v}$$

where n = number of moles of solute
v = volume of solution
C = concentration of solution

This relationship can be used to calculate the solubility.

Example 1

A saturated solution produced by dissolving hydrogen chloride gas in water is called concentrated hydrochloric acid. If 46.5 g of hydrogen chloride gas is required to prepare 100 mL of concentrated hydrochloric acid at 25°C, what is the solubility of hydrogen chloride at 25°C?

Solution

$$^n HCl_{(g)} = \frac{m_{HCl_{(g)}}}{M_{HCl_{(g)}}} = \frac{46.5 \text{ g}}{36.5 \text{ g/mol}} = 1.27 \text{ mol}$$

$$^C HCl_{(g)} = \frac{n_{HCl_{(g)}}}{v_{HCl_{(aq)}}} = \frac{1.27 \text{ mol}}{0.100 \text{ L}} = 12.7 \text{ mol/L}$$

The solubility of hydrogen chloride at 25°C is 12.7 mol/L.

$Solubitity = \frac{n}{V}$
(c)

Factors That Affect Solubility $T\uparrow$

Solid = $T\uparrow$, Solubility $\uparrow$
Gas = $T\uparrow$ Solubility $\downarrow$
Liquid = ΔT, little effect.

Gas = Pressure $\uparrow$, solubility $\uparrow$

(T) **Temperature:** An increase in temperature will increase the solubility for most solids. An increase in temperature will decrease the solubility for all gases. A change in temperature (increase or decrease) has little effect on the solubility of liquids.

(P) **Pressure:** An increase in pressure will increase the solubility of gases. Pressure has little or no effect of the solubility of solids or liquids.

Nature of Solute and Solvent: Solutes will dissolve better in some solvents than in others. This depends upon the nature of the bonds between solute and solvent. For example, grease dissolves in gasoline but not in water. Salt dissolves in water but not in gasoline.

Precipitates (solid, insoluble compound) · some (ion$^+$ + ion$^-$)

Positive Ion + negative Ion -

Sometimes when two aqueous solutions of compounds that are soluble are mixed, the positive ion (cation) of one combines with the negative ion (anion) of the other to form an insoluble compound. This insoluble compound forms a solid, which is also known as a precipitate. The reaction to form a precipitate is a double replacement reaction.

Write the net ionic equation to show the formation of a precipitate when an aqueous solutions of copper (II) sulfate and sodium sulfide are mixed.

Nonionic Equation:

$$CuSO_{4(aq)} + Na_2S_{(aq)} \rightarrow CuS_{(?)} + Na_2SO_{4(?)}$$

Is the precipitate copper (II) sulfide or sodium sulfate? A table of solubility indicates that all sodium compounds are soluble but most sulfide compounds are not. Therefore, the precipitate is CuS.

Total Ionic Equation:

$$Cu^{2+}_{(aq)} + SO_4^{2-}_{(aq)} + 2Na^+_{(aq)} + S^{2-}_{(aq)}$$
$$\rightarrow CuS_{(s)} + 2Na^+_{(aq)} + SO_4^{2-}_{(aq)}$$

Insoluble = solid.

The copper (II) sulfide is not represented as ions because the two ions have formed a solid precipitate. The sodium ions and sulfate ions remain unchanged. They are known as "spectator" ions and can be removed from the net ionic equation.

Net Ionic Equation:

$$Cu^{2+}_{(aq)} + S^{2-}_{(aq)} \rightarrow CuS_{(s)}$$

Example 2

Write the net ionic equation for the formation of a precipitate when aqueous solutions of potassium hydroxide and magnesium chloride are mixed.

Solution

Nonionic Equation:

$$2KOH_{(aq)} + MgCl_{2(aq)} \rightarrow 2KCl_{(?)} + Mg(OH)_{2(?)}$$

Is the precipitate potassium chloride or magnesium hydroxide?
A table of solubility shows that all potassium compounds are soluble, but the combination of magnesium ions with hydroxide ions is not.

Total Ionic Equation:

$$2K^+_{(aq)} + 2OH^-_{(aq)} + Mg^{2+}_{(aq)} + 2Cl^-_{(aq)}$$
$$\rightarrow Mg(OH)_{2(s)} + 2K^+_{(aq)} + 2Cl^-_{(aq)}$$

Eliminating the spectator ions give us the net ionic equation.

Net Ionic Equation:

$$Mg^{2+}_{(aq)} + 2OH^-_{(aq)} \rightarrow Mg(OH)_{2(s)}$$

ACTIVITIES

Activity 1

Title
Solubility of Ionic Compounds

Problem
Which of the given substances are soluble or insoluble in water?

Materials

ammonium nitrate	lead (II) nitrate
calcium sulfate	nickel (II) chloride
copper (I) chloride	potassium permanganate
copper (II) chloride	silver chloride
iron (III) sulfate	sodium thiosulfate

List all other materials that will be used in the activity.

Variables
List the appropriate variables.

Predictions
Write the formula of each substance and predict its solubility in water in a prediction table.

Procedure

Write a procedure that utilizes a few grains of each substance and about 20 mL of water.

Observations

Record the extent of solubility in an observation table.

Analysis

Write dissociation equations for those substances that were soluble.

PRACTICE EXERCISES

1. Operationally (empirically) define saturated, unsaturated, and supersaturated solutions.

2. Explain how you would distinguish between saturated, unsaturated, and supersaturated solutions.

3. Define solubility.

Use the following graph to answer the next question.

Solubility of Solids

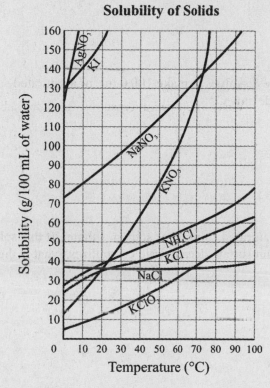

4. **a)** Which compound has the greatest solubility at 0°C?

   b) Which compound has the lowest solubility at 80°C?

   c) For which compound does temperature have little effect on solubility?

d) Make a general statement regarding the effect of temperature on the solubility of ionic compounds.

e) What is the solubility (in g/100 mL water) of

KNO_3 at 50°C?

$NaNO_3$ at 10°C?

$AgNO_3$ at 5°C?

$KClO_3$ at 85°C?

KCl at 50°C?

5. If 35.7 g of sodium chloride dissolves to make 100.0 mL of a saturated solution at 0°C, what is the solubility of sodium chloride at 0°C?

6. 50.0 mL at 30°C makes a saturated solution of sodium sulfate. If this solution is evaporated to dryness and 46.4 g of sodium sulfate decahydrate crystallizes, what is the solubility of sodium sulfate decahydrate at 30°C?

7. 40.0 g of $KCl_{(s)}$ will dissolve in 200.0 mL of solution at 40°C. What is the solubility of the KCl?

8. Use your solubility table to predict the solubility of the following solids:

   a) $NaNO_3$ **b)** $(NH_4)_2S$

   c) $CaSO_4$ **d)** Li_2SO_4

   e) $Fe(OH)_2$ **f)** $BaSO_4$

   g) $BaCl_2$ **h)** AgI

   i) $CuBr$ **j)** $CuBr_2$

9. Predict what the precipitate will be, if any, when aqueous solutions of the following compounds are mixed)

   a) lead (II) nitrate with potassium sulfide

   b) calcium nitrate with sodium sulfate

   c) sodium phosphate with calcium chloride

   d) ammonium acetate with mercury (I) nitrate

   e) zinc nitrate with lithium hydroxide

10. Write molecular, total ionic, and net ionic equations for the formation of a precipitate when the following aqueous solutions are mixed:

a) $Pb(NO_3)_{2(aq)} + NaOH_{(aq)}$

b) $Ba(NO_3)_{2(aq)} + K_2S_{(aq)}$

c) $AgNO_{3(aq)} + NaI_{(aq)}$

d) $H_3PO_{4(aq)} + Mg(NO_3)_{2(aq)}$

e) $CaCl_{2(aq)} + KOH_{(aq)}$

Lesson 5 ACIDS AND BASES

There are two special kinds of solutions, acids, and bases that have a great deal of importance and significance in our lives.

Acids are those solutions that:

- taste sour
- conduct electricity (that is, they are electrolytes)
- react with zinc or magnesium to produce hydrogen gas
- turn blue litmus red

Bases are those solutions that:

- taste bitter
- conduct electricity
- have a soapy, slippery feeling
- turn red litmus blue

Svante Arrhenius (1859–1927) was a Swedish chemist who was the first to propose a conceptual definition of acids and bases, and thereby give an explanation of these properties. According to Arrhenius, acids are those ✳ substances which increase the hydrogen ion (H^+) concentration in aqueous solution. Bases are those substances that increase the hydroxide ion (OH^-) ✳ concentration in aqueous solution.

Hydronium Ions

The hydrogen atom is the simplest of all atoms that exist in nature. Almost all hydrogen atoms (99.99%) are composed of a single proton and electron.

$$
\begin{array}{llll}
H^+ & 1 \text{ proton} & 1^+ & 1\ \mu \\
& 0 \text{ neutron} & 0 & 0\ \mu \\
& \underline{1 \text{ electron}} & \underline{1^-} & \underline{0\ \mu} \\
& & 0 \text{ charge} & 1\ \mu \text{ mass}
\end{array}
$$

A hydrogen ion is formed when the electron is stripped from the atom by an atom or group of atoms with an affinity for electrons.

$$
\begin{array}{llll}
H^+ & 1 \text{ proton} & 1^+ & 1\ \mu \\
& 0 \text{ neutron} & 0 & 0\ \mu \\
& \underline{0 \text{ electron}} & \underline{0} & \underline{0\ \mu} \\
& & 1^+ \text{ charge} & 1\ \mu \text{ mass}
\end{array}
$$

LOST e^- (electron is stripped) = hydrogen ion

Therefore, a hydrogen ion is simply a bare proton, and the terms "hydrogen ion" and "proton" mean the same thing.

Most chemists now believe that since a hydrogen ion is the smallest positive ion possible (because it has no electrons) it is strongly attracted to the negative end of the very polar water molecules.

$$H_2O_{(l)} + H^+ \rightarrow H_3O^+_{(aq)}$$

Gain one

Smallest positive ion.

Experimental evidence does not show exactly how many water molecules are bonded to each hydrogen ion (or proton) in aqueous solution. The number of water molecules may vary. Chemists use the symbol $H^+_{(aq)}$, an aqueous hydrogen ion, and $H_3O^+_{(aq)}$, an aqueous hydronium ion, to mean the same thing, a proton bonded to water molecules in aqueous solution.

Strong acids with concentrations greater than 1.0 mol/L will have a negative pH.

Strong bases with concentrations above 1.0 mol/L will have pH's above 14.

The pH Scale

The pH scale was designed by a Danish chemist, S.P.L. Sorenson in 1909. It measures the relative acidity of a solution. The term pH refers to the "potency or power of hydrogen." The pH scale is a logarithmic scale usually from 0 to 14 that gives us an indication of the nature of a solution. By definition,

$$pH = -\log_{10}[H_3O^+]$$
$$\text{and, } [H_3O^+] = 10^{-pH}$$

Acids have pH's 0 – 7

Bases have pH's 7 – 14

[H3O+] (mol/L)	pH	Nature of Solution
1.0×10^0 (1.0)	0	strongly acidic
1.0×10^{-1}	1	
1.0×10^{-5}	5	weakly acidic
1.0×10^{-6}	6	very weakly acidic
1.0×10^{-7}	7	neutral
1.0×10^{-8}	8	very weakly basic
1.0×10^{-9}	9	weakly basic
1.0×10^{-13}	13	
1.0×10^{-14}	14	strongly basic

Neutral substances have a pH of 7

Note that an increase of one integer value of pH means the solution is ten times less acidic or ten times more basic. A decrease in $[H_3O^+]$ by a factor of 10 is an increase in pH by 1 unit. An increase of 3 pH units is a decrease in $[H_3O^+]$ by a factor of 1 000. Solutions of pH 0 to just under 7 are acidic, solutions of pH 7 are neutral, and solutions of just over 7, to 14 are basic.

acidic $[H^+] > [OH^-]$

basic $[H^+] < [OH^-]$

neutral $[H^+] = [OH^-]$

156

Ions in Water

In solutions where water is the solvent (most solutions that we work with), two ions, $H_3O^+_{(aq)}$ and $OH^-_{(aq)}$, are always present.
Their concentrations at 25°C are related by the equation:

$$\left[H_3O^+_{(aq)}\right] \times \left[OH^-_{(aq)}\right] = 1.00 \times 10^{-14}$$

According to Arrhenius, as the solution becomes more acidic in behaviour its $[H_3O^+_{(aq)}]$ increases and, according to the above relationship, its $[OH^-_{(aq)}]$ must decrease. Likewise as the solution becomes more basic in behaviour its $[OH^-_{(aq)}]$ increases and its $[H_3O^+_{(aq)}]$ decreases.

if $[H_3O^+_{(aq)}] \uparrow$, $[OH^-_{(aq)}] \downarrow$ vise versa.

Example

What is the $[OH^-_{(aq)}]$ in a solution with $[H_3O^+_{(aq)}] = 2.59 \times 10^{-4}$ mol/L?

Solution

$$\left[H_3O^+_{(aq)}\right] \times \left[OH^-_{(aq)}\right] = 1.00 \times 10^{-14}$$

$$\left[OH^-_{(aq)}\right] = \frac{1.00 \times 10^{-14}}{2.59 \times 10^{-4}\,\text{mol/L}} = 3.86 \times 10^{-11}\ \text{mol/L}$$

Example

If 2.50 g of $NaOH_{(s)}$ were dissolved in water to produce 500 mL of solution, what would be $[H_3O^+_{(aq)}]$ and $[OH^-_{(aq)}]$?

Solution

$$n_{NaOH} = \frac{2.50\ \text{g}}{40.00\,\text{g/mol}} = 0.062\,5\ \text{mol}$$

$$[NaOH] = \left[OH^-_{(aq)}\right] = \frac{0.062\,5\ \text{mol}}{0.500\ \text{L}} - 0.125\ \text{mol/L} \quad \text{solution}$$

$$\left[H_3O^+_{(aq)}\right] = \frac{1.00 \times 10^{-14}}{0.125\ \text{mol/L}} = 8.00 \times 10^{-14}\ \text{mol/L}$$

[OH⁻]

Non-Integer pH

pH values will only be integers if $[H_3O^+]$ (and $[OH^-]$) have concentrations that are expressed as 1×10^{-x}.

Since most of the time $\left[H_3O^+\right] \neq 1 \times 10^{-x}$, pH will not often have an integer value. This leads to another problem. How are significant digits handled for non-integer pH values?

Formulas: $pH = -\log [H_3O^+_{(aq)}]$ and its inverse, $[H_3O^+_{(aq)}] = 10^{-pH}$.

Example

What is the pH of a solution of 0.159 mol/L $HCl_{(aq)}$?

Solution

$$-\log(0.159\ \text{mol/L}) = 0.799$$

C = H₃O

− log [H₃O⁺]

Discovery Exercise

$-\log(0.0159 \text{ mol/L}) = $? 1-799

$-\log(0.00159 \text{ mol/L}) = $? 2-799

$-\log(0.000159 \text{ mol/L}) = $? 3-799

If you try this you will get the following answers: 1.799, 2.799, and 3.799 (along with 0.799 in the previous example)

The lesson is that the pH decimal places reflect the significant digits in the concentration. The number in front of the decimal is related to the position of the decimal place.

Rule: The number of significant digits in the concentration is the number of decimal places in the pH.

When converting from pH to concentration, the same rule applies. This time the number of significant digits in the concentration comes from the number of decimal places in the pH.

Example 4

What is the $[H_3O^+]$ of a solution with pH = 2.42?

Solution

Two decimal places in the pH means two significant digits in the concentration. $\left[H_3O^+\right] = 10^{-pH} = 10^{-2.42} = 3.8 \times 10^{-3}$ mol/L

pOH

Just as pH = $-\log [H_3O^+]$ and $[H_3O^+] = 10^{-pH}$, a similar concept called pOH also exists. pOH = $-\log [OH^-]$ and $[OH^-] = 10^{-pOH}$. pOH for bases will be less than 7 and pOH for acids will be greater than 7 (the exact opposite of pH trends).

pOH values are not reported in scientific literature as pH values are. The main purpose of pOH is to easily convert between $[H_3O^+]$ and $[OH^-]$ for the same solution. The earlier relationship can be rewritten as a log relationship involving pH and pOH: pH + pOH = 14.000.

Example 5

A solution has pH = 5.75. What are the values of $[H_3O^+]$ and $[OH^-]$?

Solution

$$\left[H_3O^+_{(aq)}\right] = 10^{-pH} = 10^{-5.75} = 1.8 \times 10^{-6} \text{ mol/L}$$

$$pOH = 14.000 - 5.75 = 8.25$$

$$\left[OH^-_{(aq)}\right] = 10^{-pOH} = 10^{-8.25} = 5.6 \times 10^{-9} \text{ mol/L}$$

Alternate Solution

$$\left[H_3O^+{}_{(aq)}\right] = 10^{-pH} = 10^{-5.75} = 1.8 \times 10^{-6}\ mol/L$$

$$\left[H_3O^+{}_{(aq)}\right] \times \left[OH^-{}_{(aq)}\right] = 1.00 \times 10^{-14}$$

$$\left[OH^-{}_{(aq)}\right] = \frac{1.00 \times 10^{-14}}{1.8 \times 10^{-6}\ mol/L} = 5.6 \times 10^{-9}\ mol/L$$

Example 6

A solution has $[H_3O^+] = 1.95 \times 10^{-4}$. What are its pH, pOH, and $[OH^-]$?

Solution

$$pH = -\log\left(1.95 \times 10^{-4}\ mol/L\right) = 3.710$$

$$pOH = 14.000 - 3.710 = 10.290$$

$$\left[OH^-{}_{(aq)}\right] = 10^{-10.291} = 5.13 \times 10^{-11}\ mol/L$$

Note the handling of the significant digits in these examples

Measuring pH

pH can be measured precisely and accurately using a pH meter. In recent years the prices of pH meters have dropped dramatically, making them available in most high school laboratories. pH can also be determined from the results of tests with acid-base indicator solutions. These solutions change colour dramatically in a relatively narrow pH range. Bromothymol blue changes from yellow to blue as pH rises from 6.0 to 7.6. In the middle of this range it is green.

You will need to consult your acid/base indicator chart to understand the example and do the problems in this section.

Example 7

Separate samples of a solution of unknown pH cause the following acid/base indicator colours:
orange IV: yellow bromothymol blue: blue
phenolphthalein: colourless
What is the solution pH?

Solution

Using the indicator chart, orange IV: $pH \geq 2.8$

bromothymol blue: $pH \geq 7.6$

phenolphthalein: $pH \leq 8.2$

pH is between 7.6 and 8.2.

pH can also be measured with pH paper which is filter paper that has been soaked in a combination of indicator solutions and dried)
Each pH range produces a characteristic colour (a combination of all the indicators individual colours) which can be used to measure pH by matching against a colour chart.

NOTES

Modified Arrhenius Acids and Bases

According to the Arrhenius Theory of Acids and Bases, an acid is a substance that increases the $[H^+]$ of an aqueous solution, while a base is a substance that increases the $[OH^-]$. The original Arrhenius theory was unable to explain the acidic behaviour of chemical species like $CO_{2(aq)}$ or the basic behaviour of chemical species like $NH_{3(aq)}$.

A modification of the Arrhenius theory allows explanation of these properties. An acid is a substance that reacts with water to produce H_3O^+, while a base is a substance that reacts to produce OH^-. In each case there will be a familiar balancing species. Some examples are listed below.

$NH_{3(aq)}$:

$$NH_{3(aq)} + H_2O_{(l)} \rightarrow H_3O^+_{(aq)} + NH_2^-_{(aq)}$$
$NH_2^-_{(aq)}$ is not familiar – predict base

$$NH_{3(aq)} + H_2O_{(l)} \rightarrow OH^-_{(aq)} + NH_4^+_{(aq)}$$
$NH_4^+_{(aq)}$ is familiar – confirms prediction of base

$CO_{2(aq)}$:

$$CO_{2(aq)} + 2H_2O_{(l)} \rightarrow H_3O^+_{(aq)} + HCO_3^-_{(aq)}$$
$HCO_3^-_{(aq)}$ is familiar – predict acid

$$CO_{2(aq)} + H_2O_{(l)} \rightarrow OH^-_{(aq)} + HCO_2^+_{(aq)}$$
$HCO_2^+_{(aq)}$ is not familiar – confirms prediction of acid

$HSO_4^-_{(aq)}$:

$$HSO_4^-_{(aq)} + H_2O_{(l)} \rightarrow H_3O^+_{(aq)} + SO_4^{2-}_{(aq)}$$
$SO_4^{2-}_{(aq)}$ is familiar – predict acid

$$HSO_4^-_{(aq)} + H_2O_{(l)} \rightarrow OH^-_{(aq)} + H_2SO_{4(aq)}$$
$H_2SO_{4(aq)}$ is familiar – predict base

The last example shows the limitation of the theory. Equations can be written to explain either the acid or base behaviour of different substances, but in some cases, like the last example, the theory cannot be used to predict whether the substance is an acid or a base.

Acid-Base Neutralization

In a neutralization reaction, an acid reacts with a base to produce water and a salt (a neutral ionic compound).

An example of a neutralization reaction would be:
$$NaOH_{(aq)} + HCl_{(aq)} \rightarrow NaCl_{(aq)} + H_2O_{(l)}$$

At the ionic level, since acids produce H_3O^+, and bases produce OH^-, neutralization can be viewed as
$$H_3O^+_{(aq)} + OH^-_{(aq)} \rightarrow 2H_2O_{(l)}$$

Strengths of Acids and Bases

The strength of an acid is NOT defined in terms of how acidic its behaviour is. Instead it is defined in terms of how completely it ionizes in water to produce H^+ (or how completely it reacts with water to produce H_3O^+). A strong acid has weak bonds between H^+ and the remaining part of the acid formula (called its conjugate base). It therefore ionizes completely to produce H^+ (or reacts completely with water to produce H_3O^+). A weak acid has stronger bonds and therefore only does so partially. At equal concentration a strong acid will behave in a more acidic manner than a weak acid.

The strength of a base, in a similar manner, is defined in terms of how completely it dissociates in water to produce OH^-
(or reacts with water to produce OH^-).

To further clarify this concept, it is possible for a weak acid with a low ionization level to behave in a more acidic manner than a strong acid with a high ionization level. This may be true if the weak acid is present at much higher concentration than the strong acid. Despite this, the one that ionizes completely is still called a strong acid and the one that ionizes partially is a weak acid.

Common strong acids are $HClO_{4(aq)}$, $HBr_{(aq)}$, $HI_{(aq)}$, $HCl_{(aq)}$, $H_2SO_{4(aq)}$, $HNO_{3(aq)}$. Strong bases are ionic hydroxide compounds, for example, $NaOH_{(aq)}$.

Monoprotic and Polyprotic Acids and Bases

A monoprotic strong acid like $HCl_{(aq)}$ will ionize in water to produce one mole of H^+ per one mole of acid (or react with water to produce one mole of H_3O^+ per one mole of acid). A polyprotic strong acid like $H_2SO_{4(aq)}$ will ionize in water to produce two or more moles of H^+ per mole of acid (or react with water to produce two or more moles of H_3O^+ per mole of acid).

A monoprotic base will ionize in water or react with water to produce one mole of OH per mole of base. A polyprotic base will ionize in water or react with water to produce two or more moles of OH^- per mole of base.

NOTES

ACTIVITIES

Activity 1

Title
Properties of Acids and Bases

Materials

acid (20 mL)	$Zn_{(s)}$
base (20 mL)	$Mg_{(s)}$
spot plate	stirring rod
conductivity apparatus	litmus paper

Problem

Procedure

Observations
Prepare an observation table to include the following properties of acids and bases:

a) feel

b) electrical conductivity

c) effect on litmus paper

d) effect on the active metal zinc

e) effect on the active metal magnesium

Analysis
Write operational definitions for an acid and a base.

Activity 2

Title
Household Acids and Bases

Materials

distilled water   limewater
tap water   milk
soda pop   Alka Seltzer®
household ammonia   stirring rod
aspirin   Sani-Flush®
orange juice   baking soda
apple juice   vinegar
HCl

Set up standards showing the three indicators in acid, base, and neutral solutions.

TO COMPLETE THE EXPERIMENT, DO THE FOLLOWING:

1. Prepare the experiment in your lab book. Be sure to include all parts of the experimental write-up including the problem stated as a question.

2. Under analysis, in addition to indicating what assumptions were made when analyzing the data, prepare a summary chart of your results.

Compound	Litmus	Phenolphthalein	Bromothymol Blue
distilled water	◯	◯	◯
tap water	◯	◯	◯
soda pop (clear)	◯	◯	◯
household ammonia	◯	◯	◯
HCl	◯	◯	◯

NOTES

Compound	Litmus	Phenolphthalein	Bromothymol Blue
aspirin	◯	◯	◯
orange juice	◯	◯	◯
apple juice	◯	◯	◯
Alka-seltzer®	◯	◯	◯
Sani-Flush®	◯	◯	◯
baking soda	◯	◯	◯
vinegar	◯	◯	◯
milk	◯	◯	◯
limewater	◯	◯	◯

List the acids and bases from the above substances:

Acids   **Bases**

PRACTICE EXERCISES

1. Operationally (empirically) define:

   a) acid solution

   b) base solution

2. The following properties were observed for five solutions. From the properties identify the acids and bases (some are neither, identify those with a 0).

Solution	Conducts Electricity	Taste	Reaction With Zinc Metal	Type of Solution
V	yes	sour	gas produced	
W	yes	bitter	none observed	
X	ycs	salty	none observed	
Y	no	sweet	none observed	
Z	yes	sour	gas produced	

3. State the Arrhenius definition of an acid and a base.

4. Explain how a hydronium ion is formed in aqueous solution.

5. Explain how the nature of a solution (acid, base, or neutral) can be determined by measuring the pH of the solution.

6. Complete the following table:

Concentration of Hydronium or Hydrogen Ion	pH	Nature of the Solution
	2.0	
1.0×10^{-11} mol/L		
	8.00	
		neutral
1.0×10^{-4} mol/L		
	12.00	
1.0×10^{-9} mol/L		
	3.00	

7. a) Calculate the $[OH^-_{(aq)}]$ in a 0.050 0 mol/L $HCl_{(aq)}$ solution?

b) What is the pH of the solution in question 1? (Beware of significant digits)

8. Tomato juice has a pH of approximately 4.2. Find the $[H_3O^+_{(aq)}]$, $[OH^-_{(aq)}]$, and pOH of tomato juice.

9. 1.00 g of $Ba(OH)_{2(s)}$ are dissolved in water to make 1.00 L of solution. Find $[H_3O^+_{(aq)}]$, $[OH^-_{(aq)}]$, pH, and pOH of the solution.

10. Separate samples of a solution of unknown pH turn phenolphthalein pink, indigo carmine blue, and 1, 3, 5-trinitrobenzene colourless. What is its pH?

11. Separate samples of a solution of unknown pH turn thymol blue yellow, methyl orange red, and chlorophenol red yellow. What is its pH?

For each of the following 5 questions, write 2 equations, one which will react with water to form H_3O^+ and the other which will react with water to form OH^-. Based on whether or not the balancing species is familiar or unfamiliar, state whether the substance is predicted to be acid or base, or whether you are unable to make a prediction.

12. $CH_3COOH_{(aq)}$

$CH_3COOH_{(aq)} + H_2O_{(l)} \rightarrow$

$CH_3COOH_{(aq)} + H_2O_{(l)} \rightarrow$

Prediction

13. $HF_{(aq)}$

$HF_{(aq)} + H_2O_{(l)} \rightarrow$

$HF_{(aq)} + H_2O_{(l)} \rightarrow$

Prediction

14. $PO_4^{3-}{}_{(aq)}$ from dissolved Na_3PO_4 (use the reaction with $2H_2O_{(l)}$ for your acid prediction)

$PO_4^{3-}{}_{(aq)} + 2H_2O_{(l)} \rightarrow$

$PO_4^{3-}{}_{(aq)} + H_2O_{(l)} \rightarrow$

Prediction

15. $SO_{3(g)}$ (use the reaction with $2H_2O_{(l)}$ for your acid prediction)

$SO_{3(g)} + 2H_2O_{(l)} \rightarrow$

$SO_{3(g)} + H_2O_{(l)} \rightarrow$

Prediction

16. $HCO_3^-{}_{(aq)}$ from dissolved $NaHCO_3$

$HCO_3^-{}_{(aq)} + H_2O_{(l)} \rightarrow$

$HCO_3^-{}_{(aq)} + H_2O_{(l)} \rightarrow$

Prediction

REVIEW SUMMARY

- A solvent is any material that can dissolve a solute.

- Solutions can be liquid solutions, gaseous solutions, or solid solutions. Knowing this, it is possible to think of solvents as being not just liquids, but rather also gases and solids.

- Liquid solutions are the most common way to work with chemicals. Water is a common substance that can dissolve many solutes, and therefore is often called the 'universal solvent'.

- Energy changes take place when a solution is prepared. The formation of an aqueous solution will either release energy (be exothermic) or will absorb energy (be endothermic).

- Many ionic solutions will act as electrolytes, allowing electric current to flow through them.

- Electrolytes that dissolve in water will do so either by dissociating or by ionizing.

- Concentration is expressed in mol/L and is calculated using the relationship

$$C = \frac{n}{V}$$

- Dilution of a solution where the number of moles of solute is constant can be calculated using
$$C_1 V_1 = C_2 V_2$$

- Dynamic equilibrium: when the rates of dissolution and crystallization are equal.

- A saturated solution is achieved when the maximum amount of solute is dissolved in a given amount of solvent. If extra solute is added, the rate of dissolving of the solute equals the rate of crystallization of solute from the solution. No more solute can be dissolved, and a dynamic equilibrium is achieved.

- Supersaturation can occur if the solution is heated, allowing more solute to dissolve, or also if some solvent is allowed to evaporate.

- A material is considered to be soluble in a solvent if more than 0.1 mol of the substance can dissolve.

- A material is considered to have low solubility if less that 0.1 mol of the substance can dissolve in a solvent.

- An acid is a substance that reacts with water to produce H_3O^+, while a base is a substance that reacts to produce OH^-.

- Solutions of pH 0 to just under 7 are acidic, solutions of pH 7 are neutral, and solutions of just over 7 to 14 are basic.

- The strength of an acid is defined in terms of how completely it ionizes in water to produce H^+ (or how completely it reacts with water to produce H_3O^+).

- The strength of a base is defined in terms of how completely it dissociates in water to produce OH (or reacts with water to produce OH^-).

PRACTICE TEST

1. Define the following terms:

   a) phase

   b) homogeneous

   c) mixture

   d) solution

   e) solvent

   f) solute

2. Answer True or False to the following statements:

   A solution...

   _____   a)   can only have one phase
   _____   b)   can be solid, liquid or gas
   _____   c)   must always be colorless
   _____   d)   must always be clear, if it is a liquid or gas
   _____   e)   must have a constant composition
   _____   f)   will have a sharp melting point as it changes from solid to liquid
   _____   g)   will show a large temperature change from the point at which it starts to boil to the point at which all liquid has changed to a gas.

3. What are the three characteristics of the particles making up a solution?

4. Summarize an efficient method you would follow to determine if a liquid was pure, a heterogeneous mixture, or a homogeneous mixture (solution). State the possible conclusions you would reach at each step in your method.

5. What is the difference between solubility and miscibility?

6. What is the main difference between a solid solution, a liquid solution, and a gaseous solution?

7. How many types of possible solutions are there?

8. What is the solvent in an aqueous solution?

9. What do the terms "hydrated" and "aqueous" mean?

10. What causes the dissociation of ions or molecules?

11. Write dissociation equations for the following compounds:

   a) KCl

   b) $Al_2(SO_4)_3$

12. Define ionization.

13. Name one type of compound that is formed by the process of ionization.

Hydronium Ion.

14. Classify each of the following equations as endothermic or exothermic

   a) $KOH_{(s)} \rightarrow K^+_{(aq)} + OH^-_{(aq)} + heat$

   b) $KNO_{3(s)} \rightarrow K^+_{(aq)} + NO_3^-_{(aq)} \; \Delta t = -20°C$

   c) $NH_4NO_{3(aq)} + heat \rightarrow NH_4^+_{(aq)} + NO_3^-_{(aq)}$

   d) $NaOH_{(s)} \rightarrow Na^+_{(aq)} + OH^-_{(aq)} \; \Delta t = +15°C$

15. List the three processes that must occur for a solute to dissolve in a solvent indicating whether the temperature increases or decreases for each process.

16. Using the answer to question 15, when a solute dissolves in a solvent, the temperature of the solution will decrease if the effects of _____ are greater than the effect of _____.

17. Using the answer to question 15, a solution process is _____ if the effect of step 3 in the solution process is greater than the effects of steps 1 and 2.

18. Conceptually (or theoretically) define "electrolyte."

19. What allows the passage of an electric current through a solution?

20. Classify the following solutes as electrolytes or nonelectrolytes

a) NaCl

b) C_2H_5OH

c) $Ca(NO_3)_2$

d) $H_3PO_{4(aq)}$

e) $C_{12}H_{22}O_{11}$

21. The concentration of a _Solution_ is defined as the number of moles of _Solute_ per litre of the _Solution_ .

22. The formula for calculating concentration is C $\frac{n}{V}$.

23. The unit in which concentration is measured is C mol/l .

24. How many moles of sodium chloride are necessary to produce 2.0 L of a 0.20 mol/L solution of sodium chloride?

25. What is the concentration of a solution made by dissolving 34.22 g of sucrose in enough water to produce 500.0 mL of solution?

26. Define:

a) anion

b) cation

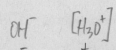

27. Calculate the anion and cation concentration for each of the following:

a) 0.50 mol/L potassium iodide solution

b) 0.25 mol/L sodium sulfate solution

c) 34.23 g of aluminium sulfate dissolved in enough water to make 100.0 mL of solution

28. What is known as caustic soda is really 19.1 mol/L sodium hydroxide solution. Caustic soda, when diluted, is used as a disinfectant. What is the concentration of a disinfectant prepared by diluting 10.0 L of caustic soda to 400.0 L?

29. a) What is meant by the term "dissolving"?

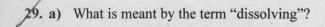

b) What is meant by the term "crystallizing"?

c) _____ _____ occurs when two _____ processes, such as dissolving and crystallizing occur, at equal rates.

30. a) i)   Operationally (empirically) define "saturated solution."

ii)   Conceptually (theoretically) define "saturated solution."

b) i)   Operationally (empirically) define "supersaturated solution."

ii)   Conceptually (theoretically) define "supersaturated solution."

c) i)   Operationally (empirically) define "unsaturated solution."

ii)   Conceptually (theoretically) define "unsaturated solution."

31. What is the difference between a qualitative and quantitative description?

expression in words only no #

expression in # based on measurement

32. Define solubility, quantitatively.

33. If 40.0 mL of 20°C saturated magnesium sulfate is evaporated to dryness and 12.0 g of magnesium sulfate is recovered, what is the solubility of magnesium sulfate at 20°C?

34. Explain the rule "like dissolves like" in reference to prediction of solubility.

35. Describe how a decrease in temperature affects the solubility of

a) solids in liquids

b) gases in liquids

c) liquids in liquids

36. Describe how pressure changes affect the solubility of:

a) solids in liquids

b) gases in liquids

c) liquids in liquids

37. List four empirical properties of acids.

38. List four empirical properties of bases.

39. State the Arrhenius definition for an acid.

40. State the Arrhenius definition for a base.

41. Name five household substances that are acids. Name four that are bases.

42. Write the nonionic, total ionic and net ionic equations for the following reactions:

a) copper (II) nitrate and sodium hydroxide

b) silver nitrate and potassium bromide

c) calcium chloride and sodium sulfate

43. A solution has a pH of 2.59. What is its pOH, $[H_3O^+]$, and $[OH^-]$?

44. Which of the following is a non-electrolyte?

A. sugar   **B.** salt
C. hydrochloric acid   **D.** sodium hydroxide

45. Substances that dissolve each other in any proportion are said to be

A. saturated   **B.** diluted
C. aqueous   **D.** miscible

46. An aqueous solution means

A. an acid has been formed   **B.** a substance has dissolved
C. dissociation has taken place   **D.** the solvent is water

47. The number of moles of cobalt (II) sulfate in 300 mL of 1.75 mol/L solution is

A. 0.171 mol   **B.** 0.525 mol
C. 0.552 mol   **D.** 5.83 mol

48. The mass of sodium hydroxide needed to prepare 1.60 L of 0.100 mol/L solution is

    A. 4.00 g   **C.** 16.0 g
    B. 6.40 g   **D.** 40.0 g

49. The concentration of a solution made by dissolving 11.7 g of sodium chloride in 500 mL of solution is

    A. 0.100 mol/L   **B.** 0.200 mol/L
    C. 0.400 mol/L   **D.** 0.800 mol/L

50. The volume of 0.100 mol/L lead (II) nitrate solution that can be prepared using 66.2 g of the pure solid is

    A. 500 mL   **B.** 1.00 L
    C. 2.00 L   **D.** 3.00 L

51. The concentration of a solution made by diluting 10.0 mL of 0.740 mol/L KCl to 250 mL is

    A. 0.033 8 mol/L   **B.** 0.029 6 mol/L
    C. 0.020 0 mol/L   **D.** 0.018 5 mol/L

52. A student was instructed to prepare 300 mL of a 0.800 mol/L solution of potassium dichromate. The correct procedure the student should follow is to dissolve

    A) 155 g of solute in 300 mL of distilled water
    B) 0.240 mol of solute in 300 mL of distilled water
    C) 70.6 g of solute in 150 mL of distilled water and then add water to a volume of 300 mL
    D) 70.6 g of solute in 300 mL of distilled water

53. A student made a 0.20 mol/L solution of ammonium sulfate $(NH_4)_2SO_4$. The ratio of the concentration of NH_4^+ ions to SO_4^- ions is

    A. 1:1   **B.** 1:2
    C. 2:1   **D.** 9:49

54. The correct term for referring to the maximum amount of solute that will dissolve under specified conditions to make a unit volume of solution is

    A. molarity   **B.** solubility
    C. dissociation   **D.** solution

55. An electrolyte is a

    A. substance which dissolves in water
    B. a nonconductor
    C. substance which forms ions in water
    D. a proton acceptor

56. The dissociation equation for the iron (III) nitrate is

    A. $Fe(NO_3)_{3(aq)} \rightarrow Fe^+_{(aq)} + 3NO_3^-_{(aq)}$
    B. $Fe(NO_3)_{3(aq)} \rightarrow Fe^{3+}_{(aq)} + NO_3^-_{(aq)}$
    C. $Fe(NO_3)_{3(aq)} \rightarrow Fe^{3+}_{(aq)} + 3NO_3^-_{(aq)}$
    D. $Fe(NO_3)_{3(aq)} \rightarrow 3Fe^{3+}_{(aq)} + 3NO_3^-_{(aq)}$

57. The property that acids and bases have in common is that they

    A. conduct electricity   **B.** turn red litmus blue
    C. turn blue litmus red   **D.** taste sour

58. A 0.1 mol/L solution that conducts electricity and turns blue litmus red is

    A. $SrCl_{2(aq)}$ **B.** $CH_3Cl_{(aq)}$
    C. $NaCl_{(aq)}$ **D.** $HCl_{(aq)}$

59. When phenolphthalein is added to a solution with a pH of 4, the resulting solution is

    A. pink   **C.** colorless
    B. blue   **D.** yellow

60. If chemically equivalent amounts of $HCl_{(aq)}$ and $NaOH_{(aq)}$ are mixed, the resulting solution will still

    A. feel slippery   **B.** turn red litmus blue
    C. taste sour   **D.** conduct electricity

61. A student gathered the following information about a cafeteria beverage:

- It tastes sour.
- Turns blue litmus red.
- Conducts an electric current.
- Reacts with $Zn_{(s)}$ to produce a gas.

The beverage is

    A. acidic   **B.** basic

    C. soapy   **D.** an alcohol

62. A similarity between solutions of a strong acid and a strong base is that both solutions

    A. taste sour   **B.** are slippery

    C. conduct electricity   **D.** turn blue litmus red

63. A mechanic is trying to clean up a spill from a leaky car battery. What common substance should be used to neutralize the effects of the spill?

    A. water   **B.** vinegar

    C. lemon juice   **D.** baking soda

64. In order to identify aqueous solutions of $NaCl$, $NaOH$, H_2SO_4 and CH_3OH, students performed a series of experiments on each solution and obtained the data below:

Solution	Electrolyte	Blue Litmus	Red Litmus	Reaction with Zn(s)
I	yes	red	red	production of $H_{2(g)}$
II	yes	blue	blue	production of a precipitate
III	yes	blue	red	no reaction
IV	no	blue	red	no reaction

According to the data, the H_2SO_4 solution is

    A. I   **B.** II

    C. III   **D.** IV

65. A base can be described as a substance that

    A.   tastes bitter   **B.**   turns blue litmus red

    C.   decreases the pH of a solution   **D.**   reacts with $Zn_{(s)}$ to produce $H_{2(g)}$

66. A student wishes to dilute some 6.00 mol/L HCl to make 5.00L of 0.010 0 mol/L HCl. The volume of 6.00 mol/L solution he should use is

    A. 50.0 mL   **B.** 12.4 mL

    C. 8.33 mL   **D.** 4.20 mL

67. In order to dilute 50.0 mL of 6.00 mol/L HCl to a concentration of 0.150 mol/L, water should be added until the final volume is

    A. 2.00 L   **B.** 2.50 L

    C. 3.00 L   **D.** 4.00 L

68. When a solution is diluted, the

    A. mass of solute remains constant

    B. number of moles of solute remains constant

    C. concentration of the solution will decrease

    D. all of the above

69. The mass of NaOH contained within a 10.0 mL sample of 0.002 50 mol/L NaOH solution would be

    A. 0.001 00 g   **B.** 0.002 50 g

    C. 0.010 0 g   **D.** 0.025 0 g

70. The following list gives the steps usually followed in preparing a solution of known concentration. The correct sequence of steps is

    1. measure out the required mass of solute

    2. calculate the mass of solute required

    3. add water to make up the total required volume of solution

    4. dissolve the solute in less than the total volume of solvent required

    A. 1, 3, 4, 4   **B.** 2, 1, 4, 3

    C. 3, 1, 2, 4   **D.** 4, 1, 2, 3

NOTES

QUANTITATIVE RELATIONSHIPS IN CHEMICAL CHANGES

When you are finished this unit, you will be able to…

- explain chemical principles, such as the conservation of mass, using quantitative analysis

- write balanced ionic and net ionic equations, including identification of spectator ions, for reactions taking place in aqueous solutions

- calculate the quantities of reactants and/or products involved in chemical reactions, using gravimetric, solution, or gas stoichiometry

- identify limiting and excess reagents in chemical reactions

- define theoretical and actual yields, and explain the discrepancy between them

- draw and interpret titration curves, using data from titration experiments involving strong monoprotic acids and strong monoprotic bases

- identify points of equivalence on strong monoprotic acid to strong monoprotic base titration curves and differentiate between the indicator end point and the equivalence point

PREREQUISITE SKILLS AND KNOWLEDGE

Prior to starting this unit, you should be able to…

- balance chemical equations in terms of atoms, molecules, and moles

- contrast quantitative and qualitative analysis

- classify and identify categories of chemical reactions

- use appropriate SI notation and significant digits

- describe WHMIS and consumer product labeling information in an experimental context

Lesson 1 MOLE-TO-MOLE PROBLEMS

The term stoichiometry comes from the Greek word stoikheion meaning element and metron meaning to measure. Stoichiometry refers to the measurement and relationship of quantities involved in chemical reactions.

All stoichiometry problems can be solved from a basic pattern:

There are four basic types of stoichiometry problems:

1. Given moles of "A", find moles of "B"
2. Given moles of "A", find quantity of "B"
3. Given quantity of "A", find moles of "B"
4. Given quantity of "A", find quantity of "B"

Solving stoichiometric problems: make sure your equation is balanced.

Mole-To-Mole Problems

This type of question involves using the mole ratio from a balanced equation to determine the moles of one substance, given the moles of another.

Steps to solve problems:

Coefficients are exact numbers and can be assigned any number of significant digits.

1. Write a balanced equation for the reaction.
2. Determine the two substances involved in the reaction, the given and the unknown.
3. Set up a mole ratio using coefficients of the balanced equation for the two substances
4. Substitute values in mole ratio for the given and unknown.
5. Solve the equation.

Example 1

How many moles of oxygen gas are needed to react completely with 3.50 mol of hydrogen gas to produce water vapor?

Solution

Step 1
Write a balanced equation for the reaction.
$$2H_{2(g)} + O_{2(g)} \rightarrow 2H_2O_{(g)}$$

Step 2
Determine the two substances required, the given and the unknown.

given: 3.50 mol of hydrogen
unknown: ? mol of oxygen

Step 3
Set up a mole ratio using coefficients of balanced equation
for the two substances

$$\frac{O_2}{H_2} = \frac{1}{2}$$

Coefficients from balanced equation

Step 4
Substitute values in mole ratio for the given and unknown.

$$\frac{x}{3.50} = \frac{1}{2}$$

Step 5
Solve for x

$$x = \frac{(1)(3.50)}{2} = 1.75 \text{ mol } O_2$$

Example 2

How many moles of ammonia gas can be produced by reacting 6.00 mol of
hydrogen gas with sufficient nitrogen gas?

Solution

Step 1
Write a balanced equation for the reaction.

$$N_{2(g)} + 3H_{2(g)} \rightarrow 2NH_{3(g)}$$

Step 2
Determine the two substances required, the given and the   unknown.
given: 6.00 mol of hydrogen
unknown: ? mol of ammonia

Step 3
Set up a mole ratio using coefficients of balanced equation for the
two substances

$$\frac{NH_3}{H_2} = \frac{2}{3}$$

Coefficients from balanced equation

Step 4
Substitute values in mole ratio for the given and unknown.

$$\frac{x}{6.00} = \frac{2}{3}$$

Step 5
Solve for x

$$x = \frac{(2)(6.00)}{3} = 4.00 \text{ mol } NH_3$$

PRACTICE EXERCISES

1. Water decomposes into its two elements, $H_{2(g)}$ and $O_{2(g)}$

   a) Balanced equation:

   b) How many moles of hydrogen gas are produced if 0.500 mol of water are decomposed?

   c) How many moles of oxygen gas are produced if 0.250 mol of water are decomposed?

2. Sulfur (S_8) reacts with barium oxide to produce barium sulfide and oxygen gas.

   a) Balanced equation:

   b) How many moles of elemental sulfur are needed if 2.00 mol of barium oxide are used?

   c) How many moles of barium sulfide are produced from 0.100 mol of sulfur?

3. The combustion of methane gas, $CH_{4(g)}$, takes place in the presence of oxygen gas, $O_{2(g)}$ to produce carbon dioxide gas and water vapor.

   a) Balanced equation:

b) How many moles of oxygen gas are needed to completely burn 3.00 mol of methane gas?

c) How many moles of water vapor are produced from 0.040 0 mol of methane gas?

4. Sodium metal and phosphorus, $P_{4(s)}$, react to form a compound.

a) Balanced equation:

b) How many moles of phosphorus are needed if 0.600 mol of sodium metal are used?

c) How many moles of sodium phosphide can be produced from 0.25 mol of sodium metal?

5. Magnesium phosphate reacts with lithium carbonate to produce magnesium carbonate and lithium phosphate.

a) Balanced equation:

b) How many moles of lithium carbonate are needed when 1.50 mol of magnesium phosphate are used?

c) How many moles of lithium carbonate are needed to produce 0.020 0 mol of magnesium carbonate?

6. Sulfur dioxide decomposes into two elements, sulfur (S_8) and oxygen gas (O_2).

    a) Balanced equation:

    b) How many moles of sulfur dioxide are needed to produce 0.30 mol of sulfur?

    c) How many moles of oxygen gas are produced when 2.1 mol of sulfur are also produced?

7. Magnesium chloride reacts with sodium metal to produce sodium chloride and magnesium metal.

    a) Balanced equation:

    b) How many moles of sodium metal are needed to react with 0.025 0 mol of magnesium chloride?

    c) How many moles of magnesium chloride would be needed to produce 3.00 mol of magnesium metal?

8. Iron (II) phosphate reacts with tin (IV) nitride to produce iron (II) nitride and tin (IV) phosphate.

    a) Balanced equation:

    b) How many moles of tin (IV) nitride are needed to produce 0.500 mol of iron (II) nitride?

c) How many moles of iron (II) phosphate are used when 0.045 mol of tin (IV) nitride also react?

9. Gasoline ($C_8H_{18(l)}$) is burned in air (O_2) to produce carbon dioxide gas and water vapor.

a) Balanced equation:

b) How many moles of carbon dioxide are produced when 3.00 mol of gasoline are completely reacted?

c) How many moles of gasoline would be needed for complete combustion if 25 mol of oxygen are used?

Lesson 2 MOLE-TO-QUANTITY PROBLEMS

In this type of question moles of one substance are given and you are asked to find a quantity such as mass, concentration, or volume.

Steps to solve problems:
1. Write a balanced equation for the reaction.
2. Determine the two substances involved in the reaction, the given and the unknown.
3. Set up a mole ratio using coefficients of the balanced equation for the two substances
4. Substitute values in mole ratio for the given and unknown. Coefficients are exact numbers and can be assigned any number of significant digits.
5. Solve the equation for unknown number of moles.
6. Convert unknown moles into mass by multiplying by the unknown's molar mass.

Example 1

Copper metal reacts with an aqueous solution of silver nitrate to produce silver metal and copper (II) nitrate. What mass of silver can be produced by reacting 0.250 mol of copper?

Solution

Step 1
Write a balanced equation for the reaction.
$$Cu_{(s)} + 2AgNO_{3(aq)} \rightarrow Cu(NO_3)_{2(aq)} + 2Ag_{(s)}$$

Step 2
Determine the two substances involved in the reaction, the given and the unknown.

given: 0.250 mol Cu
unknown: ? g Ag

Step 3
Set up a mole ratio using coefficients of the balanced equation for the two substances

$$\frac{Ag}{Cu} = \frac{1}{2}$$

Coefficients from balanced equation

Step 4
Substitute values in mole ratio for the given and unknown.

$$\frac{x}{0.250} = \frac{1}{2}$$

Step 5
Solve the equation for unknown number of moles.

$$x = \frac{(2)(0.250)}{1} = 0.500 \text{ mol Ag}$$

Step 6
Convert unknown moles into mass by multiplying by the unknown's molar mass.

$$\text{Mass of Ag} = n \times m$$
$$= (0.500 \text{ mol})(107.87 \text{ g/mol})$$
$$= 53.9 \text{ g}$$

Example 2

Sulfuric acid is neutralized by sodium hydroxide solution. What mass of sodium sulfate can be produced by reacting 0.350 mol of $NaOH_{(aq)}$?

Solution

Step 1
Write a balanced equation for the reaction.

$$H_2SO_{4(aq)} + 2NaOH_{(aq)} \rightarrow Na_2SO_{4(aq)} + 2H_2O_{(l)}$$

Step 2
Determine the two substances involved in the reaction, the given and the unknown.

given: 0.350 mol of NaOH
unknown: ? g Na_2SO_4

Step 3
Set up a mole ratio using coefficients of balanced equation for the two substances

$$\frac{Na_2SO_4}{NaOH} = \frac{1}{2}$$

Coefficients from balanced equation

Step 4
Substitute values in mole ratio for the given and unknown.

$$\frac{x}{0.350} = \frac{1}{2}$$

Step 5
Solve the equation for unknown number of moles.

$$x = \frac{(1)(0.350)}{2} = 0.175 \text{ mol } Na_2SO_4$$

Step 6
Convert unknown moles into mass by multiplying by the unknown's molar mass.
Molar mass of Na_2SO_4
$$2 \text{ mol Na} \times 22.99 \text{ g/mol} = 45.98 \text{ g}$$
$$1 \text{ mol S} \times 32.06 \text{ g/mol} = 32.06 \text{ g}$$
$$4 \text{ mol O} \times 16.00 \text{ g/mol} = 64.00 \text{ g}$$
$$1 \text{ mol} = 142.04 \text{ g}$$

$$\text{Mass of } Na_2SO_4 = n \times M$$
$$= (0.175 \text{ mol})(142.04 \text{ g/mol})$$
$$= 24.9 \text{ g}$$

PRACTICE EXERCISES

1. When 6.5 mol of potassium chlorate solid breaks down to the simpler compound of potassium chloride and oxygen gas, what mass of $KCl_{(s)}$ would be produced?

2. When 5.00 mol of methane burns in excess oxygen gas, what volume of $CO_{2(g)}$ at STP will be produced?

3. If 8.25 mol of nitrogen gas reacts with chlorine gas, what volume of nitrogen trichloride gas at 35.0°C and 98.9 kPa would be produced?

4. What volume of 1.00 mol/L $HCl_{(aq)}$ is needed to neutralize 2.50 mol of calcium hydroxide? The reaction produces calcium chloride and water.

1. 6.5 mol = n - Find m of $KCl_{(s)}$

$$2KClO_3 \rightarrow 2KCl_{(s)} + 3O_{2(g)}$$

● $K = x_2$ $K = x_2$
  $Cl = x_2$ $Cl = x_2$

  $O = x_6$ $O = x_6$

Molar
ratio 1 mol 2 3.

n   6.5 mol   X

$M \quad \dfrac{X}{2} = \dfrac{6.5}{2}$

Molar X = 6.5 mol.

$n = 6.5$ mol

$m = nM$

● $= 6.5$ mol $(74.55 g/mol)$

  $= 484.57 g$.

K 39.10
Cl $\dfrac{35.45}{74.55}$

#3. n = 8.25 mol N_2 Given. Find V.

T = 35°C $P_1 = 98.9$ kpa.

$$N_2 + 3Cl_2 \rightarrow 2N Cl_3$$

      1   3   2.

Molar
ratio.

n 8.25 mol

v   X

$PV = nRT$

$v = \dfrac{\cancel{I}}{P}$

●

5. When 5.25 mol of butane (C_4H_{10}) burns in the presence of excess oxygen gas, what volume of water vapor at SATP would be produced?

6. When an excess of silver reacts with 3.45 moles of zinc phosphate, what mass of silver phosphate would be produced? The reaction also produces zinc metal.

7. When sulfuric acid reacts with sodium hydroxide, sodium sulfate and water are produced. If 50.0 mL of $H_2SO_{4(aq)}$ react with 0.250 mol of NaOH, what is the concentration of the acid?

8. When iron (II) hydroxide reacts with cobalt (II) phosphate, iron (II) phosphate and cobalt (II) hydroxide are formed. If 3.00 mol of $Fe(OH)_{2(aq)}$ react, what mass of $Co_3(PO_4)_{2(s)}$ is needed?

9. In the neutralization of a sulfuric acid solution, 4.56 mol of sodium hydroxide was used. What mass of water would be produced in this reaction?

10. If 5.00 mol of dinitrogen pentoxide is decomposed, what volume of nitrogen gas, $N_{2(g)}$, is produced at 20.0°C and 125 kPa?

Lesson 3 QUANTITY-TO-MOLE PROBLEMS

In this type of problem a quantity of one substance such as mass, volume and concentration of solution or volume of gas is given, and you are asked to find the number of moles of another substance.

Steps to solve problems:

1 mol of and ideal gas at STP occupies 22.4 L

1 mol of an ideal gas at SATP occupies 24.8 L

1. Write a balanced equation for the reaction.
2. Determine the two substances involved in the reaction, the given and the unknown.
3. Calculate the number of moles of the given substance.
4. Set up a mole ratio using coefficients of the balanced equation for the two substances.
5. Substitute values in mole ratio for the given and unknown.
6. Solve the equation for unknown number of moles.

Example 1

How many moles of water vapor can be produced by reacting 78.4 L of oxygen gas at STP with sufficient hydrogen gas?

Solution

Step 1

Write a balanced equation for the reaction.

$$2H_{2(g)} + O_{2(g)} \rightarrow 2H_2O_{(g)}$$

Step 2

Determine the two substances involved in the reaction, the given and the unknown.

given: 78.4 L O_2
unknown: ? mol H_2O

Step 3

Calculate the number of moles of the given substance.

$$n = \frac{L}{22.4 \, L} \text{ at STP}$$
$$= \frac{78.4 \, L}{22.4 \, L}$$
$$= 3.50 \text{ mol of } O_{2(g)}$$

Step 4

Set up a mole ratio using coefficients of balanced equation for the two substances

$$\frac{H_2O}{O_2} = \frac{2}{1}$$

Coefficients from balanced equation

Step 5

Substitute values in mole ratio for the given and unknown.

$$\frac{x}{3.50} = \frac{2}{1}$$

Step 6

Solve the equation for unknown number of moles.

$$x = \frac{(2)(3.50)}{1} = 7.00 \text{ mol H}_2\text{O}$$

Example 2

How many moles of zinc are needed to produce 450.0 g of zinc chloride by reacting the zinc with an excess of hydrochloric acid?

Solution

Step 1

Write a balanced equation for the reaction.

$$\text{Zn}_{(s)} + 2\text{HCl}_{(aq)} \rightarrow \text{ZnCl}_{2(aq)} + \text{H}_{2(g)}$$

Step 2

Determine the two substances involved in the reaction, the given and the unknown.

given: 450.0 g ZnCl_2

unknown: ? mol Zn

Step 3

Calculate the number of moles of the given substance.

Molar mass of ZnCl_2:

1 mol Zn × 65.38 g/mol = 65.38
2 mol Cl × 65.45 g/mol = 70.90
1 mol = 136.28 g

Number of moles, $n = \dfrac{m}{M}$

$$= \frac{450.0 \text{ g}}{136.28 \text{ g/mol}}$$

$$= 3.302 \text{ mol}$$

Step 4

Set up a mole ratio using coefficients of balanced equation for the two substances.

$$\frac{\text{Zn}}{\text{ZnCl}_2} = \frac{1}{1}$$

Coefficients from balanced equation

Step 5

Substitute values in mole ratio for the given and unknown.

$$x = \frac{(1)(3.302)}{1} = 3.302 \text{ mol Zn}$$

PRACTICE EXERCISES

1. Iron burns in air, reacting with oxygen gas, to form the black solid, iron (III) oxide. If 5.6 g of iron are completely burned, how many moles of iron (III) oxide are formed?

2. Methane, $CH_{4(g)}$, the main constituent of natural gas, is burned. How many moles of water vapor are produced from 4.00 g of methane?

3. If potassium chlorate is heated gently, the crystals will melt. Further heating will decompose the compound to give potassium chloride and oxygen gas. If 122.6 g of potassium chloride are produced, how many moles of potassium chlorate are decomposed?

4. Black iron (III) oxide solid can be converted into a water and iron metal when it is reacted with hydrogen gas. If 125 g of iron (III) oxide are reacted, how many moles of water form?

5. Zinc is reacted with hydrochloric acid to produce hydrogen gas and an aqueous solution of zinc chloride. If 44.8 L of $H_{2(g)}$ at STP are produced, how many moles of zinc were reacted?

6. When solutions of copper (II) sulfate and potassium phosphate are mixed, solid copper (II) phosphate forms along with an aqueous solution of potassium sulfate. If 8.5 g of $Cu_3(PO_4)_{2(s)}$ form, how many moles of copper (II) sulfate reacted?

7. If solid sodium chloride is reacted with 45.0 mL of 2.00 mol/L $H_2SO_{4(aq)}$, aqueous solutions of hydrochloric acid and sodium sulfate are formed. How many moles of sodium sulfate are formed?

8. When a piece of sodium metal is lowered into a bottle of chlorine gas, a reaction forming the white solid sodium chloride takes place. How many moles of this solid will be formed from 2.3 g of sodium?

9. In the manufacture of nitric acid, nitrogen dioxide gas reacts with water to form nitric acid and nitrogen monoxide gas. How many moles of nitrogen dioxide react if 120.6 g of nitric acid are formed?

10. Solid diphosphorus pentaoxide reacts with water to form phosphoric acid. If 9.01 g of water are used, how many moles of $H_3PO_{4(aq)}$ are produced?

11. A thermite reaction is used in welding iron and steel. Solid aluminium and solid iron (III) oxide is ignited by high temperature to give aluminium oxide(s) and iron(s). If 50.0 g of aluminium is used in the reaction, how many moles of aluminium oxide will be produced?

Lesson 4 QUANTITY-TO-QUANTITY PROBLEMS

In this type of question, you are provided with a quantity of one substance and asked to calculate a quantity such as mass, volume, or concentration of another substance.

Steps to solve problems:

1.   Write a balanced equation for the reaction.
2.   Determine the two substances involved in the reaction, the given and the unknown.
3.   Calculate the number of moles of the given substance.
4.   Set up a mole ratio using coefficients of the balanced equation for the two substances
5.   Substitute values in mole ratio for the given and unknown.
6.   Solve the equation for unknown number of moles.
7.   Convert unknown moles into mass by multiplying by the unknown's molar mass, or convert moles into concentration by dividing by volume (for solutions), or convert moles into volume (for gases) using the ideal gas law (or one of the shortcuts at SATP or STP).

Example 1

What mass of aluminium oxide must be decomposed to produce 80.0 g of oxygen gas?

Solution

Step 1

Write a balanced equation for the reaction.
$$2Al_2O_{3(s)} \rightarrow 4Al_{(s)} + 3O_{2(g)}$$

Step 2

Determine the two substances involved in the reaction, the given and the unknown.

given: 80.0 g of O_2
unknown: ? g Al_2O_3

Step 3

Calculate the number of moles of the given substance.

Mass of $O_2 = 2$ mol $\times$ 16.00 g/mol
$= 32.00$ g

Number of moles O_2

$$n = \frac{m}{M}$$

$$= \frac{80.0 \text{ g}}{32.00 \text{ g/mol}}$$

$$= 2.50 \text{ mol}$$

NOTES

Step 4
Set up a mole ratio using coefficients of balanced equation for the two substances

$$\frac{Al_2O_3}{O_2} = \frac{2}{3}$$

Coefficients from balanced equation

Step 5
Substitute values in mole ratio for the given and unknown.

$$\frac{x}{2.50} = \frac{2}{3}$$

Step 6
Solve the equation for unknown number of moles.

$$x = \frac{(2)(2.50)}{3} = 1.67 \text{ mol of } Al_2O_3$$

Step 7
Convert unknown moles into mass by multiplying by the unknown's molar mass.

Molar mass Al_2O_3:

$$
\begin{array}{lll}
2 \text{ mol Al} \times 26.98 \text{ g/mol} & = 53.96 \text{ g} \\
3 \text{ mol O} \times 16.00 \text{ g/mol} & = 48.00 \text{ g} \\
1 \text{ mol} & = 101.96 \text{ g}
\end{array}
$$

Mass Al_2O_3,

$$
\begin{aligned}
m &= nM \\
&= (1.67 \text{ mol})(101.96 \text{ g/mol}) \\
&= 170 \text{ g}
\end{aligned}
$$

Example 2

An excess of zinc metal is reacted with 250.0 mL of 0.100 mol/L hydrochloric acid. What volume of hydrogen gas at 25°C and 95.0 kPa can be produced?

Step 1
Write a balanced equation for the reaction.

$$Zn_{(s)} + 2HCl_{(aq)} \rightarrow ZnCl_{2(aq)} + H_{2(g)}$$

Step 2
Determine the two substances involved in the reaction, the given and the unknown.

given: 250.0 mL of 0.100 mol/L HCl

unknown: ? g H_2

Step 3
Calculate the number of moles of the given substance.

Moles of HCl,

$$
\begin{aligned}
n &= CV \\
&= (0.100 \text{ mol/L})(0.250\,0 \text{ L}) \\
&= 0.025\,0 \text{ mol}
\end{aligned}
$$

Step 4

Set up a mole ratio using coefficients of balanced equation for the two substances

$$\frac{H_2}{HCl} = \frac{1}{2}$$

Coefficients from balanced equation

Step 5

Substitute values in mole ratio for the given and unknown.

$$\frac{x}{0.025\ 0} = \frac{1}{2}$$

Step 6

Solve the equation for unknown number of moles.

$$x = \frac{(1)(0.025\ 0)}{2} = 0.012\ 5\ \text{mol}$$

Step 7

Convert unknown moles into volume.

$$PV = nRT$$
$$V = \frac{nRT}{P}$$
$$= \frac{(0.012\ 5\ \text{mol})(8.31\ \text{L} \times \text{kPa/mol} \times \text{K})(298\ \text{K})}{95.0\ \text{kPa}}$$
$$V = 0.326\ \text{L}$$
$$= 326\ \text{mL}$$

Example 3

In a demonstration, 20.0 mL of 0.100 mol/L $H_2SO_{4(aq)}$ are completely neutralized by a 0.150 mol/L solution of $NaOH_{(aq)}$. What volume of $NaOH_{(aq)}$ would be required?

Solution

Step 1

Write a balanced equation for the reaction.

$$2\ NaOH_{(aq)} + H_2SO_{4(aq)} \rightarrow Na_2SO_{4(aq)} + 2\ H_2O_{(l)}$$

Step 2

Determine the two substances involved in the reaction, the given and the unknown.

given: 20.0 mL of 0.100 mol/L $H_2SO_{4(aq)}$

unknown: ? mL of 0.150 mol/L $NaOH_{(aq)}$

Step 3

Calculate the number of moles of the given substance.

Moles of $H_2SO_{4(aq)}$

$$n = CV$$
$$= (0.100\ \text{mol/L})\ (0.020\ 0\ \text{L})$$
$$= 0.002\ 00\ \text{mol}$$

Step 4

Set up a mole ratio using coefficients of balanced equation for the two substances

$$\frac{NaOH}{H_2SO_4} = \frac{2}{1}$$

Coefficients from balanced equation

Step 5

Substitute values in mole ratio for the given and unknown.

$$\frac{x}{0.002\,00} = \frac{2}{1}$$

Step 6

Solve the equation for unknown number of moles.

$$x = \frac{(2)(0.002\,00)}{1} = 0.004\,00 \text{ mol}$$

Step 7

Convert unknown moles into volume.

$$C = \frac{n}{v}$$

$$v = \frac{n}{C}$$

$$= \frac{0.004\,00}{0.150}$$

$$= 0.026\,7 \text{ L}$$

$$= 26.7 \text{ mL}$$

PRACTICE EXERCISES

1. Zinc metal reacts with hydrochloric acid to produce zinc chloride and hydrogen gas. What mass of zinc chloride can be produced by reacting 50.0 mL of 1.00 mol/L $HCl_{(aq)}$ with sufficient zinc?

2. Natural gas is mainly methane, $CH_{4(g)}$. What mass of methane must be burned to produce 56.0 L of $CO_{2(g)}$ at STP?

3. Aluminium metal is refined from the ore of aluminum called bauxite. In the refining process aluminium oxide decomposes to aluminum and oxygen gas. What mass of aluminium can be produced from 2.04 kg of aluminium oxide?

4. Sodium hydrogen carbonate (bicarbonate of soda) can be used to neutralize acid. Sodium hydrogen carbonate reacts with hydrochloric acid to produce sodium chloride, carbon dioxide gas, and water. What volume of carbon dioxide gas at STP can be produced by 16.8 g of sodium hydrogen carbonate?

5. Photography film is coated with silver chloride. This is produced along with sodium nitrate when silver nitrate reacts with sodium chloride. What mass of silver chloride can be made from 11.7 g of sodium chloride?

6. Ammonia, $NH_{3(g)}$, reacts with hydrochloric acid to produce ammonium chloride. What mass of ammonia is needed to produce 36.1 g of ammonium chloride?

7. Nitric acid reacts with sodium hydroxide to produce sodium nitrate and water. If 25.0 mL of the acid solution reacts with 0.600 g of the $NaOH_{(s)}$, what is the concentration of the nitric acid?

8. Sodium metal reacts vigorously with water to produce sodium hydroxide and hydrogen gas. What volume of hydrogen at 25.0°C and 113 kPa can be produced from 8.05 g of sodium?

9. In the thermite reaction aluminium reacts with iron (III) oxide to produce iron and aluminium oxide. What mass of aluminium oxide is produced along with 19.55 g of iron?

10. Sulfuric acid reacts with potassium hydroxide to produce potassium sulfate and water. What mass of potassium sulfate can be produced from 294.6 g of potassium hydroxide?

11. Sodium iodide reacts with lead (II) nitrate to produce sodium nitrate and lead (II) iodide. What mass of lead (II) nitrate will be required to produce 150 g of sodium nitrate?

12. 25.0 mL of 0.200 mol/L $Sr(OH)_2$ solution reacts completely with 15.0 mL of $HCl_{(aq)}$. What is the concentration of the $HCl_{(aq)}$?

13. A titration was performed to find the concentration of dilute $HCl_{(aq)}$. 10.00 mL of the $HCl_{(aq)}$ reached an end point with 12.5 mL of 0.250 mol/L $NaOH_{(aq)}$. What was the $HCl_{(aq)}$ concentration?

Lesson 5 QUALITATIVE AND QUANTITATIVE ANALYSIS

One of the major activities in a chemistry lab is chemical analysis. Chemical analyses can be divided into 2 major groups – qualitative and quantitative. Qualitative analysis is concerned with identifying the identity of a substance or whether or not a specific substance is present in a mixture. To remember the term think *quality*. Examples of qualitative analyses are flame tests, selective precipitation, litmus paper tests, etc.

Quantitative analysis is concerned with determining the quantity (mass or concentration most of the time) of a specific substance present in a sample. To remember the term think *quantity*. Examples of quantitative analysis include acid-base titrations, some spectroscopic tests, precipitate masses (to determine concentration of solutions), etc.

Quantitative analysis can be used to verify chemical laws like the law of conservation of mass. With careful design, an experiment can be set up to show that the mass of products equals the mass of reactants in a chemical reaction.

Limiting Reagents

Sometimes one of the two reactants is not completely used up in a chemical reaction. This type of stoichiometry question is known as a "limiting reagent" problem.

Steps to solve limiting reagent problems:

1. Write a balanced equation for the reaction.
2. Determine the two reagents (reactants) involved in the reaction.
3. Calculate the number of moles of each reagent.
4. Set up a mole ratio of the two reagents (reactants) using the coefficients from the balanced equation.
5. Find which reagent of the two will be used up first (usually will be the smallest mole amount—but be careful and check the mole ratio amounts).
6. Substitute limiting reagent mole ratio for the given and the unknown.
7. Solve the equation for the unknown number of moles.
8. Convert unknown moles into mass and multiplying by unknown's molar mass.

Example

5.00 g of $NaOH_{(s)}$ is added to 50.0 mL of 1.25 mol/L $HNO_{3(aq)}$. Calculate the mass of water that forms.

Solution

Step 1

Write and balance equation

$$NaOH_{(s)} + HNO_{3(aq)} \rightarrow NaNO_{3(aq)} + HOH_{(l)}$$

Step 2

Convert given information to moles.

$$^{n}NaOH = \frac{5.00\ g}{40.00\ g/mol} = 0.125\ mol$$

$$^{n}HNO_3 = C \times V = (1.25\ mol/L)(0.050\ 00\ L)$$
$$= 0.062\ 5\ mol$$

Step 3

Determine the limiting reagent.
From the balanced equation in step 1, the mole ratio between $NaOH$ and HNO_3 is 1:1.
Therefore, an equal number of moles are required.

Since 0.062 5 is less than 0.125 0, the HNO_3 is used up before the $NaOH$. HNO_3 is the limiting reagent.

Step 4

Find the number of moles of water when 0.062 5 moles of HNO_3 is used.

$$^{n}H2O = 0.062\ 5\ mol\ HNO_3 \times \frac{1H_2O}{1HNO_3}$$

$$= 0.062\ 5\ mol$$

Step 5

Convert moles of H_2O to mass.

$$m = 0.062\ 5\ moles \times \frac{18.02\ g}{1\ mol} = 1.13\ g$$

Example 2

If 20.0 mL of 3.0 mol/L $H_2SO_{4(aq)}$ is added to 15 mL of 5.0 mol/L $KOH_{(aq)}$, what mass of water can form?

Solution

Step 1

Balance equation:

$$H_2SO_{4(aq)} + 2KOH_{(aq)} \rightarrow K_2SO_{4(aq)} + 2H_2O_{(l)}$$

Step 2

Convert given info to moles/determine limiting reagent:

$$^nH_2SO_4 \quad = C \times V \quad = (3.0 \text{ mol/L})(0.020\,0 \text{ L})$$
$$= 0.060\,0 \text{ moles}$$

$$^nKOH \quad = C \times V \quad = (5.0 \text{ mol/L})(0.015 \text{ L})$$
$$= 0.075\,0 \text{ moles}$$

Since $0.075\,0 < 2(0.060\,0)$, KOH is limiting reagent

Step 3

Convert moles H_2O:

$$^nH_2O = 0.750 \text{ mol KOH} \times \frac{2HOH}{2KOH}$$
$$= 0.075\,0 \text{ mol}$$

Step 4

Convert to mass, H_2O

$$m = 0.075\,0 \text{ mol} \times \frac{18.02 \text{ g}}{1 \text{ mol}} = 1.35 \text{ g}$$

Example 3

350 g of $KOH_{(s)}$ is added to 1.00 L of 6.0 mol/L $H_3PO_{4(aq)}$. How many moles of which reagent is in excess?

Solution

$$H_3PO_{4(aq)} + 3KOH_{(s)} \rightarrow K_3PO_{4(aq)} + 3HOH_{(l)}$$

$$^nKOH = 350 \text{ g} \times \frac{1 \text{ mol}}{56.11 \text{ g}} = 6.237\,7 \text{ mol}$$

$$^nH_3PO_4 = C \times V = (6.0 \text{ mol/L})(1.00 \text{ L}) = 6.000 \text{ mol}$$

Since $6.237\,7 < 3(6.000)$, KOH is limiting
H_3PO_4 is in excess

$$^nH_3PO_4 \text{ reacting} = 6.237\,7 \text{ mol KOH} \times \frac{1H_3PO_4}{3KOH}$$
$$= 2.079\,24 \text{ mol}$$

Therefore, the excess $= 6.00 - 2.079\,24 = 3.9 \text{ mol}$

PRACTICE EXERCISES

1. For each of the following, write a balanced equation (including state of matter subscripts) and determine which reagent is in excess and by how many moles. Identify the limiting reagent in each.

   a) 50 mL of 1.25 mol/L $HCl_{(aq)}$ is reacted with 75 mL of 1.00 mol/L $KOH_{(aq)}$.

   b) 125 g of $NaOH_{(s)}$ is reacted with 300 mL of 10.5 mol/L nitric acid.

   c) 5.00 g of magnesium solid is reacted with 7.00 g of hydrogen chloride gas with added water.

   d) 100 mL of 0.50 mol/L $HCl_{(aq)}$ is reacted with 50 mL of 1.00 mol/L $KOH_{(aq)}$.

2. 25 mL of 0.55 mol/L phosphoric acid is reacted with 100 mL of 0.010 mol/L $NaOH_{(aq)}$. What is the maximum mass of water that can form?

3. 150 mL of 5.00 mol/L $HCl_{(aq)}$ reacts with 7.50 g of $KOH_{(s)}$. What mass of potassium chloride will form?

4. What mass of sodium hydroxide will react exactly with:

    a) 0.10 mol of $HCl_{(aq)}$

    b) 0.10 mol of $H_2SO_{4(aq)}$

    c) 0.10 mol of $H_3PO_{4(aq)}$

5. In question 4, if there are 5.0 g of sodium hydroxide, in which cases will the sodium hydroxide be in excess, and by how many moles?

6. 32.5 mL of hydrogen gas at SATP react with 0.020 0 g of oxygen gas. How many moles of which reagent is in excess?

7. In question 6, what is the mass of water that can form in the reaction?

8. 10.0 L of nitrogen gas at 105 kPa and 35°C are mixed with 33.5 L of hydrogen gas at 95.0 kPa and 40°C and ammonia gas is formed. What mass of ammonia gas will form?

Lesson 6 THEORETICAL AND ACTUAL YIELDS

When you use stoichiometry to calculate the mass of product that forms from a given quantity of limiting reagent, you are calculating the theoretical yield of the reaction. In most cases the actual yield will be smaller than the theoretical yield. (In some cases the value of the actual yield may be inflated by having a wet or impure product.)

The actual yield will be smaller than the theoretical yield for a number of reasons.

Among them are:

- impure reactants
- uncertainty in measurements
- reaction may be incomplete, either because it's a slow reaction, or because it reaches equilibrium
- various unavoidable experimental factors

Titration Curves

In acid-base titrations you might assume that the pH changes in a linear manner. For example if you are titrating an acid with a base, you might assume that the pH will get progressively larger as more base is added. This is NOT what happens. The following graphs illustrate the:

a) titration of a strong monoprotic acid with a strong base
b) titration of a strong monoprotic base with a strong acid

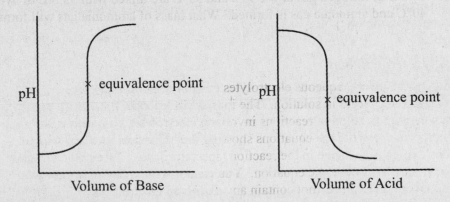

A monoprotic acid is an acid that will react on 1 to 1 basis with $NaOH_{(aq)}$
A monoprotic base is a base that will react on a 1 to 1 basis with $HCl_{(aq)}$.

The equivalence point is marked on both graphs. It is the exact centre of the rapidly rising or rapidly falling region of the graphs. At this point there will be an equal number of moles of acid and base for monoprotic strong acid to strong base titrations. The volume of titrant solution required to get to the equivalence point will be indicated by the acid-base indicator colour (next section).

The pH does not change in a linear manner during the titration of a strong monoprotic acid with a strong base because as the base is added, it is immediately neutralized by the acid. A small amount of H_3O^+ has been consumed, but it takes a 10 fold decrease in $[H_3O^+]$ to make the pH go up by 1 unit. Thus pH stays relatively constant. It does not change dramatically until almost all of the H_3O^+ has been consumed. At this point the pH rises rapidly, and at the equivalence point $[H_3O^+] = [OH^-] = 10^{-7}$ mol/L and the pH = 7. As more base is added, H_3O^+ is not present in sufficient quantity to neutralize it and the pH continues to rise. Finally the pH comes close to leveling off as it approaches the pH of the added base. It will never actually reach this pH. The titration of a strong monoprotic base with a strong acid is the exact reverse of this, and the explanation is similar.

Acid-Base Indicators

Acid-base indicators are solutions that have different colours depending on the pH of the solution they are in. There is an acid-base indicator chart in the reference tables in this book. As you view the table, you will see that different indicators change colour over different pH ranges.

For monoprotic strong acid-strong base titrations, the equivalence point always occurs at pH = 7. A suitable indicator for this type of titration is bromothymol blue which changes colour from yellow to blue over the pH range from 6.0 to 7.6. At the equivalence point of this type of titration, bromothymol blue will be a mixture of blue and yellow and therefore will appear green.

The colour of the bromothymol blue at the equivalence point is called the end point. Thus a strong monoprotic acid to strong base titration has a green bromothymol blue end point.

Net Ionic Equations

As you are aware, aqueous electrolytes exist in dissociated (ionic) or ionized (acid) form in solution. The ions act independently of each other in solution. In solution reactions involving electrolytes it is often more appropriate to write the equations showing the individual ions and to omit ions that do not change in the reaction (spectator ions). An equation of this form is called a net ionic equation. You cannot write a net ionic equation for a reaction that does not contain any dissolved electrolytes.

Steps for writing net ionic equations:

1. Write a reaction equation involving formulas. You can call this the formula equation. States of matter are important, as they will allow you to determine how to write the formulas in your next step.

2. Write a total ionic equation. In this equation all aqueous electrolytes are written in ionic form (because of dissociation or ionization). Non-aqueous electrolytes are written as formulas.

3. Cancel spectator ions in your total ionic equation to get your net ionic equation.

Example 1

Write a formula equation, a total ionic, and a net ionic equation to describe the reaction of silver metal with a copper (II) nitrate solution.

Solution
Formula equation:
$$2Ag_{(s)} + Cu(NO_3)_{2(aq)} \rightarrow Cu_{(s)} + 2AgNO_{3(aq)}$$

Total ionic equation:
$$2Ag_{(s)} + Cu^{2+}_{(aq)} + \cancel{2NO_3^-{}_{(aq)}} \rightarrow Cu_{(s)} + 2Ag^+{}_{(aq)} + \cancel{2NO_3^-{}_{(aq)}}$$

Net ionic equation:
$$2Ag_{(s)} + Cu^{2+}_{(aq)} \rightarrow Cu_{(s)} + 2Ag^+{}_{(aq)}$$

Example 2

Write a formula equation, a total ionic, and a net ionic equation to describe sodium hydroxide solution reacting with calcium nitrate solution.

Solution
Formula equation:
$$2NaOH_{(aq)} + Ca(NO_3)_{2(aq)} \rightarrow 2NaNO_{3(aq)} + Ca(OH)_{2(s)}$$

Total ionic equation:
$$\cancel{2Na^+{}_{(aq)}} + 2OH^-{}_{(aq)} + Ca^{2+}_{(aq)} + \cancel{2NO_3^-{}_{(aq)}} \rightarrow$$
$$\cancel{2Na^+{}_{(aq)}} + \cancel{2NO_3^-{}_{(aq)}} + Ca(OH)_{2(s)}$$

Net ionic equation:
$$Ca^{2+}_{(aq)} + 2OH^-{}_{(aq)} \rightarrow Ca(OH)_{2(s)}$$

Example 3

Potassium hydroxide solution is neutralized by hydrochloric acid. (Hydrochloric acid could be written in ionized form as $H^+_{(aq)}$ and $Cl^-_{(aq)}$ or $H_3O^+_{(aq)}$ and $Cl^-_{(aq)}$). Write a formula equation, a total ionic, and a net ionic equation to describe this reaction.

Solution

Formula equation:

$$KOH_{(aq)} + HCl_{(aq)} \rightarrow KCl_{(aq)} + 2H_2O_{(l)}$$

Total ionic equation:

$$\cancel{K^+}_{(aq)} + OH^-_{(aq)} + H^+_{(aq)} + \cancel{Cl^-}_{(aq)} \rightarrow \cancel{K^+}_{(aq)} + \cancel{Cl^-}_{(aq)} + H_2O_{(l)}$$

Note: by putting an extra water on each side of the equation, it could be rewritten as:

$$\cancel{K^+}_{(aq)} + OH^-_{(aq)} + H_3O^+_{(aq)} + \cancel{Cl^-}_{(aq)} \rightarrow \cancel{K^+}_{(aq)} + \cancel{Cl^-}_{(aq)} + 2H_2O_{(l)}$$

Net ionic equation:

$$H^+_{(aq)} + OH^-_{(aq)} \rightarrow H_2O_{(l)}$$
$$\text{or}$$
$$H_3O^+_{(aq)} + OH^-_{(aq)} \rightarrow 2H_2O_{(l)}$$

ACTIVITIES

Activity 1:

Title
Determining the concentration of a strong acid by titration with a strong base.

Problem
What is the concentration of a hydrochloric acid solution?

Variables
Controlled: container of base
number of drops of indicator
endpoint color

Materials
$HCl_{(aq)}$ (10.0 mL/trial)   pipette
0.10 mol/L $NaOH_{(aq)}$ pipette bulb
liquid litmus or phenolphthalein   burette
Erlenmeyer flask   burette clamp
retort stand   beakers

Procedure
1. Pipette 10.0 mL of $HCl_{(aq)}$ into an Erlenmeyer flask.
2. Add 3 drops of indicator.
3. Titrate the acid with the 0.10 mol/L $NaOH_{(aq)}$ until the endpoint is reached.
4. Measure the final volume of $NaOH_{(aq)}$.
5. Repeat steps 1–5 until three trials consistent to 0.5 mL of $NaOH_{(aq)}$ are obtained.

Safety Precautions
Rinse skin after any contact with corrosive chemicals.

Observations

Trial	Volume of NaOH(aq) (mL)
Rough	
1	
2	
3	
Average	

Analysis

Calculations

Conclusion

Sources of Error

Activity 2

Title
Acid Base Titration

Problem
What is the concentration of a solution of sulfuric acid as determined by titration with a solution of sodium hydroxide of known concentration?

Materials

burette	burette clamp
retort stand	pipette
phenolphthalein indicator	pipette bulb
sodium hydroxide solution (1.00 mol/L)	
0.10 mol/L sulfuric acid solution (10.00 mL trial)	
beakers	

Procedure

Observations
Prepare an observation table.

Analysis
Show your calculations under analysis.

Conclusion

Possible Sources of Error

Activity 3

Title
An Acid-Base Double Replacement Reaction

Problem
What are the products produced by the reaction between sulfuric acid and barium hydroxide?

Materials

1.0 mol/L $H_2SO_{4(aq)}$ (25.0 mL)	balance
1.0 mol/L $Ba(OH)_{2(aq)}$ (25.0 mL)	beaker
stirring rod	graduated cylinder
Bunsen burner	

Procedure
In your procedure, test the mass of the solid product formed.

Analysis
Calculate the theoretical yield of the reaction, and calculate the percentage difference between the theoretical yield and the actual yield.

Write the molecular, total ionic, and net ionic equations for the reaction that occurred.

Activity 4

The teacher will be demonstrating this activity.

Title
Stoichiometric Analysis

Problem
What mass of lead (II) iodide can be produced when 50.00 mL of 1.00 mol/L lead (II) nitrate is added to 50.00 mL of 2.00 mol/L sodium iodide?

Prediction
What theoretical mass of lead (II) iodide can be produced?

Materials

lead (II) nitrate (50 mL)	retort stand
sodium iodide (50 mL)	ring clamp
pipette	Bunsen burner
beakers	stirring rod
filter paper	filter funnel

Observations

Analysis
Write a balanced equation

Calculate the percent yield.

PRACTICE EXERCISES

Write a formula equation, a total ionic equation, and a net ionic equation for each of the following three questions:

1. Zinc metal reacts with lead (II) nitrate solution

   •

   •

   •

2. Zinc nitrate solution reacts with cesium sulfide solution.

   •

   •

   •

3. Chlorine gas reacts with potassium bromide solution.

   •

   •

   •

REVIEW SUMMARY

- Mole ratios from balanced equations can be used to calculate quantities in chemical reactions.
- There are four basic types of stoichiometry problems:

    1. Given moles of "A", find moles of "B"
    2. Given moles of "A", find quantity of "B"
    3. Given quantity of "A", find moles of "B"
    4. Given quantity of "A", find quantity of "B"

- Coefficients are exact numbers and can be assigned any number of significant digits.
- Limiting reagents can restrict the amount of product produced.
- Qualitative analysis = *quality*; the nature or identity of substances.
- Quantitative analysis = *quantity*; the amount of a specific substance present.
- Calculations of amounts that a reaction will produce are theoretical, in that the stoichiometric calculation indicates the maximum amount that could be produced.
- The actual yield of a reaction when performed will almost always produce an amount of product that is smaller than the theoretical yield.
- Titration curves illustrate what happens to pH of a solution as the titration progresses.
- The equivalence point is at the exact centre of the rapidly rising or rapidly falling region of a titration curve.
- A net ionic equation simplifies a reaction by omitting ions that do not change in the reaction (spectator ions).

PRACTICE TEST

1. What volume of water vapor at STP is produced when 9.6 mol of oxygen gas reacts with sufficient hydrogen gas?

2. Nitrogen monoxide gas reacts with oxygen gas to produce nitrogen dioxide gas. How many moles of nitrogen dioxide are formed if 0.530 mol of oxygen are used?

3. Ammonia gas decomposes into nitrogen gas and hydrogen gas. How many moles of ammonia are needed to produce 5.00 mol of hydrogen?

4. Nitrogen dioxide gas reacts with water to produce nitric acid and nitrogen monoxide gas. How many moles of nitrogen monoxide are formed from 0.60 mol of nitrogen dioxide gas?

5. Chlorine gas is one of the most important industrial chemicals. It is produced by the electrolysis of sodium chloride. The other product of the reaction is metallic sodium. How many moles of sodium chloride are needed to produce 4.00×10^3 L of chlorine gas at 25.0°C and 125.0 kPa?

6. Graphite, $C_{(s)}$, is one form of carbon. It can be burned in air to produce carbon monoxide. If 0.53 mol of graphite is burned, what is the mass of carbon monoxide produced?

7. Large amounts of the important metal titanium, $Ti_{(s)}$, are made by reacting titanium (IV) chloride with magnesium metal. Titanium metal and magnesium chloride are produced. What mass of magnesium is required to produce 10.5 mol of titanium?

8. Copper wire reacts with silver nitrate solution to produce silver metal and a solution of copper (II) nitrate. How many moles of metallic silver would be produced by reacting 2.37 g of copper?

9. When iron filings react with copper (II) sulfate solution metallic copper and a solution of iron (II) sulfate are produced. How many moles of copper would be produced if 2.54 g of iron react?

10. Silver metal reacts with nitric acid to produce nitrogen dioxide, silver nitrate solution, and water. How many moles of $HNO_{3(aq)}$ would be required to produce 5.00 g of $AgNO_{3(aq)}$?

11. A chemical reaction occurs between $Na_2SO_{4(aq)}$ and $Sr(NO_3)_{2(aq)}$ forming a precipitate. If 30.0 mL of 0.175 mol/L $Na_2SO_{4(aq)}$ is reacted, what is the minimum volume of 0.150 mol/L $Sr(NO_3)_{2(aq)}$ required to consume all of the $Na_2SO_{4(aq)}$?

12. In the burning of propane, C_3H_8, carbon dioxide, and water are produced. If 16.0 moles of water are produced, the number of moles of propane burned is

    A. 1.00   **B.** 4.00
    C. 12.0   **D.** 20.0

13. Sodium hydroxide, a strong monoprotic base, is titrated with hydrochloric acid. Which titration curve is correct?

A.
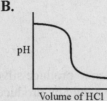
Volume of NaOH

B.
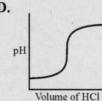
Volume of HCl

C.
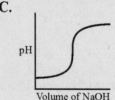
Volume of NaOH

D.

Volume of HCl

14. The production of ammonia, $NH_{3(g)}$ is given by the balanced equation

$$N_{2(g)} + 3H_{2(g)} \rightarrow 2NH_{3(g)}$$

If a chemist wishes to produce 60.0 g of $NH_{3(g)}$, the number of moles of $N_{2(g)}$ needed would be

    A. 0.880   **B.** 1.76
    C. 3.52   **D.** 7.04

15. 75.0 g of water is decomposed into oxygen gas and hydrogen gas. The number of moles of oxygen gas produced is

    A. 2.08   **B.** 4.16
    C. 37.5   **D.** 75.0

16. In a car's engine, gasoline (octane) is burned to produce carbon dioxide gas and H_2O vapor.
$$2C_8H_{18(l)} + 25O_{2(g)} \rightarrow 16CO_{2(g)} + 18H_2O_{(g)}$$

When 700 g of C_8H_{18} is burned, the mass of water vapor produced would be

    A. 6.12 g   **B.** 12.3 g
    C. 110 g   **D.** 994 g

17. Sulfuric acid is neutralized by potassium hydroxide. What mass of water will be produced when 0.445 moles of potassium hydroxide is used in the reaction?

A. 0.445 g   B. 0.890 g
C. 8.02 g   D. 16.0 g

18. When 6.50 moles of propane gas, $C_3H_{8(g)}$, burns in air, what volume of $CO_{2(g)}$ would be produced at STP?

A. 6.50 L   B. 19.5 L
C. 146 L   D. 437 L

19. When 7.00 g of copper solid is immersed into 400 mL of 0.650 mol/L silver nitrate solution, a single replacement reaction takes place.

$$Cu_{(s)} + 2AgNO_{3(aq)} \rightarrow Cu(NO_3)_{2(aq)} + 2Ag_{(s)}$$

The mass of $Ag_{(s)}$ produced is:

HINT: limiting reagent reaction.

A. 4.28 g   B. 11.9 g
C. 23.8 g   D. 28.0 g

20. Methane gas, $CH_{4(g)}$ can be decomposed into $C_{(s)}$ and $H_{2(g)}$. What volume of $CH_{4(g)}$ at 110 kPa and 25°C would be needed to produce 86.0 g of $H_{2(g)}$.

A. 21.3 L   B. 479 L
C. 958 L   D. 191 6 L

21. Zinc metal is put in 400 mL of 0.550 mol/L $HCl_{(aq)}$. The mass of $Zn_{(s)}$ required to fully react with the HCl is?

A. 0.110 g   B. 0.220 g
C. 7.19 g   D. 14.4 g

NOTES

Answers

and

Solutions

REVIEW OF SCIENCE 10 CHEMISTRY

Lesson 1—Review of Atoms and Ions

PRACTICE EXERCISES—ANSWERS AND SOLUTIONS

1.

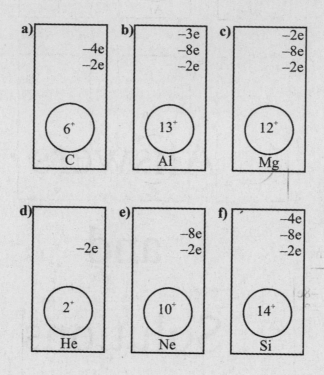

3.

Isotope	Atomic Number	Protons	Electrons	Neutrons	Mass Number
$^{40}_{18}Ar$	18	18	18	22	40
$^{7}_{3}Li$	3	3	3	4	7
$^{16}_{8}O$	16	8	8	8	16
$^{52}_{24}Cr$	24	24	24	28	52
$^{1}_{1}H$	1	1	1	0	1
$^{27}_{13}Al$	13	13	13	14	27
$^{28}_{13}Al$	13	13	13	15	28
$^{63}_{29}Cu$	29	29	29	34	63

5.

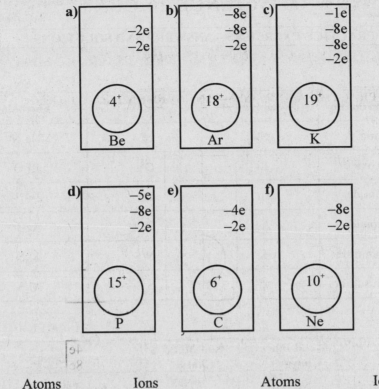

a) −2e −2e 4⁺ Be

b) −8e −8e −2e 18⁺ Ar

c) −1e −8e −8e −2e 19⁺ K

d) −5e −8e −2e 15⁺ P

e) −4e −2e 6⁺ C

f) −8e −2e 10⁺ Ne

7.

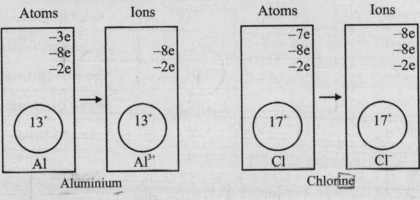

Atoms

−3e −8e −2e 13⁺ Al

Ions

−8e −2e 13⁺ Al³⁺

Aluminium

Atoms

−7e −8e −2e 17⁺ Cl

Ions

−8e −8e −2e 17⁺ Cl⁻

Chlorine

9.

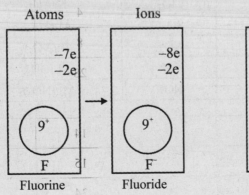

Atoms

−7e −2e 9⁺ F

Ions

−8e −2e 9⁺ F⁻

Fluorine Fluoride

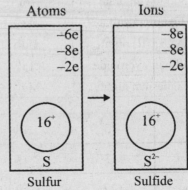

Atoms

−6e −8e −2e 16⁺ S

Ions

−8e −8e −2e 16⁺ S²⁻

Sulfur Sulfide

Lesson 2—Review of Chemical Nomenclature

PRACTICE EXERCISES—ANSWERS AND SOLUTIONS

1.

Compound Name	Metal Ion (+)	Non Metal Ion (–)	Formula
Sodium nitride	Na^+	N^{3-}	Na_3N
Lithium oxide	Li^+	O^{2-}	Li_2O
Zinc chloride	Zn^{2+}	Cl^-	$ZnCl_2$
Silver bromide	Ag^+	Br^-	$AgBr$
Potassium nitride	K^+	N^{3-}	K_3N
Aluminium sulfide	Al^{3+}	S^{2-}	Al_2S_3

3.

Formula	Metal Ion Charge	Non-Metal Charge	Name
$NiCl_3$	Ni^{3+}	Cl^-	nickel (III) chloride
MnO	Mn^{2+}	O^{2-}	manganese (II) oxide
Cr_2O_3	Cr^{3+}	O^{2-}	chromium (III) oxide
$CuCl_2$	Cu^{2+}	Cl^-	copper (II) chloride
PbO_2	Pb^{4+}	O^{2-}	lead (IV) oxide

5.

Name	Positive Ion Charge	Negative Ion Charge	Formula
Sodium chlorate	Na^+	ClO_3^-	$NaClO_3$
Aluminium sulfate	Al^{3+}	SO_4^{2-}	$Al_2(SO_4)_3$
Copper (II) nitrate	Cu^{2+}	NO_3^-	$Cu(NO_3)_2$
Lithium hydroxide	Li^+	OH^-	$LiOH$
Magnesium nitrate	Mg^{2+}	NO_3^-	$Mg(NO_3)_2$

7.

Name	Formula
sulfur dioxide	SO_2
carbon monoxide	CO
hydrogen sulfide	H_2S
sulfur dichloride	SCl_2
tetraphosphorus decaoxide	P_4O_{10}

9.

Formula	Binary or Oxy	Name
$HCl_{(aq)}$	B	hydrochloric acid
$H_2SO_{4(aq)}$	O	sulfuric acid
$H_3BO_{3(aq)}$	O	boric acid
$HNO_{2(aq)}$	O	nitrous acid

11.

Name	Formula	Type
sodium bromide	$NaBr$	i
iron (II) chloride	$FeCl_2$	i
calcium hydroxide	$Ca(OH)_2$	i
potassium sulfite	K_2SO_3	i
magnesium sulfide	MgS	i
Phosphorus trichloride	PCl_3	m
glucose	$C_6H_{12}O_6$	m
ammonium sulfate	$(NH_4)_2SO_4$	i
cobalt (II) nitrate	$Co(NO_3)_2$	i

Name	Formula	Type
dinitrogen tetraoxide	N_2O_4	m
sulfurous acid	$H_2SO_{3(aq)}$	a
hydrochloric acid	$HCl_{(aq)}$	a
ammonia	NH_3	m
hypochlorous acid	$HClO_{(aq)}$	i
hydrobromic acid	$HBr_{(aq)}$	a
phosphoric acid	$H_3PO_{4(aq)}$	a
chloric acid	$HClO_{3(aq)}$	a
carbon monoxide	CO	m

Lesson 3—Chemical Equations

PRACTICE EXERCISES—ANSWERS AND SOLUTIONS

1. **a)** F $N_{2(g)} + 3\ H_{2(g)} \rightarrow 2\ NH_{3(g)}$

    b) F $2Na_{(s)} + Cl_{2(g)} \rightarrow 2\ NaCl_{(s)}$

    c) S.D. $2\ H_2O_{(l)} \rightarrow 2\ H_{2(g)} + O_{2(g)}$

    d) S.R. $2\ Na_{(s)} + 2\ H_2O_{(l)} \rightarrow 2\ NaOH_{(aq)} + H_{2(g)}$

    e) S.R. $Zn_{(s)} + 2\ HCl_{(aq)} \rightarrow ZnCl_{2(aq)} + H_{2(g)}$

    f) H.C. $CH_{4(g)} + 2\ O_{2(g)} \rightarrow CO_{2(g)} + 2\ H_2O_{(g)}$

    g) F $P_{4(s)} + 10\ Cl_{2(g)} \rightarrow 4\ PCl_{5(s)}$

    h) S.R. $CoCl_{2(aq)} + 2\ Na_{(s)} \rightarrow 2\ NaCl_{(aq)} + Co_{(s)}$

    i) D.R. $2\ Na_3PO_{4(aq)} + 3\ MgCl_{2(aq)} \rightarrow Mg_3(PO_4)_{2(s)} + 6\ NaCl_{(aq)}$

    j) H.C. $2\ C_4H_{10(g)} + 13\ O_{2(g)} \rightarrow 8\ CO_{2(g)} + 10\ H_2O_{(g)}$

    k) S.D. $2\ P_2O_{5(s)} \rightarrow P_{4(s)} + 5\ O_{2(g)}$

    l) S.D. $2\ Al_{(s)} + 3\ Cu(NO_2)_{2(aq)} \rightarrow 3\ Cu_{(s)} + 2\ Al(NO_2)_{3(aq)}$

    m) D.R. $CaCl_{2(aq)} + H_2SO_{4(aq)} \rightarrow CuSO_{4(s)} + 2HCl_{(aq)}$

3. $2\ H_{2(g)} + O_{2(g)} \rightarrow 2H_2O_{(g)}$

5. $3\ MgCl_{2(aq)} + Al_2O_{3(s)} \rightarrow 3MgO_{(aq)} + 2AlCl_{3(aq)}$

7. $KCl_{(aq)} + AgNO_{3(aq)} \rightarrow KNO_{3(aq)} + AgCl_{(s)}$

Lesson 4—Moles

PRACTICE EXERCISES—ANSWERS AND SOLUTIONS

1.

Formula	Name	Molar Mass (g/mol)
Na_2SO_4	sodium sulfate	22.99×2 $32.07 \times 1 = 142.05$ g/mol 16.00×4
$Ca(NO_3)_2$	calcium nitrate	40.08×1 $14.01 \times 2\ = 164.10$ g/mol 16.00×6
N_2O_5	dinitrogen pentaoxide	14.01×2 $16.00 \times 5\ = 108.02$ g/mol

Formula	Name	Molar Mass (g/mol)
$K_2Cr_2O_7$	potassium dichromate	39.10×2 $52.00 \times 2 = 294.20$ g/mol 16.00×7
Al_2O_3	aluminium oxide	26.98×2 16.00×3 $= 101.96$ g/mol
$(NH_4)_2SO_4$	ammonium sulfate	14.01×2 1.01×8 32.07×1 $= 132.17$ g/mol 16.00×4

3.

Compound	Name	Molar Mass (g/mol)	Number Of Moles (mol)	Mass (g)
$CH_{4(g)}$	methane	16.05	2.16	34.7
$CuCl_{2(s)}$	copper (II) chloride	134.45	0.855	115
$Ca(NO_3)_{2(s)}$	calcium nitrate	164.10	2.77	455
$CO_{2(g)}$	carbon dioxide	44.01	0.153	6.75
$ZnS_{(s)}$	zinc sulfide	97.46	9.08	885
$(NH_4)_2SO_{4(s)}$	ammonium sulfate	132.17	0.567	75.0
$C_2H_{6(g)}$	ethane	30.08	2.55	76.7
$MgBr_{2(s)}$	magnesium bromide	184.11	25.5	4.69×10^3
$NiCl_{2(s)}$	nickel (II) chloride	129.59	33.4	4.33×10^3
$Fe_2O_{3(s)}$	iron (III) oxide	159.70	0.115	18.4
$HCl_{(g)}$	hydrogen chloride	36.46	5.75	210
$K_2Cr_2O_{7(s)}$	potassium dichromate	294.20	0.012 5	3.68

PRACTICE TEST

PRACTICE TEST—ANSWERS AND SOLUTIONS

1.

Symbol	Name
C	carbon
Al	aluminium
Li	lithium
F	fluorine
Ne	neon
O	oxygen
Au	gold

Symbol	Name
Ag	silver
Mg	magnesium
Cl	chlorine
Ni	nickel
Na	sodium
Fe	iron
K	potassium

3.

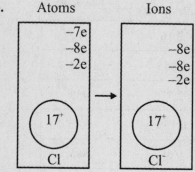

Atoms   Ions

5.

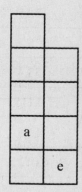

7.

Formula	Name
$CH_{4(g)}$	methane
$NH_{3(g)}$	ammonia
$H_2SO_{4(aq)}$	sulfuric acid
$HF_{(aq)}$	hydrofluoric acid
$Cu(ClO_3)_{2(s)}$	copper (II) chlorate
$CH_3OH_{(l)}$	methanol
$C_{12}H_{22}O_{11(s)}$	sucrose

Formula	Name
$Al_2O_{3(s)}$	aluminium oxide
$Fe_2O_{3(s)}$	Iron (III) oxide
$Na_2CO_{3(s)}$	sodium carbonate
$Mg(NO_3)_{2(s)}$	magnesium nitrate
$P_4O_{10(s)}$	tetraphosphorous decaoxide
$HCl_{(aq)}$	hydrochloric acid
$O_{3(g)}$	ozone

9.
a) D.R. $2NaOH_{(aq)} + H_2SO_{4(aq)} \rightarrow Na_2SO_{4(aq)} + 2H_2O_{(l)}$
b) S.D. $2H_2O_{(l)} \rightarrow 2H_{2(g)} + O_{2(g)}$
c) F $P_{4(s)} + 10Cl_{2(g)} \rightarrow 4PCl_{5(s)}$

11. molar mass = 342.34 g/mol

a) 1.7×10^2 g
b) 3.01×10^{23}
c) 3.61×10^{24}

13. Assume 100 atoms

$$(16.0)(122) = 1\,952$$
$$(72.6)(118) = 8\,566.8$$
$$(11.4)(115) = 1\,311$$
$$\frac{11\,829.8}{100} = 188$$

THE DIVERSITY OF MATTER AND CHEMICAL BONDING

Lesson 1—What is a Chemical Bond

PRACTICE EXERCISES—ANSWERS AND SOLUTIONS

1.

Name	Electron Dot Diagram	Number of Lone Pairs	Number of Bonding Electrons
Na	Na •	0	1
C	• C •	0	4
N	• N •	1	3
Ar	: Ar :	4	0

Lesson 2— Ionic, Covalent, and Metallic Bonding

PRACTICE EXERCISES—ANSWERS AND SOLUTIONS

1. $[Al]^{3+}$ $\begin{bmatrix} : \ddot{F} : \end{bmatrix}$ $\begin{bmatrix} : \ddot{F} : \end{bmatrix}$ $\begin{bmatrix} : \ddot{F} : \end{bmatrix}^{-}$ Mg_3N_2 AlF_3

   $[Mg]^{2+} [Mg]^{2+} [Mg]^{2+}$ $\begin{bmatrix} : \ddot{N} : \end{bmatrix}^{3-} \begin{bmatrix} : \ddot{N} : \end{bmatrix}^{3-}$

3.

H •							He:
Li •	Be •		• B •	• C •	• N •	• O :	: F •	: Ne :
Na •	Mg •		• Al •	• Si •	• P •	• S •	: Cl •	: Ar :
K •	Ca •						

5. a) Bonding electrons are electrons that are transferred or shared to complete an outside energy level. In a Lewis dot diagram they are unpaired electrons

$$\underset{\bullet\bullet}{\overset{\bullet\bullet}{\text{:}}} \text{Br} \, \square \longleftarrow \text{bonding electron}$$

b) Lone pairs are paired electrons in an energy level; they are generally not involved in bond formation

$$\bullet \, \text{S} \, \square \longleftarrow \text{sulfur has two lone pairs}$$

7. a)

Atom	Group Number	Gain or Loss	Name of Ion	Formula of Ion
Na	1	L	sodium ion	Na^+
Mg	3	L	magnesium ion	Mg^{2+}
S	16	G	sulfide ion	S^{2-}
Cl	17	G	chloride run	Cl^-

b) Na_2S sodium sulfide
$NaCl$ sodium chloride
MgS magnesium sulfide
$MgCl_2$ magnesium chloride

9. a) In a covalent bond, electrons are shared between atoms to attain noble gas configuration.

b) Groups of elements that are likely to form covalent bonds are on the right hand side of the periodic table and the right side of the staircase.

11.

Molecule	Covalent	Ionic	Metallic
$KCl_{(s)}$		✓	
$Mg_{(s)}$			✓
$CaO_{(s)}$		✓	
$O_{2(g)}$	✓		
$NO_{2(g)}$	✓		
$Ag_{(s)}$			✓
$BaCl_{2(s)}$		✓	
$S_{8(s)}$	✓		
$SO_{2(g)}$	✓		
$CsF_{(s)}$		✓	

Lesson 3—Bond Types and Electronegativity

PRACTICE EXERCISES—ANSWERS AND SOLUTIONS

1. Electronegativity is the measure of an atom's attraction for electrons in a bond.

3. **a)** Electronegativity is 1.7 or greater
   b) Electronegativity is smaller than 1.7

5. **a)** Electrons shared equally. Electronegativity difference = 0
   b) Electrons shared unequally. Electronegativity difference is greater than 0 but less than 1.7.

7.

Pairs of Atoms	Electronegativity Difference	Type of Bond
H–H	0	non-polar covalent
C–H	0.4	polar covalent
K–K	0	metallic
Li–Br	1.8	ionic
C–S	0	polar covalent
Zn–Br	1.2	polar covalent
S–S	0	non-polar covalent
N–I	0.5	polar covalent
Fr–F	3.3	ionic
V–V	0	metallic

Lesson 4— Molecular Shapes (Stereochemistry) and Polarity

PRACTICE EXERCISES—ANSWERS AND SOLUTIONS

1.

Molecule	Lewis Structure	Molecular Shape	Shape Diagram	Polarity
NF_3		pyramidal		polar
CH_2Cl_2		tetrahedral		polar
CS_2		triatomic linear	$S = C = S$	non-polar
CBr_4		tetrahedral		non-polar
HCl		diatomic linear	$H-Cl$	polar
H_2Te		v-shaped (bent)		polar
O_2		diatomic linear	$O=O$	non-polar
$CHCl_3$		tetrahedral		polar
CH_3OH		tetrahedral		polar
CO_2		triatomic linear	$O = C = O$	non-polar

3.

Formula	Lewis Diagram	Shape	Polarity	Types of Intermolecular Bond
NH_3	H – N – H with H below	pyramidal	polar	Hydrogen, dipole-dipole, London dispersion
CBr_4	Br – C – Br with Br above and below	tetrahedral	non-polar	London dispersion
H_2S	H – S – H	v-shaped (bent)	polar	London dispersion, dipole-dipole
PCl_3	Cl – P – Cl with Cl below	pyramidal	polar	London dispersion, dipole-dipole
BCl_3	Cl – B – with Cl above and Cl Cl below	trigonal planar	non-polar	London dispersion, dipole-dipole
NH_4^+	[H – N – H with H above and below]$^+$	tetrahedral		
HBr	H – Br	linear	polar	London dispersion, dipole-dipole
OCl_2	Cl – O – Cl	v-shaped (bent)	polar	London dispersion, dipole-dipole
NI_3	I – N – I with I below	pyramidal	polar	London dispersion
SO_4^{2-}	[O – S – O with O above and below]$^{-2}$	tetrahedral		
SBr_2	Br – S – Br	bent	polar	London dispersion, dipole-dipole
GeH_4	H – Ge – H with H above and below	tetrahedral	non-polar	London dispersion
H_2Te	H – Te – H	bent	polar	London dispersion, dipole-dipole
NF_3	F – N – F with F below	pyramidal	polar	London dispersion, dipole-dipole

Formula	Lewis Diagram	Shape	Polarity	Types of Intermolecular Bond
H_2Se	H–Se–H	bent	polar	London dispersion, dipole-dipole
$SnBr_4$	Br–Sn–Br with Br above and Br below	tetrahedral	non-polar	London dispersion
SO_3^{2-}	[O–S–O with O below]$^{2-}$	pyramidal		
CO_2	O=C=O	triatomic linear	non-polar	London dispersion
PO_4^{3-}	[O–P–O with O above and O below]$^{3-}$	tetrahedral		

5.

Name	Formula	Solid	Type of Bonding
sodium chloride	NaCl	B	ionic
silicon carbide	SiC	D	covalent
iron	Fe	E	metallic
sulfur	S_8	A	London dispersion
1,3-dichlorobenzene	$C_6H_4Cl_2$	C	London dispersion, dipole-dipole

PRACTICE TEST

PRACTICE TEST—ANSWERS AND SOLUTIONS

1.
d) ionic bond **h)** covalent bond **j)** electronegativity
c) polar covalent bond **g)** non-polar covalent bond **i)** metallic bond
f) dipole-dipole attraction **b)** London dispersion force **a)** bonding electron
e) lone pair electrons

3.

Formula	Lewis Structure Diagram	Shape Diagram	Shape Description	Intermolecular Attraction
CH_4	H–C–H with H above and H below	C with H atoms tetrahedral	tetrahedral	London dispersion
OF_2	F–O–F	O with F, F	bent	London dispersion, dipole-dipole
NCl_3	Cl–N–Cl with Cl below	N with Cl, Cl, Cl	pyramidal	London dispersion, dipole-dipole
BI_3	I–B–I with I below	I–B–I with I below	trigonal planar	London dispersion
CO_2	O=C=O	O=C=O	triatomic linear	London dispersion
C_2H_4	H–C=C–H with H's	C=C with H's	trigonal planar	London dispersion
H_2O	H–O–H	H, H, O	bent	London dispersion, dipole-dipole, hydrogen
SiH_4	H–Si–H with H above and H below	Si with H atoms	tetrahedral	London dispersion
SCl_2	Cl–S–Cl	Cl, Cl, S	bent	London dispersion, dipole-dipole
C_2H_2	H–C≡C–H	H–C≡C–H	linear	London dispersion
PBr_3	Br–P–Br with Br above	P with Br, Br, Br	pyramidal	London dispersion, dipole-dipole
H_2Te	H–Te–H	H, H, Te	v-shaped (bent)	London dispersion, dipole-dipole

5. If the electronegativity difference is 1.7 or greater, it is said to be an ionic bond. If it is 0 it is non-polar covalent between 0 and 1.7 it is polar covalent.

7.	B)	**9.**	B)	**11.**	C)	**13.**	B)
15.	B)	**17.**	C)	**19.**	A)	**21.**	C)
23.	B)	**25.**	D)	**27.**	B)		

FORMS OF MATTER—GASES

Lesson 1—Gas Laws

PRACTICE EXERCISES—ANSWERS AND SOLUTIONS

1. $P_1V_1 = P_2V_2$

    $V_2 = \dfrac{P_1V_1}{P_2}$

    $\quad = \dfrac{(75.0 \text{ kPa})(450.0 \text{ mL})}{96.5 \text{ kPa}}$

    $\quad = 350 \text{ mL}$

3. $P_1V_1 = P_2V_2$

    $P_2 = \dfrac{P_1V_1}{V_2}$

    $\quad = \dfrac{(775 \text{ mm Hg})(3.25 \text{ L})}{2.90 \text{ L}}$

    $\quad = 869 \text{ mm Hg}$

5. $P_1V_1 = P_2V_2$

    $V_2 = \dfrac{P_1V_1}{P_2}$

    $\quad = \dfrac{(85.0 \text{ kPa})(35.0 \text{ L})}{65.0 \text{ kPa}}$

    $\quad = 45.8 \text{ L}$

Lesson 2—Charles' Law and Temperature Scales

PRACTICE EXERCISES—ANSWERS AND SOLUTIONS

1. a) $35°C = 308 \text{ K}$
    b) $-196°C = 77 \text{ K}$
    c) $212 \text{ K} = -61°C$
    d) $450 \text{ K} = 177°C$

3. STP $T = 273.0$ K

$$\frac{V_1}{T_1} = \frac{V_2}{T_2}$$

$$V_2 = \frac{V_1 T_2}{T_1}$$

$$= \frac{(345 \text{ mL})(293 \text{ K})}{273 \text{ K}}$$

$$= 370 \text{ mL}$$

5. $17.0°C = 290$ K

$$\frac{V_1}{T_1} = \frac{V_2}{T_2}$$

$$T_2 = \frac{V_1 T_2}{V_1}$$

$$= \frac{(65.0 \text{ L})(290 \text{ K})}{45.0 \text{ L}}$$

$$= 419 \text{ K or } 146°C$$

Lesson 3—Combined Gas Law

PRACTICE EXERCISES—ANSWERS AND SOLUTIONS

1. $25.0°C = 298$ K

   $45.0°C = 318$ K

$$\frac{P_1 V_1}{T_1} = \frac{P_2 V_2}{T_2}$$

$$V_2 = \frac{P_1 V_1 T_2}{T_1 P_2}$$

$$= \frac{(110.0 \text{ kPa})(24.5 \text{ L})(318 \text{ K})}{(298 \text{ K})(95.0 \text{ kPa})}$$

$$= 30.3 \text{ L}$$

3. $775 \text{ mm Hg} = 103.3$ kPa

$$\frac{P_1 V_1}{T_1} = \frac{P_2 V_2}{T_2}$$

$$V_2 = \frac{P_1 V_1 T_2}{T_1 P_2}$$

$$= \frac{(103.3 \text{ kPa})(50.0 \text{ L})(273 \text{ K})}{(101.3 \text{ kPa})(303 \text{ K})}$$

$$= 45.9 \text{ L}$$

5. $\dfrac{P_1V_1}{T_1} = \dfrac{P_2V_2}{T_2}$

$V_2 = \dfrac{P_1V_1T_2}{T_1P_2}$

$= \dfrac{(660 \text{ mm Hg})(775 \text{ mL})(318 \text{ K})}{(885 \text{ mm Hg})(248 \text{ K})}$

$= 741 \text{ mL}$

7. Gas molecules have the freedom to move anywhere, thus can go anywhere, and will always fill the container.

9. Gas molecules have the freedom to move.

Lesson 4—The Ideal Gas Law

PRACTICE EXERCISES—ANSWERS AND SOLUTIONS

1. $PV = nRT$

$V = \dfrac{nRT}{P}$

$= \dfrac{(2.50 \text{ mol})(8.31 \text{ L} \times \text{kPa}/\text{mol} \times \text{K})(298 \text{ K})}{95.0 \text{ kPa}}$

$= 65.2 \text{ L}$

3. $PV = nRT$ 　　　　　$= \dfrac{(0.757 \text{ mol})(8.31 \text{ L} \times \text{kPa}/\text{mol} \times \text{K})(318 \text{ K})}{95.0 \text{ kPa}}$

$V = \dfrac{nRT}{P}$ 　　　　　$= 21.1 \text{ L}$

$n - \dfrac{44.0 \text{ g}}{58.149 \text{ g}/\text{mol}} = 0.757 \text{ mol}$

5. $n = \dfrac{PV}{RT}$

$= \dfrac{(96.5 \text{ kPa})(48.0 \text{ L})}{(8.31 \text{ L} \times \text{kPa}/\text{mol} \times \text{K})(328 \text{ K})}$

$= 1.70 \text{ mol}$

$m = n \times M$

$= (1.70 \text{ mol})(32.0 \text{ g}/\text{mol})$

$= 54.4 \text{ g}$

PRACTICE TEST

PRACTICE TEST—ANSWERS AND SOLUTIONS

1. For a constant amount of gas at constant temperature, the pressure varies inversely with the volume.

3. For a constant amount of gas at constant pressure, the absolute temperature and volume vary directly.

5. **a)** temperature, amount of gas
   b) pressure, amount of gas
   c) amount of gas
   d) none

7. STP—standard temperature (0°C) and pressure (101.3 kPa)
   SATP—standard ambient temperature (25°C) and pressure (100 kPa)

9. $PV = nRT$

$$n = \frac{PV}{RT}$$

$$= \frac{(150 \text{ kPa})(0.150)}{\left(8.314 \frac{\text{L}\times\text{kPa}}{\text{mol}\times\text{K}}\right)(303 \text{ K})}$$

since $n = \frac{m}{M}$; $\quad M = \frac{m}{n}$

$$= \frac{0.456 \text{ g}}{0.008\,931\,6 \text{ mol}}$$

$$= 51.1 \text{ g/mol}$$

11. d)   **13. c)**   **15. b)**

MATTER AS SOLUTIONS, ACIDS AND BASES

Lesson 1—Definitions of Solutions, Acids and Bases

PRACTICE EXERCISES—ANSWERS AND SOLUTIONS

1. **a)** solute: The substance present in smaller quantity in a solution.
   b) solvent: The substance present in larger quantity in a solution.
   c) solution: A uniform (single phase) mixture of two or more substances.

3. **a)** A solution is a homogeneous mixture, a single phase uniform mixture of two or more substances

   A heterogeneous mixture is a multi phase, non-uniform
   mixture of two or more substances

   b) A solution is a homogeneous, single phase, uniform system containing two or more pure substances mixed together.

   A pure substance is a homogeneous, single phase, uniform system containing only one pure substance, itself.

5. The ability of one substance to completely dissolve in another.

7.

Solution	Type
sugar and water	liquid
air	gaseous
copper and zinc	solid
carbonated beverage	liquid
alcohol and water	liquid
table salt and water	liquid

Lesson 2—Aqueous Solutions

PRACTICE EXERCISES—ANSWERS AND SOLUTIONS

1. a) $Na_2SO_{4(g)} \rightarrow 2Na^+_{(aq)} + SO_4^{2-}_{(aq)}$
   b) $CaCl_{2(s)} \rightarrow Ca^{2+}_{(aq)} + 2Cl^-_{(aq)}$
   c) $Cu(NO_3)_{2(s)} \rightarrow Cu^{2+}_{(aq)} + 2NO_3^-_{(aq)}$
   d) $BaCl_{2(s)} \rightarrow Ba^{2+}_{(aq)} + 2Cl^-_{(aq)}$
   e) $ZnSO_{4(s)} \rightarrow Zn^{2+}_{(aq)} + SO_4^{2-}_{(aq)}$
   f) $LiOH_{(s)} \rightarrow Li^+_{(aq)} + OH^-_{(aq)}$
   g) $MgBr_{2(s)} \rightarrow Mg^{2+}_{(aq)} + 2Br^-_{(aq)}$
   h) $K_2S_{(s)} \rightarrow 2K^+_{(aq)} + S^{2-}_{(aq)}$
   i) $Al_2(SO_4)_{3(s)} \rightarrow 2Al^{3+}_{(aq)} + 3SO_4^{2-}_{(aq)}$
   j) $MgI_{2(s)} \rightarrow Mg^{2+}_{(s)} + 2I^-_{(aq)}$

3. a) A solution with water as the solvent.
   b) A change which causes the temperature of the surroundings to increase.
   c) A change which causes the temperature of the surrounding to decrease.
   d) A solute in an aqueous solution which conducts electricity
   e) A solute in an aqueous solution which does not conduct electricity.

5. A solution is a homogeneous mixture of two or more substances. The particles in a solution are referred to as solute, those present in smaller quantity, and solvent, those are present in a larger quantity. All particles are molecular in size, scattered uniformly throughout the solution and constantly in motion.

7. Solvent molecules attract the surface particles of the solute. The solute particles that are removed from the surface become surrounded by the solvent molecules.

9. Dissociation:

   During dissolving, regularly ordered crystals of ionic solids break apart into positive and negative ions which are widely separated from each other by the solvent.

   Ionization:

   During dissolving, neutral molecules react with the solvent to produce ions. These new ions are then widely separated from each other by the remainder of the solvent.

11. a) hydrogen bromide $HBr_{(g)} + HOH_{(l)} \rightarrow H_3O^{1+}_{(aq)} + Br^{1-}_{(aq)}$
    b) methanoic acid $HCOOH_{(aq)} + HOH_{(l)} \rightarrow H_3O^{1+}_{(aq)} + HCOO^{1-}_{(aq)}$
    c) sulfuric acid $H_2SO_{4(aq)} + HOH_{(l)} \rightarrow H_3O^{1+}_{(aq)} + HSO_4^{1-}_{(aq)}$
    d) carbonic acid $H_2CO_{3(aq)} + HOH_{(l)} \rightarrow H_3O^{1+}_{(aq)} + HCO_3^{1-}_{(aq)}$
    e) nitric acid $HNO_{3(aq)} + HOH_{(l)} \rightarrow H_3O^{1+}_{(aq)} + NO_3^{1-}_{(aq)}$
    f) chlorous acid $HClO_{2(aq)} + HOH_{(l)} \rightarrow H_3O^{1+}_{(aq)} + ClO_2^{1-}_{(aq)}$

PRACTICE EXERCISES—ANSWERS AND SOLUTIONS

1. a)
$$\text{Moles} = C \times V$$
$$C = \frac{\text{mol}}{V}$$
$$= \frac{3.44 \text{ mol}}{0.450 \text{ L}}$$
$$= 7.64 \text{ mol/L}$$

b)
$$\text{Moles} = C \times V$$
$$C = \frac{\text{mol}}{V}$$
$$= \frac{0.766 \text{ mol}}{0.675 \text{ L}}$$
$$= 1.13 \text{ mol/L}$$

c)
$$\text{Moles} = C \times V$$
$$C = \frac{\text{mol}}{V}$$
$$= \frac{7.11 \text{ mol}}{2.25 \text{ L}}$$
$$= 3.16 \text{ mol/L}$$

d)
$$\text{Moles} = C \times V$$
$$C = \frac{\text{mol}}{V}$$
$$= \frac{8.25 \times 10^{-2} \text{ mol}}{0.0250 \text{ L}}$$
$$= 3.30 \text{ mol/L}$$

3. a) moles $= C \times V$
$$= (1.25 \text{ mol/L}) (0.035\ 0 \text{ L})$$
$$= 0.043\ 8 \text{ mol}$$

b) moles $= C \times V$
$$= (0.122 \text{ mol/L}) (0.565 \text{ L})$$
$$= 0.068\ 9 \text{ mol}$$

c) moles $= C \times V$
$$= (2.22 \text{ mol/L}) (0.085\ 0 \text{ L})$$
$$= 0.189 \text{ mol}$$

d) moles $= C \times V$
$$= (0.175 \text{ mol/L}) (0.125\ 0 \text{ L})$$
$$= 0.021\ 9 \text{ mol}$$

5. a)

$$Na_3PO_{4(aq)} \rightarrow 3Na^+_{(aq)} + PO_4^{3-}_{(aq)}$$

$$\frac{Na_3PO_4}{Na^+} = \frac{1}{3} = \frac{0.091}{(3)(0.091)}$$

$$= \left[Na^+\right] = 0.273 \text{ mol/L}$$

$$= \frac{Na_3PO_4}{PO_4^{3-}} = \frac{1}{1} = \frac{0.019}{0.019}$$

$$\left[PO_4^{3-}\right] = 0.019 \text{ mol/L}$$

b)

$$NaHCO_{3(aq)} \rightarrow Na^+_{(aq)} + HCO_3^-_{(aq)}$$

$$\frac{NaHCO_3}{Na^+} = \frac{1}{3} = \frac{0.014\ 3}{0.014\ 3}$$

$$= \left[Na^+\right] = 0.014\ 3 \text{ mol/L}$$

$$= \frac{NaHCO_3}{HCO_3^-} = \frac{1}{1} = \frac{0.014\ 3}{0.014\ 3}$$

$$\left[HCO_3^-\right] = 0.014\ 3 \text{ mol/L}$$

c)

$$Fe_2O_{3(aq)} \rightarrow 2Fe^{3+}_{(aq)} + 3O^{2-}_{(aq)}$$

$$\frac{Fe_2O_3}{Fe^{3+}} = \frac{1}{2} = \frac{0.250}{(2)(0.250)}$$

$$= \left[Fe^{3+}\right] = 0.500 \text{ mol/L}$$

$$= \frac{Fe_2O_3}{O^{2-}} = \frac{1}{3} = \frac{0.250}{(3)(0.250)}$$

$$\left[O^{2-}\right] = 0.750 \text{ mol/L}$$

d)

$$Mn(CH_3COO)_{4(s)} \rightarrow Mn^{4+}_{(aq)} + 4CH_3COO^-_{(aq)}$$

$$Mn(CH_3COO)_4 = 291.14 \text{ g/mol}$$

$$moles = \frac{50.0 \text{ g}}{291.14 \text{ g/mol}}$$

$$= 0.172 \text{ mol}$$

$$C = \frac{mol}{V}$$

$$= \frac{0.172 \text{ mol}}{3.00 \text{ L}}$$

$$= 0.057\ 2 \text{ mol/L}$$

$$\frac{Mn(CH_3COO)_4}{Mn^{4+}} = \frac{1}{1} = \frac{0.057\ 2}{0.057\ 2}$$

$$= \left[Mn^{4+}\right] = 0.057\ 2 \text{ mol/L}$$

$$= \frac{Mn(CH_3COO)_4}{CH_3COO^-} = \frac{1}{4} = \frac{0.057\ 2}{(4)(0.057\ 2)}$$

$$\left[CH_3COO^-\right] = 0.229 \text{ g/mol}$$

e)

$$Ga_2(C_2O_4)_{3(aq)} \rightarrow 2Ga^{3+}{}_{(aq)} + 3C_2O_4{}^{2-}{}_{(aq)}$$

$$Ga(C_2O_4)_3 = 403.54 \text{ g/mol}$$

$$moles = \frac{100.0 \text{ g}}{403.54 \text{ g/mol}}$$

$$= 0.247\,8$$

$$C = \frac{mol}{V}$$

$$= \frac{0.247\,8 \text{ mol}}{5.0 \text{ L}}$$

$$= 0.049\,6 \text{ mol/L}$$

$$\frac{Ga(C_2O_4)_3}{2Ga^{3+}} = \frac{1}{2} = \frac{0.049\,6}{(2)(0.049\,6)}$$

$$= \left[2Ga^{3+}\right] = 0.991 \text{ mol/L}$$

$$= \frac{Ga(C_2O_4)_3}{C_2O_4{}^{2-}} = \frac{1}{3} = \frac{0.049\,6}{(3)(0.049\,6)}$$

$$\left[C_2O_4{}^{2-}\right] = 0.149 \text{ mol/L}$$

7. a)

$$moles = C \times V$$

$$= (3.00 \text{ mol/L})(0.0250 \text{ L})$$

$$= 0.0750 \text{ mol}$$

$$new\ C = \frac{mol}{V}$$

$$= \frac{0.075 \text{ mol}}{0.065\,0 \text{ L}}$$

$$= 1.15 \text{ mol/L}$$

b)

$$moles = C \times V$$

$$= (1.75 \text{ mol/L})(0.450\,0 \text{ L})$$

$$= 0.788 \text{ mol}$$

$$new\ C = \frac{mol}{V}$$

$$= \frac{0.788 \text{ mol}}{0.675\,0 \text{ L}}$$

$$= 1.17 \text{ mol/L}$$

c)

$$moles = C \times V$$

$$= (6.00 \text{ mol/L})(0.035\,0 \text{ L})$$

$$= 0.210 \text{ mol}$$

$$new\ C = \frac{mol}{V}$$

$$= \frac{0.210 \text{ mol}}{0.125 \text{ L}}$$

$$= 1.68 \text{ mol/L}$$

d)

$$moles = C \times V$$

$$= (4.50 \text{ mol/L})(1.25 \text{ L})$$

$$= 5.63 \text{ mol}$$

$$new\ C = \frac{mol}{V}$$

$$= \frac{5.63 \text{ mol}}{3.45 \text{ L}}$$

$$= 1.63 \text{ mol/L}$$

Lesson 4—Solubility

PRACTICE EXERCISES—ANSWERS AND SOLUTIONS

1. A saturated solution contains the maximum amount of solute that can remain dissolved in a given solvent at a particular temperature.

    An unsaturated solution contains less than the maximum amount of solute than can dissolve in a given amount of solvent at a particular temperature.

    A supersaturated solution contains more dissolved solute than it would if it were saturated.

3. A certain amount of solute dissolving in water until it becomes saturated.

5.
$$NaCl = 58.44 \text{ g/mol}$$

Therefore, $\dfrac{35.7 \text{ g}}{58.44 \text{ g/mol}} = 0.611 \text{ mol}$

$$C = \frac{\text{mol}}{V}$$

$$= \frac{0.611 \text{ mol}}{0.100 \text{ L}}$$

$$= 6.11 \text{ mol/L}$$

7.
$$KCl = 74.55 \text{ g/mol}$$

Therefore, $\dfrac{40.0 \text{ g}}{74.55 \text{ g/mol}} = 0.537 \text{ mol}$

$$C = \frac{\text{mol}}{V}$$

$$= \frac{0.537 \text{ mol}}{0.200 \text{ L}}$$

$$= 2.68 \text{ mol/L}$$

9. **a)** $PbS_{(s)}$ **b)** $CaSO_{4(s)}$ **c)** $Ca_3(PO_4)_{2(s)}$ **d)** none **e)** $Zn(OH)_{2(s)}$

PRACTICE EXERCISES—ANSWERS AND SOLUTIONS

1. **a)**   turns litmus red, tastes sour, feels squeaky, conducts an electric current, reacts with active metals
    b)   turns litmus blue, tastes bitter, feels slippery, conducts an electric current, does not react with active metals

3.   An acid is a substance that increases the hydrogen ion (H^+) the concentration in aqueous solution.
     A base is a substance that increases the hydroxide ion (OH^-) concentration in aqueous solution.

5.   pH 7   neutral
     pH > 7   base
     pH < 7   acid

7.   **a)** $\left[H_3O^+_{(aq)} \right] = 5.00 \times 10^{-2}$ mol/L

     $pH = -\log\left(5.00 \times 10^{-2} \text{ mol/L} \right)$

     $\quad = 1.301$

     $pOH = 14.000 - 1.301$

     $\quad = 12.968$

     $\left[OH^-_{(aq)} \right] = 10^{-12.698}$

     $\quad\quad = 2.00 \times 10^{-13}$

     b) $pH = 1.301$

9.

$\quad Ba(OH)_{2(s)}$

$Ba = 137.33$ g/mol

$2O = 2 \times 16.00$ g/mol

$2H = 2 \times 1.00$ g/mol

$137.33 + 32.00 + 2.02 = 171.35$ g/mol

$\quad n = \dfrac{m}{M}$

$C = \dfrac{n}{V} \quad \dfrac{1.00\,g}{171.35\,g/mol} = 5.84 \times 10^{-3}$ mol

$\left[OH^-_{(aq)} \right] = \dfrac{2 \times \left(5.84 \times 10^{-3} \text{ mol} \right)}{1.00 \text{ L}}$

$\quad\quad = \dfrac{1.17 \times 10^{-2} \text{ mol}}{1.00\,L} = 1.17 \times 10^{-2} \dfrac{\text{mol}}{L}$

$$pOH = -\log\left[OH^-_{(aq)}\right]$$
$$= -\log\left(1.17 \times 10^{-2}\right)$$
$$= 1.932$$
$$pH = 14.000 - 1.932$$
$$= 12.067$$
$$\left[H_3O^+_{(aq)}\right] = 10^{-pH}$$
$$= 10^{-12.067}$$
$$= 8.55 \times 10^{-13} \frac{mol}{L}$$

11. thymol blue = yellow; the pH is between 2.8 and 8.0
    methyl orange = red; the pH is below 3.2
    chlorophenol red = yellow; the pH is below 5.2

    Therefore, the pH of the solution is between 2.8 and 3.2

13. $HF_{(aq)} + H_2O_{(l)} \rightarrow H_3O^+_{(aq)} + F^-_{(aq)}$
    $F^-_{(aq)}$ is familiar; prediction = acid
    $HF_{(aq)} + H_2O_{(l)} \rightarrow OH^-_{(aq)} + H_2F^+_{(aq)}$
    $H_2F^+_{(aq)}$ is not familiar; prediction supported

15. $SO_{3(g)} + 2H_2O_{(l)} \rightarrow H_3O^+_{(aq)} + HSO_4^-_{(aq)}$
    $HSO_4^-_{(aq)}$ is familiar; prediction = acid
    $SO_{3(g)} + H_2O_{(l)} \rightarrow OH^-_{(aq)} + HSO_3^+_{(aq)}$
    $HSO_3^+_{(aq)}$ is not familiar; prediction supported

PRACTICE TEST

PRACTICE TEST—ANSWERS AND SOLUTIONS

1. **a)** Any region with a uniform set of priorities.
    b) The same or uniform throughout.
    c) A combination of two or more pure substances, each of which retains its own chemical and physical properties
    d) A homogeneous mixture.
    e) The substance present in larger quantity in a solution.
    f) The substance present in smaller quantity in a solution.

3. The particles in a solution are: molecular in size, scattered randomly, but uniformly, throughout the solution, and constantly in motion.

5. Solubility refers to a situation in which two substances dissolve in each other only to a certain extent. Miscibility refers to a situation in which two substances dissolve in each other in all proportions.

7. There are nine types of possible solutions:

s in s	l in s	g in s
s in l	l in l	g in l
s in g	l in g	g in g

9. "Hydrated" and "aqueous" mean surrounded by water.

11. **a)** $KCl_{(s)} \xrightarrow{H_2O} K^{1+}{}_{(aq)} + Cl^{1-}{}_{(aq)}$

    b) $Al_2(SO_4)_{3(s)} \xrightarrow{H_2O} 2Al^{3+}{}_{(aq)} + 3SO_4{}^{2-}{}_{(aq)}$

13. Hydronium ions are formed by the process of ionization.

15. The three steps in the solution process model are:
    1. The solvent particles separate from each other, temperature decreases.
    2. The solute particles separate from each other, temperature decreases.
    3. Solvent particles attract solute particles, temperature increases.

17. exothermic

19. Ions allow the passage of an electric current through a solution.

21. solution, solute, solution

23. mol/L

25. Find the molar mass of $C_{12}H_{22}O_{11}$:

$$12C = (12 \text{ mol})(12.01 \text{ g/mol}) = 144.12 \text{ g}$$
$$22H = (22 \text{ mol})(1.01 \text{ g/mol}) = 22.22 \text{ g}$$
$$11O = (11 \text{ mol})(16.00 \text{ g/mol}) = 176.00 \text{ g}$$
$$\text{molar mass} = 342.34 \text{ g/mol}$$

$$n = \frac{34.22 \text{ g}}{342.24 \text{ g/mol}} = 0.100 \text{ mol}$$

$$C = \frac{0.100 \text{ mol}}{0.500 \, 0 \text{ L}} = 0.200 \, \frac{\text{mol}}{\text{L}}$$

27. a) $KI_{(aq)} \rightarrow K^{1+}_{(aq)} + I^{1-}_{(aq)}$

$$[KI] = 0.50 \text{ mol/L}$$
$$\left[K^{1+}\right] = 1 \times 0.50 \text{ mol/L} = 0.50 \text{ mol/L}$$
$$\left[I^{1-}\right] = 1 \times 0.50 \text{ mol/L} = 0.50 \text{ mol/L}$$

b) $Na_2SO_{4(aq)} \rightarrow 2Na^{1+}_{(aq)} + SO_4^{2-}_{(aq)}$

$$[Na_2SO_4] = 0.25 \text{ mol/L}$$
$$\left[Na^{1+}\right] = 2 \times 0.25 \text{ mol/L} = 0.50 \text{ mol/L}$$
$$SO_4^{2-} = 1 \times 0.25 \text{ mol/L} = 0.25 \text{ mol/L}$$

c) Find molar mass $Al_2(SO_4)_3$:

$$2Al = (2 \text{ mol})(26.98 \text{ g/mol}) = 53.96 \text{ g}$$
$$3S = (3 \text{ mol})(32.06 \text{ g/mol}) = 96.18 \text{ g}$$
$$12O = (12 \text{ mol})(16.00 \text{ g/mol}) = 192.00 \text{ g}$$
$$\text{molar mass} = 342.14 \text{ g}$$
$$M_{Al_2(SO_4)_3} = 342.14 \text{ g/mol}$$

Find moles $Al_2(So_4)_3$:

$$\frac{342.14 \text{ g}}{1 \text{ mol}} = \frac{34.23 \text{ g}}{?}$$

$$? = 0.100 \, 0 \text{ mol}$$

Find $[Al_2(So_4)_3]$:

$$\frac{0.100 \, 0 \text{ mol}}{0.100 \text{ L}} = \frac{?}{1 \text{ L}}$$

$$? = 1.00 \text{ mol}$$
$$C = 1.00 \text{ mol/L}$$

$$\left[Al_2(SO_4)_3\right] \rightarrow 2Al^{3+}_{(aq)} + 3SO^{2-}_{(aq)}$$

$$\left[Al_2(SO_4)_3\right] = 1.00 \text{ mol/L}$$

$$\left[Al^{3+}\right] = 2 \times 1.00 \text{ mol/L} = 2.00 \text{ mol/L}$$

$$\left[SO_4^{2-}\right] = 3 \times 1.00 \text{ mol/L} = 3.00 \text{ mol/L}$$

29. a) Dissolving refers to particles of solute leaving the surface of the solute and moving into the solvent.

b) Crystallizing refers to particles of solute leaving the solvent and sticking on the surface of the solute.

c) dynamic equilibrium, opposing

31. A qualitative description is one expressed in words only; no measurements are made so no numbers are used. A quantitative description is one expressed in terms of numbers based on measurements.

33. Find molar mass of $MgSO_4$:

$$1Mg = (1 \text{ mol})(24.31 \text{ g/mol}) = 24.31 \text{ g}$$

$$1S = (1 \text{ mol})(32.06 \text{ g/mol}) = 32.06 \text{ g}$$

$$4O = (4 \text{ mol})(16.00 \text{ g/mol}) = 64.00 \text{ g}$$

molar mass $= 120.36$ g

$$M_{MgSO_4} = 120.37 \text{ g/mol}$$

Find moles of $MgSO_4$:

$$\frac{120.37}{1 \text{ mol}} = \frac{12.0 \text{ g}}{?}$$

$$? = 0.099\ 7 \text{ mol}$$

Find concentration

$$\frac{0.099\ 7 \text{ mol}}{0.040 \text{ L}} = \frac{?}{1 \text{ L}}$$

$$? = 2.5 \text{ /mol}$$

Therefore, the solubility of $MgSO_4$ at 20°C is 2.49 mol/L

35. a) Solids will be less soluble in liquids

b) Gases will be more soluble in liquids

c) No effect on the solubility of liquids in liquids

37. pHs less than 7 taste sour, react with active metals, conduct electricity, turn litmus paper red

39. An acid is a substance that produces hydrogen (or hydronium) ions in a solution.

41. Household acids: vinegar, all citrus juices & fruits, aspirin, Alka-Seltzer, Saniflush, sour milk products, etc.

Household base: baking soda, Draino, ammonia, bleach, etc.

43. pH = 2.59

$$\left[H_3O^+_{(aq)}\right] = 10^{-2.59}$$

$$= 2.6 \times 10^{-3} \frac{\text{mol}}{\text{L}}$$

$$pOH = 14.000 - 2.59$$

$$= 11.41$$

$$\left[OH^-_{(aq)}\right] = 10^{-11.41}$$

$$= 3.9 \times 10^{-12} \frac{\text{mol}}{\text{L}}$$

45. d) **47. b)** **49. c)** **51. b)**

53. c) **55. c)** **57. a)** **59. c)**

61. a) **63. d)** **65. a)** **67. a)**

69. a)

QUANTITATIVE RELATIONSHIPS IN CHEMICAL CHANGES

Lesson 1—Mole-to-Mole Problems

PRACTICE EXERCISES—ANSWERS AND SOLUTIONS

1. **a)** $2H_2O_{(l)} \rightarrow 2H_{2(g)} + O_{2(g)}$

    b) $\dfrac{H_2O}{H_2} = \dfrac{2}{2} = \dfrac{0.500 \text{ mol}}{x}$

    $x = 0.500$ mol

    mol $H_2 = 0.500$ mol

    c) $\dfrac{H_2O}{O_2} = \dfrac{2}{1} = \dfrac{0.250 \text{ mol}}{x}$

    $x = 0.125$ mol

    mol $O_2 = 0.125$ mol

3. **a)** $CH_{4(g)} + 2O_{2(g)} \rightarrow 2H_2O_{(g)} + CO_{2(g)}$

    b) $\dfrac{O_2}{CH_4} = \dfrac{2}{1} = \dfrac{x}{3.00 \text{ mol}}$

    $x = 6.00$ mol

    mol $O_2 = 6.00$ mol

    c) $\dfrac{H_2O}{CH_4} = \dfrac{2}{1} = \dfrac{x}{0.040\,0 \text{ mol}}$

    $x = 0.080\,0$ mol

    mol $H_2O = 0.080\,0$ mol

5. **a)** $Mg(PO_4)_2 + 3Li_2CO_3 \rightarrow 3MgCO_3 + 2Li_3PO_4$

    b) $\dfrac{Li_2CO_3}{Mg_3(PO_4)_2} = \dfrac{3}{1} = \dfrac{x}{1.50 \text{ mol}}$

    $x = 4.50$ mol

    mol $Li_2CO_3 = 4.50$ mol

    c) $\dfrac{Li_2CO_3}{MgCO_3} = \dfrac{3}{3} = \dfrac{x}{0.020\,0 \text{ mol}}$

    $x = 0.020\,0$ mol

    mol $Li_2CO_3 = 0.020\,0$ mol

7. a) $MgCl_{2(s)} + 2Na_{(s)} \rightarrow 2NaCl_{(s)} + Mg_{(s)}$

b) $\dfrac{Na}{MgCl_2} = \dfrac{2}{1} = \dfrac{x}{0.025\,0\ mol}$

$$x = 0.050\,0\ mol$$

$$mol\ Na = 0.050\,0\ mol$$

c) $\dfrac{MgCl_2}{Mg} = \dfrac{1}{1} = \dfrac{x}{3.00\ mol}$

$$x = 3.00\ mol$$

$$mol\ MgCl_2 = 3.00\ mol$$

9. a) $2C_8H_{18(l)} + 25O_{2(g)} \rightarrow 16CO_{2(g)} + 18H_2O_{(l)}$

b) $\dfrac{CO_2}{C_8H_{18}} = \dfrac{16}{2} = \dfrac{x}{3.00\ mol}$

$$x = 24.0\ mol$$

$$mol\ CO_2 = 24.0\ mol$$

c) $\dfrac{C_8H_{18}}{O_2} = \dfrac{2}{25} = \dfrac{x}{25\ mol}$

$$x = 2.00\ mol$$

$$mol\ C_8H_{18} = 2.00\ mol$$

Lesson 2—Mole-To-Quantity Problems

PRACTICE EXERCISES—ANSWERS AND SOLUTIONS

1. $2KClO_{3(s)} \rightarrow 2KCl_{(s)} + 3O_{2(g)}$

$$\dfrac{KCl}{KClO_3} = \dfrac{2}{2} = \dfrac{x}{6.5\ mol}$$

$$KCl = 6.5\ mol$$

$$KCl = (39.10 + 35.45)\ g/mol$$

$$= 74.55\ g/mol$$

$$mol\ KCl = (6.5\ mol)(74.55\ g/mol)$$

$$= 485\ g$$

$$= 4.8 \times 10^2\ g$$

3. $N_{2(g)} + 3Cl_{2(g)} \rightarrow 2NCl_{3(g)}$

$$\dfrac{N_2}{NCl_3} = \dfrac{1}{2} = \dfrac{8.25\ mol}{x}$$

$$mol\ NCl_3 = 16.5\ mol$$

$$V = \dfrac{nRT}{P}$$

$$= \dfrac{(16.5\ mol)\left(8.314\,\dfrac{L \times kPa}{mol \times K}\right)(308\ K)}{98.9\ kPa}$$

$$= 427\ L$$

5. $2C_4H_{10(l)} + 13O_{2(g)} \rightarrow 8CO_{2(g)} + 10H_2O_{(g)}$

$$\frac{H_2O}{C_4H_{10}} = \frac{10}{2} = \frac{x}{5.25 \text{ mol}}$$

mol $H_2O = 26.3$ mol

$$V = \frac{nRT}{P}$$

$$= \frac{(26.3 \text{ mol})\left(8.314 \frac{L \times kPa}{mol \times K}\right)(298 \text{ K})}{100 \text{ kPa}}$$

$$= 650 \text{ L}$$

7. $H_2SO_{4(aq)} + 2NaOH_{(aq)} \rightarrow Na_2SO_{4(aq)} + 2HOH_{(l)}$

$$\frac{H_2SO_4}{NaOH} = \frac{1}{2} = \frac{x}{0.250 \text{ mol}}$$

mol $H_2SO_4 = 0.125$ mol

$$C = \frac{n}{V}$$

$$= \frac{0.125 \text{ mol}}{0.050\,0 \text{ L}}$$

$$= 2.50 \text{ mol/L}$$

9. $2NaOH_{(aq)} + H_2SO_{4\,(aq)} \rightarrow Na_2SO_{4(aq)} + 2HOH_{(l)}$

$$\frac{H_2O}{NaOH} = \frac{2}{2} = \frac{x}{4.56 \text{ mol}}$$

mol $H_2O = 4.56$ mol

$$\text{mass} = (\text{mol})(M)$$

$$= (4.56)18.02 \text{ g/mol}$$

$$= 82.2 \text{ g}$$

Lesson 3—Quantity-To-Mole Problems

PRACTICE EXERCISES—ANSWERS AND SOLUTIONS

1. $4Fe_{(s)} + 3O_{2(g)} \rightarrow 2Fe_2O_{3(g)}$

$$\text{mol Fe}_{(s)} = \frac{5.6 \text{ g}}{55.85 \text{ g/mol}}$$

$$= 0.10 \text{ mol}$$

$$\frac{Fe}{Fe_2O_3} = \frac{4}{2} = \frac{2}{1} = \frac{0.10 \text{ mol}}{x}$$

$$x = \frac{0.10 \text{ mol}}{2}$$

mol $Fe_2O_3 = 0.050$ mol

3. $2KClO_{3(s)} + 2KCl_{(g)} \rightarrow 3O_{2(g)}$

$$mol\ KCl = \frac{122.6\ g}{74.55\ g/mol}$$

$$= 1.64\ mol$$

$$\frac{KClO_3}{KCl} = \frac{2}{2} = \frac{1}{1} = \frac{x}{1.64\ mol}$$

$$x = 1.64\ mol$$

$$mol\ KClO_3 = 1.64\ mol$$

5. $Zn_{(s)} + 2HCl_{(aq)} \rightarrow H_{2\ (g)} + ZnCl_{2(s)}$

$$mol\ H_2 = \frac{44.8\ L}{22.4\ L/mol}$$

$$= 2.00\ mol$$

$$\frac{Zn}{H_2} = \frac{1}{1} = \frac{x}{2.00\ mol}$$

$$x = 2.00\ mol$$

$$mol\ Zn = 2.00\ mol$$

7. $2NaCl_{(s)} + H_2SO_{4(aq)} \rightarrow 2HCl_{(aq)} + Na_2SO_{4(aq)}$

$$mol\ H_2SO_4 = C \times V$$

$$= (2.00\ mol/L)(0.045\ 0\ L)$$

$$= 0.090\ 0\ mol$$

$$\frac{H_2SO_4}{Na_2SO_4} = \frac{1}{1} = \frac{0.090\ 0\ mol}{x}$$

$$x = 0.090\ 0\ mol$$

$$mol\ H_2SO_4 = 0.090\ 0\ mol$$

9. $3NO_{2(g)} + H_2O_{(l)} \rightarrow 2HNO_{3(;)} + NO_{(g)}$

$$mol\ HNO_3 = \frac{120.6\ g}{63.02\ g/mol}$$

$$- 1.914\ mol$$

$$\frac{NO_2}{HNO_3} = \frac{3}{2} = \frac{x}{1.914\ mol}$$

$$x = \frac{(3)(1.914\ mol)}{2}$$

$$mol\ NO_2 = 2.871\ mol$$

11. $2Al_{(s)} + Fe_2O_{3(s)} \rightarrow Al_2O_{3(s)} + 2Fe_{(s)}$

$$mol\ Al = \frac{50.0\ g}{26.98\ g/mol}$$

$$= 1.85\ mol$$

$$\frac{Al}{Al_2O_3} = \frac{2}{1} = \frac{1.85\ mol}{x}$$

$$x = \frac{1.85\ mol}{2}$$

$$mol\ Al_2O_3 = 0.927\ mol$$

Lesson 4—Quantity-To-Quantity Problems

PRACTICE EXERCISES—ANSWERS AND SOLUTIONS

1. $Zn_{(s)} + 2HCl_{(aq)} \rightarrow ZnCl_{2(aq)} + H_{2(g)}$

    $mol\ HCl = C \times V$

    $\qquad = (1.00\ mol/L)(0.050\ 0\ L)$

    $\dfrac{HCl}{ZnCl_2} = \dfrac{2}{1} = \dfrac{0.050\ 0\ mol}{x}$

    $\qquad x = \dfrac{0.050\ 0\ mol}{2}$

    $\qquad = 0.025\ 0\ mol$

    $mass\ ZnCl_2 = (0.025\ 0\ mol)(136.28\ g/mol)$

    $\qquad = 3.41\ g$

3. $2Al_2O_{3(s)} \rightarrow 4Al_{(s)} + 3O_{2(g)}$

    $mol\ Al_2O_3 = \dfrac{2\ 040\ g}{101.96\ g/mol}$

    $\qquad = 20.0\ mol$

    $\dfrac{Al_2O_3}{Al} = \dfrac{2}{4} = \dfrac{1}{2} = \dfrac{20.0\ mol}{x}$

    $\qquad x = 40.0\ mol$

    $mass\ Al = (40.0\ mol)(26.98\ g/mol)$

    $\qquad = 1079\ g$

    $\qquad = 1.08\ kg$

5. $AgNO_{3(aq)} + NaCl_{(aq)} \rightarrow AgCl_{(s)} + NaNO_{3(aq)}$

    $mol\ NaCl = \dfrac{11.7\ g}{58.44\ g/mol}$

    $\qquad = 0.200\ mol$

    $\dfrac{NaCl}{AgCl} = \dfrac{1}{1} = \dfrac{0.200\ mol}{x}$

    $\qquad x = 0.200\ mol$

    $mass\ AgCl = (0.200\ mol)(143.32\ g/mol)$

    $\qquad = 28.7\ g$

7. $HNO_{3(aq)} + NaOH_{(s)} \rightarrow NaNO_{3(aq)} + HOH_{(l)}$

$$\text{mol NaOH} = \frac{0.60 \text{ g}}{40.00 \text{ g/mol}}$$

$$= 0.015 \text{ 0 mol}$$

$$\frac{HNO_3}{NaOH} = \frac{1}{1} = \frac{x}{0.015 \text{ 0 mol}}$$

$$x = 0.015 \text{ 0 mol } HNO_3$$

$$C = \frac{0.015 \text{ 0 mol}}{0.025 \text{ 0 L}} = 0.600 \ \frac{\text{mol}}{\text{L}}$$

$$= 11.5 \text{ g}$$

9. $2Al_{(s)} + Fe_2O_{3(s)} \rightarrow 2Fe_{(s)} + Al_2O_{3(s)}$

$$\text{mol Fe} = \frac{19.55 \text{ g}}{55.85 \text{ g/mol}}$$

$$= 0.350 \text{ 0 mol}$$

$$\frac{Fe}{Al_2O_3} = \frac{2}{1} = \frac{0.350 \text{ 0 mol}}{x}$$

$$x = 0.175 \text{ mol}$$

$$\text{mass } Al_2O_3 = (0.175 \text{ 0 mol})(101.96 \text{ g/mol})$$

$$= 17.85 \text{ g}$$

11. $2NaI_{(aq)} + Pb(NO_3)_{(aq)} \rightarrow 2NaNO_{3(aq)} + PbI_{(s)}$

$$\text{mol NaNO}_3 = \frac{150 \text{ g}}{85.00 \text{ g/mol}}$$

$$= 1.76 \text{ mol}$$

$$\frac{Pb(NO_3)_2}{NaNO_3} = \frac{1}{2} = \frac{x}{1.76 \text{ mol}}$$

$$x = 0.882 \text{ mol}$$

$$\text{mass } Pb(NO_3)_2 = (0.882 \text{ mol})(331.21 \text{ g/mol})$$

$$= 292 \text{ g}$$

13. $HCl_{(aq)} + NaOH_{(aq)} \rightarrow HOH_{(l)} + NaCl_{(aq)}$

Mol NaOH=0.250 mol/L2HCl = 0.0031 mol

$$\text{mol NaOH} = 0.250 \ \frac{\text{mol}}{\text{L}} \times 0.012 \text{ 5 L} = 0.000 \text{ 313 mol}$$

$$\frac{HCl}{NaOH} = \frac{1}{1} = \frac{x}{0.003 \text{ 13}}$$

$$x = 0.003 \text{ 13 mol } HCl$$

$$C = \frac{0.003 \text{ 13 mol}}{0.010 \text{ 00 L}} = 0.313 \ \frac{\text{mol}}{\text{L}} \text{ of } HCl_{(aq)}$$

Lesson 5—Qualitative and Quantitative Analysis

PRACTICE EXERCISES—ANSWERS AND SOLUTIONS

1. **a)** $HCl_{(aq)} + KOH_{(aq)} \rightarrow KCl_{(aq)} + H_2O_{(aq)}$

moles of $HCl_{(aq)} = C \times V$

$$= (1.25 \text{ mol/L})(0.050 \text{ L})$$

$$= 0.062\ 5 \text{ moles}$$

moles of $KOH_{(aq)} = C \times V$

$$= (1.00 \text{ mol/L})(0.075\ L)$$

$$= 0.075\ 0 \text{ moles}$$

The mole ratio between the two reagents is 1:1

Therefore, $HCl_{(aq)}$ is the limiting reagent

$KOH_{(aq)}$ is in excess by

$$0.075\ 0 \text{ mol} - 0.062\ 5 \text{ mol} = 0.012\ 5 \text{ mol}$$

$$= 0.013 \text{ mol}$$

b) $NaOH_{(s)} + HNO_{3(aq)} \rightarrow NaNO_{3(aq)} + H_2O_{(l)}$

moles of $NaOH_{(s)} = \dfrac{mass}{molar\ mass}$

$$= \dfrac{125 \text{ g}}{40.00 \text{ g/mol}}$$

$$= 3.125 \text{ mol}$$

moles of $HNO_3 = 10.5\ \dfrac{mol}{L} \times 0.300 \text{ L}$

$$= 3.15 \text{ mol}$$

The mole ratio between the two reagents is 1:1

Therefore, $NaOH_{(s)}$ is the limiting reagent

$HNO_{3(aq)}$ is in excess by

$$3.150 \text{ mol} - 3.125 \text{ mol} = 0.025 \text{ mol}$$

c) $Mg_{(s)} + 2HCl_{(aq)} \rightarrow MgCl_{2\ (aq)} + H_{2(g)}$

moles of $Mg_{(s)} = \dfrac{mass}{molar\ mass}$

$$= \dfrac{5.00 \text{ g}}{24.31 \text{ g/mol}}$$

$$= 0.206 \text{ mol}$$

moles of $HCl_{(aq)} = \dfrac{mass}{molar\ mass}$

$$= \dfrac{7.00 \text{ g}}{36.46 \text{ g/mol}}$$

$$= 0.192 \text{ mol}$$

The molar ratio between the two reagents is 1:2.

Since you need 2× as many moles of $HCl_{(aq)}$ (0.384 moles), $HCl_{(aq)}$ is the limiting reagent because there is not that amount of $HCl_{(aq)}$ to react with 0.206 mol $Mg_{(s)}$.

When all the $HCl_{(aq)}$ reacts (0.192 mol), you will need half of 0.192 mol = 0.0960 moles of $Mg_{(s)}$

d) $HCl_{(aq)} + KOH_{(aq)} \rightarrow KCl_{(aq)} + H_2O_{(l)}$

$$\text{moles of } HCl_{(aq)} = C \times V$$
$$= (0.50 \text{ mol/L})(0.100 \text{ L})$$
$$= 0.0500 \text{ mol}$$

$$\text{moles of } KOH_{(aq)} = C \times V$$
$$= (1.00 \text{ mol/L})(0.0500 \text{ L})$$
$$= 0.0500 \text{ mol}$$

The mole ratio between the two reagents is 1:1

Since both reagents have the same number of moles, there is not a limiting reagent.

3. $HCl_{(aq)} + KOH_{(aq)} \rightarrow KCl_{(aq)} + H_2O_{(l)}$

$$\text{moles of } HCl_{(aq)} = C \times V$$
$$= (5.00 \text{ mol/L})(0.150 \text{ L})$$
$$= 0.750 \text{ mol}$$

$$\text{moles of } KOH_{(aq)} = \frac{\text{mass}}{\text{molar mass}}$$
$$= \frac{7.50 \text{ g}}{56.11 \text{ g/mol}}$$
$$= 0.134 \text{ mol}$$

The mole ratio between the two reagents is 1:1

Therefore, $KOH_{(s)}$ is the limiting reagent

$$\frac{KOH_{(s)}}{KCl_{(aq)}} = \frac{1}{1} = \frac{0.134 \text{ mol}}{x}$$

$$x = 0.134 \text{ mol of } KCl_{(aq)}$$

$$\text{mass } KCl_{(aq)} = (\text{moles})(\text{molar mass})$$
$$= (0.134 \text{ mol})(74.55 \text{ g/mol})$$
$$= 9.96 \text{ g}$$

5. a) $NaOH_{(s)} + HCl_{(aq)} \rightarrow NaCl_{(aq)} + H_2O_{(l)}$

Mole ratio between the two reagents is 1:1

$$\text{moles of } NaOH_{(s)} = \frac{\text{mass}}{\text{molar mass}}$$
$$= \frac{5.0 \text{ g}}{40.00 \text{ g/mol}}$$
$$= 0.125 \text{ mol}$$

$$\text{moles of } HCl_{(aq)} (\text{from 4 a}) = 0.10 \text{ mol}$$

$$\text{excess of } NaOH_{(s)} \text{ by } 0.125 \text{ mol} = 0.025 \text{ mol}$$

b) $2NaOH_{(s)} + H_2SO_{4(aq)} \rightarrow Na_2SO_{4(aq)} + 2H_2O_{(l)}$

Mole ratio between two reagents is 2:1

$$\text{moles of NaOH}_{(s)} = \frac{\text{mass}}{\text{molar mass}}$$

$$= \frac{5.0 \text{ g}}{40.00 \text{ g/mol}}$$

$$= 0.125 \text{ mol}$$

moles of $H_2SO_{4(aq)}$ (from 4 b) = 0.10 mol

Since we need 2 times as many moles of $NaOH_{(s)}$, we will need 0.20 moles. We do not have enough $NaOH_{(s)}$.

c) $3NaOH_{(s)} + H_3PO_{4(aq)} \rightarrow Na_3PO_{4(aq)} + 3H_2O_{(l)}$

Mole ratio between two reagents is 3:1

$$\text{moles of NaOH}_{(s)} = \frac{\text{mass}}{\text{molar mass}}$$

$$= \frac{5.0 \text{ g}}{40.00 \text{ g/mol}}$$

$$= 0.125 \text{ mol}$$

moles of $H_3PO_{4(aq)}$ (from 4 c) = 0.10 mol

Since we need 3 times as many moles of NaOH(s), we will need 0.30 moles. We do not have enough $NaOH_{(s)}$

7. $2H_{2(g)} + O_{2(g)} \rightarrow 2H_2O_{(g)}$

$$\frac{O_{2(g)}}{H_2O_{(l)}} = \frac{1}{2} = \frac{6.25 \times 10^{-4} \text{ mol}}{x}$$

$$x = 1.25 \times 10^{-3} \text{ mol of } H_2O_{(l)}$$

$$\text{mass of } H_2O = (\text{moles})(\text{molar mass})$$

$$= \left(1.25 \times 10^{-3} \text{ mol}\right)(18.02 \text{ g/mol})$$

$$= 0.0225 \text{ g}$$

Lesson 6—Theoretical and Actual Yields

PRACTICE EXERCISES—ANSWERS AND SOLUTIONS

1. Formula Equation:

    $$Zn_{(s)} + Pb(NO_3)_{2(aq)} \rightarrow Zn(NO_3)_{2(aq)} + Pb_{(s)}$$

    Total Ionic Equation:

    $$Zn_{(s)} + Pb^{2+}_{(aq)} + 2\cancel{NO_3^-} \rightarrow Pb_{(s)} + Zn^{2+}_{(aq)} + 2\cancel{NO_3^-}$$

    Net Ionic Equation:

    $$Zn_{(s)} + Pb^{2+}_{(aq)} \rightarrow Zn^{2+}_{(aq)} + Pb_{(s)}$$

3. Formula Equation:

    $$Cl_{2(g)} + 2KBr_{(aq)} \rightarrow 2KCl_{(aq)} + 2Br^-_{(aq)}$$

    Total Ionic Equation:

    $$Cl_{2(g)} + 2\cancel{K^+}_{(aq)} + 2Br^-_{(aq)} \rightarrow 2Cl^-_{(aq)} + 2\cancel{K^+}_{(aq)} + Br_{2(aq)}$$

    Net Ionic Equation:

    $$Cl_{2(g)} + 2Br^-_{(aq)} \rightarrow 2Cl^-_{(aq)} + Br_{2(aq)}$$

PRACTICE TEST

PRACTICE TEST—ANSWERS AND SOLUTIONS

1. $2H_{2(g)} + O_{2(g)} \rightarrow 2H_2O_{(g)}$

    $$\frac{H_2O}{O_2} = \frac{2}{1} = \frac{x}{9.6 \text{ mol}}$$

    $$\text{mol } H_2O = 19.2 \text{ mol}$$

    $$V = \frac{nRT}{P}$$

    $$= \frac{(19.2 \text{ mol})\left(8.314 \dfrac{L \times kPa}{mol \times K}\right)(273 \text{ K})}{101.3 \text{ kPa}}$$

    $$= 430 \text{ L}$$

    $$= 4.3 \times 10^2 \text{ L}$$

3. $2NH_{3(g)} \rightarrow N_{2(g)} + 3H_{2(g)}$

    $$\frac{NH_3}{H_2} = \frac{2}{3} = \frac{x}{0.50 \text{ mol}}$$

    $$\text{mol } NH_3 = 3.33 \text{ mol}$$

5. $2NaCl_{(l)} \rightarrow 2Na_{(l)} + Cl_{2(g)}$

$$nCl_2 = \frac{PV}{RT}$$

$$= \frac{(125 \text{ kPa})(4\,000 \text{ L})}{\left(8.314 \dfrac{\text{L} \times \text{kPa}}{\text{mol} \times \text{K}}\right)(298 \text{ K})}$$

$$= 202 \text{ mol}$$

7. $TiCl_{4(aq)} + 2Mg_{(s)} \rightarrow Ti_{(s)} + 2MgCl_{2(aq)}$

$\phantom{TiCl_{4(aq)} +}$?g $\phantom{+ 2Mg_{(s)} \rightarrow}$ 10.5 mol

$$\frac{Mg}{Ti} = \frac{2}{1} = \frac{x}{10.5 \text{ mol}}$$

$$\text{mol Mg} = 21.0 \text{ mol}$$

$$\text{mass Mg} = (21.0 \text{ mol})(24.31 \text{ g/mol})$$

$$= 511 \text{ g}$$

9. $Fe_{(s)} + CuSO_{4(aq)} \rightarrow Cu_{(s)} + FeSO_{4(aq)}$

2.54 g $\phantom{+ CuSO_{4(aq)} \rightarrow}$? mol

$$nFe = (2.54 \text{ g})\left(\frac{1 \text{ mol}}{55.85 \text{ g}}\right)$$

$$\text{mol Cu} = 0.455 \text{ mol}$$

11. $Na_2SO_{4(aq)} + Sr(NO_3)_{2(aq)} \rightarrow SrSO_{4(s)} + 2NaNO_{3(aq)}$

$\phantom{Na_2SO_{4(aq)} + Sr(NO_3)_{2(aq)}}$ $V = ?$

$$\text{mol Na}_2\text{SO}_4 = 0.03 \text{ L} \times 0.175 \text{ mol/L}$$

$$= 5.25 \times 10^{-3} \text{ mol}$$

$$\text{mol Sr(NO}_3)_2 = 5.25 \times 10^{-3} \text{ mol}$$

$$V = \frac{n}{C}$$

$$= \frac{5.25 \times 10^{-3} \text{ mol}}{0.150 \text{ mol/L}}$$

$$= 5.50 \times 10^{-2} \text{ L}$$

$$= 35.0 \text{ mL}$$

13. b)   **15. a)**   **17. c)**   **19. c)**   **21. c)**

CHEMISTRY 20—FORMULA SHEETS

COMMON FORMULAS AND UNITS OF MEASUREMENT

- *STP conditions*: 0°C (273.15 K) and 1 atm (101.325 kPa) pressure.

- *SATP conditions*: 25°C (298.15 K) and 100 kPa pressure.

- *Molar Volumes*: $V_{STP} = 22.4$ L and $V_{SATP} = 24.8$ L

- 1 atm = 101.325 kPa = 760 mm Hg = 760 torr

- $T(K) = T(°C) + 273.15$

- *Ideal Gas Law*: $PV = nRT$

- *Combined Gas Law*: $\dfrac{P_1 V_1}{T_1} = \dfrac{P_2 V_2}{T_2}$

- *The Gas Constant*: $R = 8.314 \dfrac{L \cdot kPa}{mol \cdot K}$ or $0.082\,06 \dfrac{L \cdot atm}{mol \cdot K}$

- *Avogadro's Number*: $N_A = 6.022 \times 10^{23}$

- $K_W = 1.0 \times 10^{-14} \left(\dfrac{mol}{L} \right)^2$ at 25° C

- $pH = -\log \left[H^+_{(aq)} \right]$ *note*: $\left(\left[H^+_{(aq)} \right] \text{ in } \dfrac{mol}{L} \right)$

- $\left[H^+_{(aq)} \right] = 10^{-pH}$

- $C_1 V_1 = C_2 V_2$ (for dilution only)

SOLUBILITY OF SOME COMMON IONIC COMPOUNDS IN WATER AT 298.15 K (25°C)

ION	Group IA NH_4^+ $H^+(H_3O^+)$	ClO_3^- NO_3^- ClO_4^-	CH_3COO^-	Cl^- Br^- I^-	SO_4^{2-}	S^{2-}	OH^-	PO_4^{3-} SO_3^{2-} CO_3^{2-}
Solubility greater than or equal to 0.1 mol/L (very soluble)	all	all	most	most	most	Group IA Group IIA NH_4^+	Group IA NH_4^+ Sr^{2+} Ba^{2+} Tl^+	Group IA NH_4^+
Solubility less than 0.1 mol/L (slightly soluble)	none	none	Ag^+ Hg^+	Ag^+ Pb^{2+} Hg^+ Cu^+ Tl^+	Ca^{2+} Sr^{2+} Ba^{2+} Ra^{2+} Pb^{2+} Ag^+	most	most	most

COLOR CHART OF COMMON AQUEOUS IONS

ION	SYMBOL	COLOR
chromate	CrO_4^{2-}	yellow
chromium(III)	Cr^{3+}	green
chromium(II)	Cr^{2+}	blue
cobalt(II)	Co^{2+}	pink
copper(I)	Cu^+	green
copper(II)	Cu^{2+}	blue
dichromate	$Cr_2O_7^{2-}$	orange
iron(II)	Fe^{2+}	pale green
iron(III)	Fe^{3+}	pale yellow
manganese(II)	Mn^{2+}	pale pink
permanganate	MnO_4^-	purple

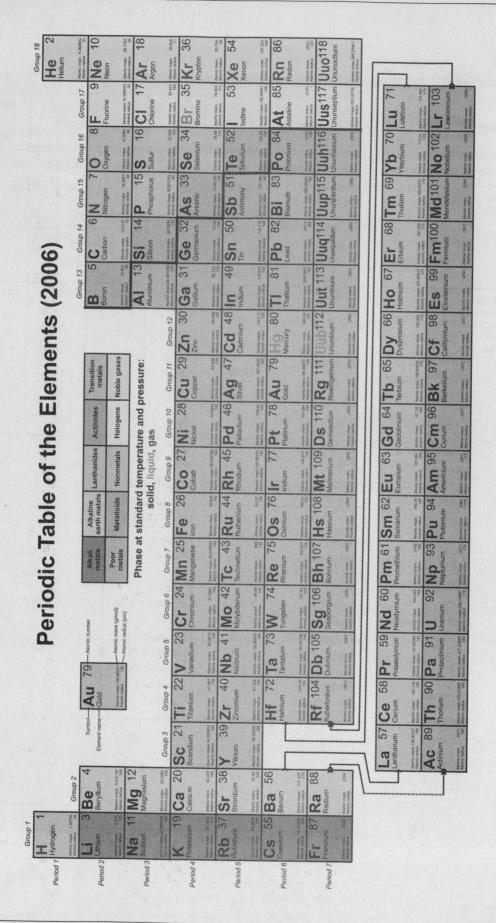

Periodic Table of the Elements (2006)

PERIODIC CHART OF IONS

TABLE OF POLYATOMIC IONS

acetate	CH_3COO^-	dichromate	$Cr_2O_7^{2-}$	dihydrogen phosphate	$H_2PO_4^-$
ammonium	NH_4^+	cyanide	CN^-	silicate	SiO_3^{2-}
benzoate	$C_6H_5COO^-$	hydroxide	OH^-	sulphate	SO_4^{2-}
borate	BO_3^{3-}	iodate	IO_3^-	sulphite	SO_3^{2-}
carbonate	CO_3^{2-}	nitrate	NO_3^-	hydrogen sulphide	HS^-
hydrogen carbonate	HCO_3^-	nitrite	NO_2^-	hydrogen sulphate	HSO_4^-
chlorate	ClO_3^-	oxalate	$OOCCOO^{2-}$	hydrogen sulphite	HSO_3^-
hypochlorite	ClO^-	permanganate	MnO_4^-	thiocyanate	SCN^-
chromate	CrO_4^{2-}	phosphate	PO_4^{3-}	thiosulphate	$S_2O_3^{2-}$
		hydrogen phosphate	HPO_4^{2-}		

KEY

atomic number → 26 Fe^{3+} ← ion charge
iron(III) ← stock name (IUPAC)
Fe^{2+} ← symbol
iron(II)

Main group and transition elements

1 H^+ hydrogen

3 Li^+ lithium
4 Be^{2+} beryllium

11 Na^+ sodium
12 Mg^{2+} magnesium

19 K^+ potassium
20 Ca^{2+} calcium
21 Sc^{3+} scandium
22 Ti^{4+} titanium(IV) / Ti^{3+} titanium(III)
23 V^{3+} vanadium(V) / V^{4+} vanadium(IV)
24 Cr^{2+} chromium(III) / Cr^{2+} chromium(II)
25 Mn^{2+} manganese(II) / Mn^{4+} manganese(IV)
26 Fe^{3+} iron(III) / Fe^{2+} iron(II)
27 Co^{2+} cobalt(II) / Co^{3+} cobalt(III)
28 Ni^{2+} nickel(II) / Ni^{3+} nickel(III)
29 Cu^{2+} copper(II) / Cu^+ copper(I)
30 Zn^{2+} zinc

37 Rb^+ rubidium
38 Sr^{2+} strontium
39 Y^{3+} yttrium
40 Zr^{4+} zirconium
41 Nb^{5+} niobium(V) / Nb^{3+} niobium(III)
42 Mo^{6+} molybdenum
43 Tc^{7+} technetium
44 Ru^{3+} ruthenium(III) / Ru^{2+} ruthenium(IV)
45 Rh^{3+} rhodium
46 Pd^{2+} palladium(II) / Pd^{4+} palladium(IV)
47 Ag^+ silver
48 Cd^{2+} cadmium

55 Cs^+ cesium
56 Ba^{2+} barium
57-71
72 Hf^{4+} hafnium
73 Ta^{5+} tantalum
74 W^{6+} tungsten
75 Re^{6+} rhenium
76 Os^{4+} osmium
77 Ir^{4+} iridium
78 Pt^{4+} platinum(IV) / Pt^{2+} platinum(II)
79 Au^{3+} gold(III) / Au^+ gold(I)
80 Hg^{2+} mercury(II) / Hg_2^{2+} mercury(I)

87 Fr^+ francium
88 Ra^{2+} radium
89-103

5 B boron
13 Al^{3+} aluminum
31 Ga^{3+} gallium
49 In^{3+} indium
81 Tl^+ thallium(I) / Tl^{3+} thallium(III)

6 C carbon
14 Si silicon
32 Ge^{4+} germanium
50 Sn^{4+} tin(IV) / Sn^{2+} tin(II)
82 Pb^{2+} lead(II) / Pb^{4+} lead(IV)

7 N^{3-} nitride
15 P^{3-} phosphide
33 As^{3-} arsenide
51 Sb^{3+} antimony(III) / Sb^{5+} antimony(V)
83 Bi^{3+} bismuth(III) / Bi^{5+} bismuth(V)

8 O^{2-} oxide
16 S^{2-} sulphide
34 Se^{2-} selenide
52 Te^{2-} telluride
84 Po^{2+} polonium(II) / Po^{4+} polonium(IV)

1 H^- hydride
9 F^- fluoride
17 Cl^- chloride
35 Br^- bromide
53 I^- iodide
85 At^- astatide

2 He helium
10 Ne neon
18 Ar argon
36 Kr krypton
54 Xe xenon
86 Rn radon

Lanthanides

57 La^{3+} lanthanum
58 Ce^{3+} cerium
59 Pr^{3+} praseodymium
60 Nd^{3+} neodymium
61 Pm^{3+} promethium
62 Sm^{3+} samarium(III) / Sm^{2+} samarium(II)
63 Eu^{3+} europium(III) / Eu^{2+} europium(II)
64 Gd^{3+} gadolinium
65 Tb^{3+} terbium
66 Dy^{3+} dysprosium
67 Ho^{3+} holmium
68 Er^{3+} erbium
69 Tm^{3+} thulium
70 Yb^{3+} ytterbium(III) / Yb^{2+} ytterbium(II)
71 Lu^{2+} lutetium

Actinides

89 Ac^{3+} actinium
90 Th^{4+} thorium
91 Pa^{5+} protactinium(V) / Pa^{4+} protactinium(IV)
92 U^{6+} uranium(VI) / U^{4+} uranium(IV)
93 Np^{5+} neptunium
94 Pu^{5+} plutonium(V) / Pu^{6+} plutonium(VI)
95 Am^{3+} americium(III) / Am^{4+} americium(V)
96 Cm^{3+} curium
97 Bk^{3+} berkelium(III) / Bk^{4+} berkelium(IV)
98 Cf^{3+} californium
99 Es^{3+} einsteinium
100 Fm fermium
101 Md^{2+} mendelevium(II) / Md^{3+} mendelevium(III)
102 No^{2+} nobelium(II) / No^{3+} nobelium(III)
103 Lr^{3+} lawrencium

PERIODIC TABLE OF ELECTRONEGATIVITY
USING THE PAULING SCALE

→ Atomic radius decreases → Ionization energy increases → Electronegativity increases →

Group (vertical)	1	2	3	4	5	6	7	8	9	10	11	12	13	14	15	16	17	18
Period (horizontal)																		
1	H 2.20																	He
2	Li 0.98	Be 1.57											B 2.04	C 2.55	N 3.04	O 3.44	F 3.98	Ne
3	Na 0.93	Mg 1.31											Al 1.61	Si 1.90	P 2.19	S 2.58	Cl 3.16	Ar
4	K 0.82	Ca 1.00	Sc 1.36	Ti 1.54	V 1.63	Cr 1.66	Mn 1.55	Fe 1.83	Co 1.88	Ni 1.91	Cu 1.90	Zn 1.65	Ga 1.81	Ge 2.01	As 2.18	Se 2.55	Br 2.96	Kr 3.00
5	Rb 0.82	Sr 0.95	Y 1.22	Zr 1.33	Nb 1.6	Mo 2.16	Tc 1.9	Ru 2.2	Rh 2.28	Pd 2.20	Ag 1.93	Cd 1.69	In 1.78	Sn 1.96	Sb 2.05	Te 2.1	I 2.66	Xe 2.67
6	Cs 0.79	Ba 0.89	*	Hf 1.3	Ta 1.5	W 2.36	Re 1.9	Os 2.2	Ir 2.20	Pt 2.28	Au 2.54	Hg 2.00	Tl 1.62	Pb 2.33	Bi 2.02	Po 2.0	At 2.2	Rn
7	Fr 0.7	Ra 0.9	**	Rf	Db	Sg	Bh	Hs	Mt	Ds	Rg	Uub	Uut	Uuq	Uup	Uuh	Uus	Uuo

Lanthanides	*	La 1.1	Ce 1.12	Pr 1.13	Nd 1.14	Pm 1.13	Sm 1.17	Eu 1.2	Gd 1.2	Tb 1.1	Dy 1.22	Ho 1.23	Er 1.24	Tm 1.25	Yb 1.1	Lu 1.27
Actinides	**	Ac 1.1	Th 1.3	Pa 1.5	U 1.38	Np 1.36	Pu 1.28	Am 1.13	Cm 1.28	Bk 1.3	Cf 1.3	Es 1.3	Fm 1.3	Md 1.3	No 1.3	Lr

ACID BASE INDICATOR CHART

Indicator	pH Range	Quantity per 10 ml	Acid	Base
Thymol Blue	1.2-2.8	1-2 drops 0.1% soln. in aq.	red	yellow
Pentamethoxy red	1.2-2.3	1 drop 0.1% soln. in 70% alc.	red-violet	colorless
Tropeolin OO	1.3-3.2	1 drop 1% aq. soln.	red	yellow
2,4-Dinitrophenol	2.4-4.0	1-2 drops 0.1% soln. in 50% alc.	colorless	yellow
Methyl yellow	2.9-4.0	1 drop 0.1% soln. in 90% alc.	red	yellow
Methyl orange	3.1-4.4	1 drop 0.1% aq. soln.	red	orange
Bromphenol blue	3.0-4.6	1 drop 0.1% aq. soln.	yellow	blue-violet
Tetrabromphenol blue	3.0-4.6	1 drop 0.1% aq. soln.	yellow	blue
Alizarin sodium sulfonate	3.7-5.2	1 drop 0.1% aq. soln.	yellow	violet
α-Naphthyl red	3.7-5.0	1 drop 0.1% soln. in 70% alc.	red	yellow
p-Ethoxychrysoidine	3.5-5.5	1 drop 0.1% aq. soln.	red	yellow
Bromcresol green	4.0-5.6	1 drop 0.1% aq. soln.	yellow	blue
Methyl red	4.4-6.2	1 drop 0.1% aq. soln.	red	yellow
Bromcresol purple	5.2-6.8	1 drop 0.1% aq. soln.	yellow	purple
Chlorphenol red	5.4-6.8	1 drop 0.1% aq. soln.	yellow	red
Bromphenol blue	6.2-7.6	1 drop 0.1% aq. soln.	yellow	blue
p-Nitrophenol	5.0-7.0	1-5 drops 0.1% aq. soln.	colorless	yellow
Azolitmin	5.0-8.0	5 drops 0.5% aq. soln.	red	blue
Phenol red	6.4-8.0	1 drop 0.1% aq. soln.	yellow	red
Neutral red	6.8-8.0	1 drop 0.1% soln. in 70% alc.	red	yellow
Rosolic acid	6.8-8.0	1 drop 0.1% soln. in 90% alc.	yellow	red
Cresol red	7.2-8.8	1 drop 0.1% aq. soln.	yellow	red
α-Naphtholphthalein	7.3-8.7	1-5 drops 0.1% soln. in 70% alc.	rose	green
Tropeolin OOO	7.6-8.9	1 drop 0.1% aq. soln.	yellow	rose-red
Thymol blue	8.0-9.6	1-5 drops 0.1% aq. soln.	yellow	blue
Phenolphthalein	8.0-10.0	1-5 drops 0.1% soln. in 70% alc.	colorless	red
α-Naphtholbenzein	9.0-11.0	1-5 drops 0.1% soln. in 90% alc.	yellow	blue
Thymolphthalein	9.4-10.6	1 drop 0.1% soln. in 90% alc.	colorless	blue
Nile blue	10.1-11.1	1 drop 0.1% aq. soln.	blue	red
Alizarin yellow	10.0-12.0	1 drop 0.1% aq. soln.	yellow	lilac
Salicyl yellow	10.0-12.0	1-5 drops 0.1% soln. in 90% alc.	yellow	orange-brown
Diazo violet	10.1-12.0	1 drop 0.1% aq. soln.	yellow	violet
Tropeolin O	11.0-13.0	1 drop 0.1% aq. soln.	yellow	orange-brown
Nitramine	11.0-13.0	1-2 drops 0.1% soln in 70% alc.	colorless	orange-brown
Poirrier's blue	11.0-13.0	1 drop 0.1% aq. soln.	blue	violet-pink
Trinitrobenzoic acid	12.0-13.4	1 drop 0.1% aq. soln.	colorless	orange-red

NOTES

NOTES

NOTES

ORDERING INFORMATION

SCHOOL ORDERS

Please contact the Learning Resource Centre (LRC) for school discount and order information.

THE KEY Study Guides are specifically designed to assist students in preparing for unit tests, final exams, and provincial examinations.

THE KEY Study Guides – $29.95 each plus G.S.T.

SENIOR HIGH		JUNIOR HIGH	ELEMENTARY
Biology 30	Biology 20	English Language Arts 9	English Language Arts 6
Chemistry 30	Chemistry 20	Math 9	Math 6
English 30-1	English 20-1	Science 9	Science 6
English 30-2	Mathematics 20-1	Social Studies 9	Social Studies 6
Applied Math 30	Physics 20	Math 8	Math 4
Pure Math 30	Social Studies 20-1	Math 7	English Language Arts 3
Physics 30	English 10-1		Math 3
Social Studies 30-1	Math 10 Combined		
Social Studies 30-2	Science 10		
	Social Studies 10-1		

Student Notes and Problems (SNAP) Workbooks contain complete explanations of curriculum concepts, examples, and exercise questions.

SNAP Workbooks – $29.95 each plus G.S.T.

SENIOR HIGH		JUNIOR HIGH	ELEMENTARY
Biology 30	Biology 20	Math 9	Math 6
Chemistry 30	Chemistry 20	Science 9	Math 5
Applied Math 30	Mathematics 20-1	Math 8	Math 4
Pure Math 30	Physics 20	Science 8	Math 3
Math 31	Math 10 Combined	Math 7	
Physics 30	Science 10	Science 7	

Visit our website for a tour of resource content and features or order resources online at
www.castlerockresearch.com

#2340, 10180 – 101 Street
Edmonton, AB Canada T5J 3S4
e-mail: learn@castlerockresearch.com

Phone: 780.448.9619
Toll-free: 1.800.840.6224
Fax: 780.426.3917

CASTLE ROCK
RESEARCH CORP

ORDER FORM

THE KEY	QUANTITY
Biology 30	
Chemistry 30	
English 30-1	
English 30-2	
Applied Math 30	
Pure Math 30	
Physics 30	
Social Studies 30-1	
Social Studies 30-2	
Biology 20	
Chemistry 20	
English 20-1	
Mathematics 20-1	
Physics 20	
Social Studies 20-1	
English 10-1	
Math 10 Combined	
Science 10	
Social Studies 10-1	
English Language Arts 9	
Math 9	
Science 9	
Social Studies 9	
Math 8	
Math 7	
English Language Arts 6	
Math 6	
Science 6	
Social Studies 6	
Math 4	
English Language Arts 3	
Math 3	

Student Notes and Problems Workbooks	QUANTITY	
	SNAP Workbooks	Solution Manuals
Math 31		
Biology 30		
Chemistry 30		
Applied Math 30		
Pure Math 30		
Physics 30		
Biology 20		
Chemistry 20		
Mathematics 20-1		
Physics 20		
Chemistry 20		
English 20-1		
Mathematics 20-1		
Math 9		
Science 9		
Math 8		
Science 8		
Math 7		
Science 7		
Math 6		
Math 5		
Math 4		
Math 3		

TOTALS
KEYS
SNAP WORKBOOKS
SOLUTION MANUALS
SOLUTION MANUALS

Learning Resources Centre

Castle Rock Research is pleased to announce an exclusive distribution arrangement with the Learning Resources Centre (LRC). Under this agreement, schools can now place all their orders with LRC for order fulfillment. As well, these resources are eligible for applying the Learning Resource Credit Allocation (LRCA), which gives schools a 25% discount off LRC's selling price. Call LRC for details.

Orders may be placed with LRC by
Telephone: 780.427.2767
Fax: 780.422.9750
Internet: www.lrc.education.gov.ab.ca
Or mail: 12360 – 142 Street NW
Edmonton, AB T5L 4X9

PAYMENT AND SHIPPING INFORMATION

Name: _____
School Telephone: _____
SHIP TO
School: _____
Address: _____
City: _____ Postal Code: _____
PAYMENT
☐ by credit card
VISA/MC Number: _____
Expiry Date: _____
Name on card: _____
☐ enclosed cheque
☐ invoice school   P.O. number: _____

CASTLE ROCK
RESEARCH CORP

#2340, 10180 – 101 Street, Edmonton, AB T5J 3S4   **Phone:** 780.448.9619 **Fax:** 780.426.3917
Email: learn@castlerockresearch.com   **Toll-free:** 1.800.840.6224
www.castlerockresearch.com